The
Childcare
Answer
Book

LINDA H. CONNELL
Attorney at Law

SPHINX® PUBLISHING
AN IMPRINT OF SOURCEBOOKS, INC.®
NAPERVILLE, ILLINOIS
www.SphinxLegal.com

First Edition: 2005

Published by: Sphinx® Publishing, An Imprint of Sourcebooks, Inc.®

Naperville Office
P.O. Box 4410
Naperville, Illinois 60567-4410
630-961-3900
Fax: 630-961-2168
www.sourcebooks.com
www.SphinxLegal.com

This publication is designed to provide accurate and authoritative information in regard to the subject matter covered. It is sold with the understanding that the publisher is not engaged in rendering legal, accounting, or other professional service. If legal advice or other expert assistance is required, the services of a competent professional person should be sought.

From a Declaration of Principles Jointly Adopted by a Committee of the American Bar Association and a Committee of Publishers and Associations

This product is not a substitute for legal advice.

Disclaimer required by Texas statutes.

Library of Congress Cataloging-in-Publication Data
Connell, Linda H.
  The childcare answer book / by Linda H. Connell.-- 1st ed.
    p. cm.
  ISBN 1-57248-482-9 (pbk. : alk. paper)
  1. Child care--United States--Handbooks, manuals, etc. 2. Child care services--United States--Handbooks, manuals, etc. 3. Children of working parents--Care--United States--Handbooks, manuals, etc. I. Title.

HQ778.63.C63 2005
362.71'2'0973--dc22
                                                                2005014027

Printed and bound in the United States of America.

VP 10 9 8 7 6 5 4 3 2 1

Acknowledgment

I would like to thank my husband, Bill, for his assistance and support in my efforts to keep working, *and* for being my own family's dedicated childcare provider during the many days and nights it took me to complete this book.

Contents

Section I: Overview *1*

Chapter 1: Your Family's Need for Childcare *5*
    Making the Cost/Benefit Analysis
    Dealing with the Guilty Parent Syndrome

Chapter 2: Childcare Alternatives *11*
    Day Care Centers
    Family Day Care
    Preschools
    Nannies
    Au Pairs
    Babysitters
    Relatives

Chapter 3: The Importance of Quality Childcare. *15*
    Quality of Care

Section II: Childcare Outside of the Home *19*

Chapter 4: Day Care Centers and Preschools *21*
Day Care Centers
Preschools
Montessori Programs

Chapter 5: Family Day Care *27*
Disadvantages
Locating Family Day Care
Costs of Family Day Care
Unlicensed Family Day Care Homes

Chapter 6: Evaluating Out-of-Home Care *31*
Licensing and Accreditation
Checking Out Potential Day Care Centers and Family Day Care Homes
Preliminary Questions
  • *Director and Staff*
  • *Premises*
  • *Daily Activities*
  • *Policies*
  • *Interactions with the Staff*
  • *Safety and Security Concerns*
  • *Emergencies*
  • *Miscellaneous Concerns*

Section III: Childcare Inside the Home. *49*

Chapter 7: Locating Nannies *51*
Agencies
Finding a Nanny on Your Own
Nanny Training Programs

Chapter 8: The Hiring Process *57*
    Application
    Interview Discussion
    References and Background Checks

Chapter 9: Employment Issues *65*
    The Employment Agreement
    Nanny Taxes
    Employment Eligibility Verification
    Minimum Wage and Overtime Laws

Chapter 10: Au Pairs *79*
    Locating an Au Pair
    Exchange Visitor Visa Providers
    Cost of an Au Pair

Chapter 11: Using Relatives as Childcare Givers *85*
    Availability and Reliability of the Relative
    Ability of the Relative
    Family Issues
    Compensation

Section IV: Occasional or Part-Time Childcare *91*

Chapter 12: After-School Care *93*
    Day Care Centers and Family Day Care
    Sitters
    After-School Programs

Chapter 13: Childcare During Summer Vacation *97*
    Sitters
    Summer Camp

Chapter 14: Childcare Options for the Night Shift *101*

Chapter 15: Backup Childcare *105*
   Sources for Backup Childcare
   Sick Child Day Care

Section V: Paying for Childcare *109*

Chapter 16: Government Assistance *111*
   Tax Credits
   State Tax Benefits
   Temporary Assistance for Needy Families
   Child Care and Development Funds
   Head Start
   State Departments of Human Services and Telephone Numbers
   State Child Care and Development Programs

Chapter 17: Employer Assistance *133*
   On-Site Day Care
   Dependent Care Assistance Plans
   Subsidies

Section VI: Your Child's Well-Being in the Childcare Setting *137*

Chapter 18: Helping Your Child Adjust *139*
   Out-of-Home Care
   In-Home Care

Chapter 19: Maintaining a Good Relationship with the Childcare Provider *145*
   Out-of-Home Caregivers
   In-Home Caregivers

Section VII: Handling Difficulties in the Childcare Relationship *149*

Chapter 20: Monitoring the Childcare Situation *151*
Visits to the Childcare Facility
Networking with Other Families
Nanny Cams

Chapter 21: Resolving Problems with the Caregiver *155*
Philosophical Differences
When the Childcare Provider is Unreasonable or Unreliable

Chapter 22: Harmful or Abusive Situations *159*
Preventing the Harmful Environment
Avoiding Child Abuse in Childcare
Addressing Abuse or Neglect
Child Abuse Hotline Telephone Numbers

Chapter 23: Terminating the Childcare Relationship *167*
Put It in Writing
In-Home Care Terminations
Problems the In-Home Caregiver Can Create
Termination by the Childcare Provider
Your Child's Reaction
Set Up a Replacement

Section VIII: Additional Childcare Issues *173*

Chapter 24: The Special Needs Child *175*
Locating Specialized Childcare
Deciding on the Type of Childcare
Evaluating Special Needs Childcare Options

Americans with Disabilities Act
Cost Considerations

Chapter 25: The Work-at-Home Parent............................ *181*
Finding Childcare so You Can Work
Using Other WAHMs for Childcare
National Parenting-Related Organizations

Chapter 26: The Single Parent............................... *185*
Finding Support

Chapter 27: Transportation During Childcare *189*

Conclusion... *193*

Glossary *195*

Appendix A: State Childcare Licensing Offices.......... *201*

Appendix B: Child Care Resource and
            Referral Agencies...................... *209*

Appendix C: Websites *273*

Appendix D: Sample Forms......................... *279*

Index.. *289*

About the Author *294*

Section I

Overview

This book is intended for use by both parents who are contemplating whether to place their child with a childcare provider, and by parents who already have made that decision and are now looking for help in finding a more suitable arrangement. I have been in both places — trying to decide whether to return to full-time work after having a baby, and then searching for the best possible childcare situation for a 12-week-old to spend ten hours a day, five days a week. It was hard to know where to turn for answers to all of my questions. You are doing the right thing by reading up on the subject. Information is the key to making good childcare decisions.

Many factors play a part in determining childcare. Not the least of these are the financial considerations regarding whether, when, where, and how to work. Some families have few choices in these areas. For them, nonparental childcare is a given. The main concern is how to pay for it. For those who have trouble affording quality childcare, help in various forms may be available from an employer or a public or private agency. Learning about your options is the way to make the childcare equation work for your family.

Decisions about who is looking after the children and where the care is to be provided are of much importance. Childcare may be available in the family's home, at other peoples' homes, or at separate day care centers. In-home care can be provided by a caregiver who comes and goes each day or who lives in your home. The cost differences among all of these options may be great. Moreover, hiring someone to come into your home adds an entire subset of issues—employment taxes, labor laws, work contracts—about which you would then have to educate yourself.

Once you have found a suitable childcare situation, you will need to see that your child makes the adjustment to the new circumstances. Even after he or she seems to be comfortable with the day care provider, continued monitoring is a must. Working in partnership with the caregiver also is important to ensure that any problems arising with your child—whether at home or in day care—are addressed promptly and in a constructive manner.

There are occasions when the childcare arrangement you have chosen does not work out. It could be a difference of opinion between you and the caregiver on a parenting issue. It might be a change of life circumstance for one of you, such as a reduction in work hours for you or a return to school for your nanny. In some cases, the childcare situation may actually pose a danger due to unsafe premises or even a neglectful or abusive caregiver. It is important to know how to proceed in the unfortunate event that your family is in such a position.

Some families have special circumstances, such as a child with a disability, a single parent, or unusual work hours, that make the search for quality childcare particularly challenging. In other cases, a childcare arrangement that is already in place does not seem to be working for the family for some reason or another, and suddenly a whole new set of decisions needs to be made. Even if none of these are dilemmas for your family, you should be aware of them for future reference. There are solutions out there—even for difficult situations.

When I was in the position of looking for childcare, the decisions seemed overwhelming. On top of all of the usual worries that go along with having a newborn, there were so many mixed feelings about leaving a little one in somebody else's care all day. With this book, I hope to offer some help for others who have to sort through all the options and make the best choice for their family.

• • • • •

Please note that in this book I refer to the childcare providers using feminine pronouns. This is not to make a statement of any kind, but simply reflects the reality that the vast majority of childcare workers are women.

Chapter 1

Your Family's Need for Childcare

Recent United States Census reports show that more than 8 million children under the age of five spend some part of their day in the care of someone other than their parents. Many of these parents had to make tough decisions regarding the care of their children.

Making the Cost/Benefit Analysis

For many parents, there is no question as to whether a childcare arrangement is necessary. Financial or other situational limitations require both parents to work full-time. Many other families, however, must weigh the costs — both monetary and emotional — of making childcare arrangements against the benefits of remaining employed. To make the cost/benefit analysis, start with a piece of paper. Make two columns, one representing the monetary expenses and other sacrifices of working, the other for the financial as well as nonfinancial gains from continuing to work. List the *costs* and *benefits* in their appropriate columns. Having both sides of the equation laid out right in front of you may help make the decision, if not easier, at least a bit more clear and well-reasoned.

Benefits of remaining employed may be tangible. Examples are the paycheck you receive and the health insurance or 401(k) plans your employer provides. There are other, intangible advantages too, such as the personal satisfaction a person receives from a job well done. Benefits may include the following:

- staying on a career path;
- keeping up with advances within your profession;
- having contact with other adults;
- travel (although this is a benefit to some and a detriment to others); and,
- social perks, such as lunches and recreational outings.

The most obvious financial cost of working and placing children in a day care setting is the fees for the childcare itself. However, there are other expenses of being employed as well. For example, many employers have a certain dress code they require employees to adhere to, which means employees must spend part of their income on suitable clothing for the workplace. Some employees are expected to eat out on their lunch breaks, resulting in more expense. Transportation costs, such as gasoline or train fare, also must be factored into a cost/benefit equation. Moreover, a significant portion of the second income may be eaten up by income tax, particularly if the primary earner's income puts the household into the highest tax bracket.

Besides the regular paycheck and nonmonetary perks, there are other forms of financial compensation that a second income-earner gives up to remain home raising children. A company may provide a 401(k) plan for its employees, but typically will have vesting requirements that dictate the employee remain with the company for a certain number of years before being entitled to the money. Leaving a job before vesting occurs can cost a high price in later retirement income.

Another cost can come in the form of missed opportunity to pay into Social Security. Many agree that this federal system of retirement benefits is seriously flawed and might not be available ten or twenty years from now. However, leaving paid employment to stay home with children might seriously affect a person's entitlement to Social Security benefits down the road.

Whether you are eligible to receive benefits at all depends upon how many *credits* you have earned, which in turn is based upon how much you earn in a year and the number of years you contributed to the fund. The amount of the monthly Social Security payment a retiree receives depends, in general, on average earnings over the course of his or her career. Taking a hiatus from working, even for just a few years, cuts into this fund. The difference in benefits later on may determine whether you can fully retire or will need to supplement your income even after becoming eligible for Social Security.

Nonmonetary costs are harder to evaluate. If your child is attending childcare outside of your own home, you must consider the stress of having to get him or her fed, dressed, and ready to go every day before you leave for work. You have to leave enough time to drop him or her off so that you are not late for work. Even if you have in-home childcare, if there is a crisis at work and you need to stay after your regular day is over, you must have a back-up plan for picking up your child from the day care provider. And you always have to be prepared for the possibility that either your child will be sick or the day care provider will not be available for some reason. The most important consideration, of course, is whether your child will thrive in a childcare setting—a factor that is discussed later in this book.

Start with the Monetary Expenses

While the childcare decision is not usually strictly a financial one, it is easiest to start by tallying up the monetary expenses. First, calculate your household's tax liability. Figure your taxable income (including your spouse's, if applicable) by subtracting all deductions and exemptions to which you are entitled. Consult the IRS tax tables, found in the instructions accompanying Form 1040 or 1040A, to determine your tax. Then subtract from that amount all tax credits for which you are eligible. (Tax credits related to children and childcare are discussed in Chapter 16.) Add to the total any other taxes you may owe, such as FICA (Social Security and Medicare taxes) and state income tax (if any). This amount is your total tax liability.

To your tax liability amount, add the yearly expenses that you incur solely because of the fact that you work. These costs include the gas money you spend to get to work and the parking fees you would not have to pay if you did not drive every day. Add extra expenditures that you make for items such as work clothes and lunch that you would not be purchasing if you did not work away from home. Include in your total either the amount that you already spend or the estimate of what you would spend for your childcare arrangement. (See Section V for a general discussion of childcare costs.)

After adding up taxes paid and work-related expenses incurred, subtract that total from your gross income. Now you have what this book will call your *net cash benefit*, which is the annual dollar amount you have, free and clear, as a result of your hard work.

Example: In 2004, Hank and Wendy have two children, ages 12 months and 5 years. Hank earns an annual salary of $60,000; Wendy's is $40,000. Wendy has a short drive to work, and eats lunch out only a few times a month. As a result, she has only a little more than $1,000 worth of nontax, work-related expenses. The breakdown of their financial situation, both with and without the second income, is as follows.

Assumption	Two Incomes	One Income
Gross income	$100,000	$60,000
Less: Standard deduction and exemptions	($22,100)	($22,100)
Taxable income	$77,900	$37,900
Tax (according to tax table)	$12,956	$4,974
Less: Child Tax Credit and Credit for		
Child and Dependent Care Expenses	($3,200)	($2,000)
Net federal income tax due	$9,756	$2,974
Plus: FICA and State income tax	$10,450	$6,270
Total tax liability	$20,206	$9,244
Plus: Day care expenses	$13,000	n/a
Commuting expenses	$1,605	$1,070
Extra lunch/clothing expenses	$1,500	$1,000
Total work-related expenses	$36,311	$11,314

When you subtract the combined work-related expenses from gross income in this example, you arrive at a net cash benefit of $63,689 for the two-income family and $48,686 for the single-income family. The difference in net cash benefit from giving up the second income of $40,000, therefore, is about $15,000.

Evaluate Your Results

Once you have figured out the financial benefit from both parents continuing to work, the more difficult part of the equation comes into play. Is the net cash benefit, the missed contributions to pension plans, 401(k)s, and Social Security, and the passed-up opportunities for advancement, plus the other, intangible advantages of working, worth the costs and sacrifices of continuing to work and placing your child with a day care provider?

For some families struggling to make ends meet, the net cash benefit is really the only consideration—they cannot afford the loss of income from one parent staying home to care for the child. In the case of single-parent families, there is not even a second income to give up.

It is hard to know ahead of time whether a long-term hiatus from outside employment would be right for you. For some people, staying home with their children sounds like a vacation. Trips to the zoo and walks in the park with your kids are great—who would not choose a day spent reading to your little one over eight hours at a desk job? The reality for the majority of us, however, is that full-time parenting at home is no picnic. Even being home for several months on a maternity or paternity leave will not give you a clear picture of life as a stay-at-home parent.

Dealing with the Guilty Parent Syndrome

Some parents may be guilt-ridden because they have chosen to work and have placed their children in a day care setting. Others feel guilty because they do not have the choice of staying home. Some segments of our society frown upon mothers working outside the home. *Normal* families are often portrayed as having a stay-at-home parent, typically the mother. This implies that two-income families are unusual or less desirable. Of course, nothing could be further from the truth.

In Chapter 3, you will find a discussion of an important study of the effects of childcare on various aspects of the family dynamic, such as the impact on the parent-child relationship and on the child's ability to socialize later on. In summary, children do well in life if they have high-quality childcare, and not as well if they are in lower-quality childcare. This, it would seem, is not a surprising result.

Working parents provide many benefits for their children beyond just the financial ones. Having working parents helps to instill a strong work ethic in children. Seeing their mothers work is a good thing for children. This is particularly the case for girls, who need positive female role models in many areas — including parenthood — to instill that they have choices as adults.

If you really feel that your children would be better off if you were home with them, but you still need your income to make ends meet, consider whether you can afford the compromise of part-time work. *Flextime*, the rearrangement of an employee's work hours to better suit the schedule of family responsibilities, is becoming a very common perk offered by companies to retain good employees. *Job sharing*, the splitting of a single shift or a work week by two employees, who each work part of the shift, is another option at a large number of companies.

From the Expert
By working part-time, you could end up with the best of both worlds—more time for your children, plus the many advantages of paid employment.

Most importantly, remember that all children are different and will respond in their own way to a given situation. Many children thrive in a childcare setting where they are exposed to new experiences and have lots of other children with whom to play. Others benefit from having not just a set of parents who love them, but a nanny or another family member with whom they can also interact on a regular basis. The best advice is to follow your instincts in making childcare decisions.

Chapter 2

Childcare Alternatives

Although some families do not have many choices when it comes to their childcare options, it is important to understand the various alternatives available to working parents. Informed decision-making benefits parents and children alike.

Whichever alternative your family is contemplating, begin your search for childcare early. If you are already expecting your first child and plan to return to work three months after the blessed event, now is definitely not too soon to start making phone calls. You can learn from my mistake—I contacted the first childcare providers on my list six months before I needed one, and found myself shut out of almost all of the locations I called. If the same thing happens to you, ask to be placed on a waiting list, then keep in touch to see if any spots have opened up for your child.

Day Care Centers

Day care centers provide professional childcare, sometimes in an institutional-type setting, for larger groups of children. Children are often placed in different rooms or areas of the facility according to age or grade level. For example, there may be an infant room for children under the age of 2; a toddler room for 2- and 3-year-olds; a preschool or prekindergarten room for children up to the age of 5 or 6; and then rooms for early elementary-aged children (up to age 8 or 9).

Many parents who choose a large center for childcare do so because they want their children to have a number of other children to play with. In addition, centers are not dependent on one caregiver, so parents do not have to worry about finding other childcare when one of the day care staff is unable to come to work on a particular day. With a greater number of staff watching over the children, it is less likely that any incidents of abuse will occur in a day care center, although there is no guarantee of this in any childcare setting. (Day care centers are discussed fully in Chapter 4.)

Family Day Care

Family day care is childcare that is provided in the caregiver's home. Under most states' regulations, there are limits to the number of children that may be enrolled in any one family day care program, although more may be allowed if the caregiver has an aide. According to the *National Association for Family Child Care* (NAFCC), more than 4 million American children spend part of their week in a family day care setting.

Working parents often choose family day care because they want their children in a childcare setting that is similar to their own home, with a *mom* figure caring for them, a backyard to play in, and other children around to socialize with. They prefer a smaller setting to a large day care center that has many more children and the greater potential for the passing around of illness. Family day care also tends to be less expensive than care in a center, but that is not a hard and fast rule. (Family day care programs are considered in Chapter 5.)

Preschools

Preschools provide childcare in a school-type setting that serves to get children ready for elementary school. Preschools may be independently run or may be run in conjunction with a school, a religious program, or a park district.

While preschools are preferred by some parents because of the educational leaning of the daily activities, these often are only part-day or half-day programs. This makes them unsuitable for the needs of many working parents, unless they are utilized in conjunction with some other type of childcare arrangement. (Preschools are discussed more thoroughly in Chapter 4.)

Nannies

A nanny is an employee hired specifically to care for children in your home. The employment relationship may include housekeeping or whatever other terms to which you and the nanny agree. Some nannies distinguish themselves from babysitters by limiting their ranks to those who have completed rigorous childcare training programs. (For purposes of this book, any household childcare provider who works a regular schedule will be considered a nanny.) Nannies may be hired as live-in help, or may come and go on a daily basis.

Nannies are favored by parents who want one-on-one care for their children. However, nanny care tends to be quite expensive compared with out-of-home care. For families with many children, however, a nanny can end up costing less than paying day care tuition separately for each child. (The locating and hiring of nannies is discussed in greater detail in Chapter 7.)

Au Pairs

An *au pair* is a young person from another country, who comes to the United States to study and to live with a family. In exchange, the au pair provides childcare services to the family in their home. As is the case with nannies, the au pair *may* agree to take on light housekeeping duties as well. The family provides room and board, and also agrees to pay the au pair a stipend to cover additional expenses while the au pair is in the country. Other possible benefits the au pair may receive include exclusive use of a family vehicle and assistance with educational expenses.

Au pairs are often less pricey than nannies, which makes them an attractive childcare option for working parents. Some families are hesitant to take on an au pair, however, due to the fact that au pairs are fairly young, may be inexperienced in childcare, and live in the family's home as a member of the household (although this last consideration is a definite plus for some families). (Au pairs are explained further in Chapter 10.)

Babysitters

Babysitters also provide childcare in the child's home, but differ from au pairs and nannies in that they usually work under a less formal arrangement. Moreover, they are less likely to have been schooled in childcare or early childhood education. They are not as likely to be bound by any sort of written agreement, and they are usually paid in cash. As a result, Social Security, Medicare, and income taxes are rarely withheld from the babysitter's pay by the parents.

Relatives

The availability of relatives as childcare providers can be favorable to working parents, but such an arrangement must be thought through fully and objectively. Relatives can be less costly childcare providers, and may help to avoid separation anxiety in the children because they are familiar figures. On the other hand, grandparents, aunts, uncles, and the like may have their own ideas about child-rearing, which may be at odds with the parents' plans. Because she does not have an arms-length employment relationship with the working parents, the family member childcare provider may be less willing to follow the parents' instructions as to discipline, naps, and so on. (Issues related to childcare by relatives is considered in detail in Chapter 11.)

Chapter 3

The Importance of Quality Childcare

Beginning in the early 1990s, the *National Institute of Child Health and Human Development* (NICHD) embarked upon a landmark comprehensive study of the effects of childcare. The children studied spanned a wide range of demographic groups, including different ages, ethnicities, family situations, family incomes, and geographic regions. Importantly, the study followed these children for a course of eight years, allowing assessment of longer-term effects of various types of childcare arrangements.

Not surprisingly, the research indicated that children in high-quality childcare situations show greater cognitive and social development than do children receiving lower-quality childcare. Interestingly, however, the type of childcare arrangement itself did not seem to have much effect on children's development. [Non-maternal care and family factors in early development: An overview of the NICHD Study of Early Child Care. Journal of Applied Developmental Psychology, Vol. 22, pp.457-492 (2001).] In other words, day care centers or family day care homes did not impact development any more or less than a nanny or other in-home caregiver, provided the quality of care itself was consistent.

Another finding of the NICHD study was that, in general, the emotional attachment between mother and child is not affected by having the child in day care, unless the day care and the care the child receives from his mother are both substandard. [The Effects of Infant Care on Infant-Mother Attachment Security: Results of the NICHD Study of Early Child Care. Child Development, Vol. 68, No. 5, pp. 860-879 (1997).] Put another way, the child who receives poor parenting will be more negatively affected by lower-quality childcare than a child in a similar childcare environment who is well cared-for by his or her parents.

Quality in childcare is often determined by examining factors such as the responsiveness of the caregiver to the child's needs, the level of training the caregiver has, and the ratio of caregivers to children in a particular setting. Other factors relate to the childcare program itself, looking at the types of activities to which children are exposed and the socialization skills that are encouraged in the children. (These and other indicators of childcare quality are examined further in Chapter 6, which discusses how to evaluate out-of-home childcare providers, and in Chapter 8, which covers interview topics for in-home caregivers.)

Quality of Care

The issue of quality becomes problematic when you consider the overall state of childcare in the United States. The general consensus among childcare experts seems to be that, in many areas of this country, there is plenty of room for improvement in the quality of available childcare. Although most day care facilities avoid being classified as *substandard*, there are not that many facilities that are considered *excellent*, either. The vast majority are simply *adequate*. Thus, though children do well developmentally when they are placed in high-quality childcare, most children are not receiving that level of care.

From the Expert

For cost reasons, most day care providers will provide only as much staff as they are legally required, even if it would be to the children's benefit to have more caregivers available.

The dilemma for those advocating high-quality childcare options is how to improve the state of day care, particularly in rural areas. There are three important factors affecting the quality of childcare at present, and these factors are interrelated. The first is the ratio of children per caregiver in day care centers and homes. Although most states have laws limiting the number of children that may be cared for by a single childcare worker, the laws do not always reflect the recommendations of various professional organizations that *accredit*, or give approval to, day care programs.

The second main element of the quality of childcare is the level of training that the staff or caregiver has achieved. Most states also regulate the educational qualifications required of childcare workers in each state and the requirements can vary quite a bit. In some states, a certain number of college-level early childhood education coursework is necessary, while in others, only a high school diploma is required. Those who complete the coursework for a degree in early childhood education are usually qualified for more desirable teaching positions with better pay. Having lower educational standards for childcare workers leads to having fewer qualifications for the work involved.

The third — and possibly most important — component affecting childcare quality is the low pay that is typical in the profession. Day care workers typically earn only a little more than minimum wage, which keeps many well-qualified individuals from entering the childcare field. As previously discussed, college graduates with degrees in early childhood education are much more likely to bypass childcare as a career in favor of jobs as preschool or elementary school teachers.

Finding an Answer

So what is the answer? Raising the educational bar for childcare workers without increasing the financial rewards will not attract candidates. On the contrary, it may harm the childcare profession by making it too difficult for some potential caregivers to qualify to enter the field. Day care facilities can be encouraged to increase pay to staff or can be required by law to hire more staff per enrolled children, but both of these solutions will result in higher costs for childcare, which many working families will have trouble affording.

The simple solution is *money*. Funding is needed to improve the number and quality of childcare staff. The difficult part is figuring out where the money should come from. Many people in this country who are not faced with the issue of day care quality would howl at the suggestion that the government should fund programs to improve childcare. Their answer would be to put the burden on the working families who actually need high-quality day care.

Perhaps the solution lies somewhere in the middle such as a combination of government involvement in the form of increased standards for staffing and training, increased subsidies for working families, and increased subsidies for students seeking to enter the early childhood education profession. Unfortunately, there is no substantial movement at the present time toward real improvement of childcare in this country. The quality day care dilemma is a tricky problem that appears to have no easy solution on the horizon.

Section II

Childcare Outside of the Home

Out-of-home childcare generally refers to day care centers and smaller family day care settings. Working parents who choose one of these options often do so because it is more affordable than in-home care. Many also prefer out-of-home care because they want their children to have more socialization opportunities. Some feel that day care centers in particular are a safer environment than leaving children in the care of only one person—a situation that may be more difficult for the parents to monitor.

Day care centers and family day care homes are discussed separately in the chapters that follow. (Chapter 6 gives guidance to parents in evaluating their out-of-home childcare alternatives.) A great indicator of quality in childcare is whether the facility is *accredited*, which means a nationally recognized organization has certified that the program meets certain high standards. Hopefully, your childcare choices will be accredited by the appropriate agency. At the very least, you should expect the facilities you are considering to be *licensed*, which means they have met minimum state standards and are approved to operate by your state authorities.

No licensing or accreditation process, however, can take the place of your own investigation of a potential childcare provider. This should include contact with your state licensing agency about the provider and several visits to the facility to check it out for yourself.

Chapter 4

Day Care Centers
and Preschools

Day care centers, as well as preschools, typically are institutional settings similar to elementary schools. Often, children are grouped in classroom-type arrangements according to age, with one or more teachers or aides. Each class usually will follow a lesson plan similar to those used in grade schools. These school-like surroundings are one of the main differences from family day care.

Day Care Centers

Day care centers provide supervision to children in a larger group environment during set hours. A typical center might remain open from 6:00 a.m. until 6:00 p.m., Monday through Friday, although there are any number of variations on opening hours for different facilities. Some programs provide care into the evening, overnight, or on weekends.

Another major advantage to choosing a day care center is that centers are able to remain open if one of the employees is ill. In a family day care setting, discussed in Chapter 5, there may only be one caregiver, forcing the need to make other arrangements if the caregiver is sick. Absent a facility-wide outbreak of an illness, a day care center can be relied upon to remain open on all of its regular business days.

Day care centers also are seen by some as safer than family day care or in-home situations, mainly because of the number of people present in the facility. With a greater number of staff, not to mention all of the parents coming and going throughout the day, it is less likely that a situation of abuse or neglect toward any child would occur without anyone noticing.

Disadvantages

On the flip side, there are several disadvantages with day care centers, mainly related to the number of staff members and the number of children. The biggest problem has to do with children-to-staff ratios. Higher numbers of children per staff member generally correlates with lower quality of care. Unfortunately, in many cases, day care center staff is underpaid, leading to unfilled positions and high turnover. This results in higher children-to-staff ratios than are desirable, and possibly to less stability in the care that the children receive.

The sheer number of children in day care centers is also seen as a disadvantage by many parents. If there are four, five, or even more rooms, even if there are fewer than ten children per room, there are far more children present than there would be in a family day care setting. More children means more germs, and of course, a greater chance that your child will come home with a nasty cold, strep throat, or worse.

Another potential sticking point for families is the philosophy of the *individual program*. Sometimes, day care centers tend to be play-based rather than educationally focused. This is seen as a deficiency by some parents, who prefer that their children are provided with scholastic experiences when in childcare situations. At the same time, there are plenty of day care centers that provide an actual curriculum for enrolled children. Check for *National Association for the Education of Young Children* (NAEYC) accreditation, which is discussed in Chapter 6. If the facility is accredited, it has a curriculum that meets NAEYC standards.

Locating Day Care Centers

Probably the best starting place in a search for a day care center is through your local *Child Care Resource and Referral agency* (CCRR). CCRRs are organizations that assist working parents in finding quality childcare. They also help train new day care providers so there are more childcare openings available for children of working parents. The *National Association of Child Care Resource and Referral Agencies* (NACCRRA) is the nationwide network of local CCRRs and can provide a great deal of useful information for parents with questions pertaining to their childcare search. (Appendix B provides a list of all local CCRRs operating in the country at the time of writing.)

Typically, a CCRR will charge a small fee for a list of local day care centers and family day care homes. For that fee, you will be able to utilize the CCRR's services for a certain time period, such as six months. This is useful in case you try a day care situation, and it ends up not working out. You can receive an updated listing in order to locate a new provider. For lower-income families, the fee may be either waived or prorated on a sliding scale according to household income. A CCRR can tell you which programs are accredited, the age ranges of children that each program accepts, and the operating hours of each.

> **From the Expert**
>
> Using a CCRR is highly recommended as a starting point in a childcare search. It may be all the help you need.

Referrals from Friends, Family, and Coworkers

Of course, no referral agency can take the place of a recommendation from someone you trust. Talk to friends, relatives, or people you know from church or work and ask them about their search for childcare. They will give you much more than a name or address. If you know a family currently using the same type of childcare arrangement that you are considering, talk to them about their experiences. For example, if it is family day care, ask if they would recommend the provider. See if there is anything they would change about this provider or arrangement. It may even turn out that their childcare provider would suit your family's needs, in which case, you may have to look no further. Even if that caregiver would not work for you, your friends might be able to talk to the provider about other caregivers who might be suitable for your family. Repeat this process with anyone else you can think of who might be able to connect you with the right childcare setting. This type of networking is a great way to find childcare leads.

Another source of referrals, especially if you work for an employer of a large number of people, is your company's human resources personnel. HR departments exist in part to provide employees with solutions to problems that keep them from realizing their full potential with the company. While they may or may not have a formal day care referral program, chances are they will at least be able to give you useful suggestions about finding qualified caregivers in the area.

Costs of Day Care Centers

The expense of day care centers varies according to geographic region, services provided to children, and ratio of staff to children. It is reasonable to expect full-time care to cost anywhere from $250 to $1,000 per month in a center. Costs are more likely to be less in a small town than in a large urban area. Generally, centers charge more for infants than they do for toddlers, and more for toddlers than for school-age children.

The following are some examples of monthly costs found in a random sampling of day care facilities.

Oklahoma (rural area)	$420/month for infants; $300/month for preschoolers
New England (small urban area)	$780/month for infants; $620/month for preschoolers
Northwest (urban area)	$1030/month for infants; $790/month for preschoolers

The sample expenses listed are only an illustration of what you might find where you live. Keep in mind that for an exclusive childcare facility, with a very low ratio of children to staff, the sky may be the limit when it comes to tuition. On the other hand, a church-based day care program for children of parishioners, for example, may cost much less than the norm.

Preschools

Preschools are usually educationally-based programs with developed lesson plans and teachers specializing in early childhood education. Preschools are more likely to be limited in their operating hours. Although some preschools remain open from early morning until evening, they are much more likely to be either half-day programs, or at the most, run approximately the same hours as a regular full school day.

Some states provide free preschool for certain qualified children from low-income families. Two states—Georgia and Oklahoma—offer free preschool to all children residing in the state.

If you are looking for an academic program with full-time day care hours, however, your choices are more likely to be limited. This is true particularly if you are not in a large, urban area. In addition, be prepared to pay a premium for a program with an emphasis on education over play. Oftentimes, these types of schools will offer extras, such as music or foreign language classes, which may or may not be included in the basic tuition.

Whether an academic or a play-based preschool is preferable for children is something of a hot topic these days. As families feel more and more pressure to ensure that their children succeed in school, some parents want an academic childcare environment in order to give their children an advantage over their peers in later years. It is important, however, not to overlook the growing body of evidence that emotional intelligence is a more accurate indicator of life success than cognitive intellect or *book smarts*.

Emotional intelligence refers to social and personal abilities that a person has, which help him or her get along with others, make good decisions, and achieve satisfaction with his or her circumstances and environment. As a result of this relatively new way of looking at child development, some people believe that a play-based environment, with emphasis on social and emotional growth, is the best way to prepare young children for success in school.

At this point in time, the play and academic factions will probably have to simply agree to disagree as to which is better. It may be best to look for a balance between the two. A well-rounded full-time program will include plenty of time for play, as well as opportunities for learning.

Montessori Programs

One type of educational program that often operates full time similarly to day care centers is the Montessori school. Montessori refers to the philosophy of the program, which was developed by Dr. Maria Montessori in the early part of the last century. A *very general* summary of the Montessori method is that children are placed in an environment in which they take the initiative for their own learning. Teachers are present as guides in the learning process, rather than as the main focus of the room. Teachers allow children to pursue the concepts that interest them, rather than standing at the front of the room and directing what the children are learning. Large group learning is not a significant part of the program; children work individually more often than not. A great emphasis is placed on the use of concrete objects in learning. Some critics believe that this is at the expense of more abstract concepts. All academic subjects are integrated in the learning process. Rather than a math lesson, followed by geography, then science, for instance, the Montessori method encourages the child to incorporate many disciplines into a single pursuit.

Some parents do not favor Montessori education. One reason is—in the program's pure form—pretend play is not encouraged. Also, some parents are not comfortable with the teachers taking such a hands-off stance with regard to the children's learning. They prefer to have a teacher be the educator rather than the guide, with the children instructed in a more traditional manner.

One thing to be noted is that the Montessori method is not patented and the Montessori name is not trademarked. This means that any program can call itself a Montessori school, whether or not it adheres to the original principles. As a result, you should take a good look at the actual operations of a Montessori school you are considering to see if you agree with the particular methods the program is using.

Chapter 5

Family Day Care

Those who choose family day care for their children are most likely to cite the *homey* atmosphere of the family day care setting as their main reason for doing so. With few others being supervised by the childcare provider, children in family day care tend to receive more one-on-one attention.

At the same time, family day care also gives children a chance to socialize, just with a much smaller group of other children than they would be exposed to in a center. The ability to spend time with other kids makes the family day care home a more attractive option to some working parents than having in-home care, such as a nanny. With the in-home caregiver, the child might end up feeling isolated, with fewer opportunities for social interaction. The possibility of the caregiver becoming isolated may be a concern as well.

Disadvantages

The biggest problems with family day care arise from the fact that there is usually only one care provider, possibly two. One difficulty occurs if the provider or her own children become ill. In that case, the parents will have to make other arrangements for the care of their children.

From the Expert

A good family day care provider will have a network of other caregivers to whom she can refer families when she is unable to care for your child.

Another disadvantage to having only one person as a day care provider is that it may be difficult to monitor how the children are faring in the childcare setting. If the children are older and are sufficiently able to express themselves, then it will be easier to determine if there is a problem situation, such as physical or verbal abuse or neglect. Neglect can particularly be a problem when childcare is given in the provider's own home, because the provider may be tempted to tend to her own business when she should be supervising the children.

An additional complication to consider with the family day care situation is the caregiver's other family members who may be present in the home during the course of a typical day. The caregiver's spouse, and perhaps other adult relatives, may be in the home while your child is attending day care there. If this is the case, you will want make a point of asking the names of all of those people who may be on the premises at the same time as your child. Then, you will want to perform background checks on all of those people, as well as on the provider herself. You will have to obtain written consent from all concerned in order to obtain the checks. A sample consent form that can be adapted to this situation is provided in Appendix D. (Criminal checks, credit reports, and other background checks are discussed in Chapter 8.)

Locating Family Day Care

As is the case with day care centers, your local Child Care Resource and Referral agency (CCRR) can be an invaluable source of information in a search for a family day care. (See Chapter 4.) CCRRs are organizations that connect families with suitable childcare, provide day care homes and centers assistance with start-up needs, staff training, and other help that ensures quality care for children. CCRRs across the nation are listed in Appendix B, and you can check for updated information at **www.childcareaware.org**.

There are a number of other online resources for a family day care search. A few examples are: **www.childcare.net**; **www.daycare.com**; and, **www.metrodaycare.com**. These organizations probably do not screen the facilities listed in their database. If you are considering any family child-care provider, do a thorough background check.

As with day care centers, referrals from people you trust can be your best tool in a search for family day care. Start with family and friends, but do not limit yourself to these people. Anyone you know with ties to your community may be able to set you in the right direction.

Costs of Family Day Care

The cost of family day care tends to be less than that of a day care center. However, as with day care centers, the monthly rate will differ according to the location of the program and the number of staff per child. In a random sample of facilities nationwide, the rates were in the range of $400-$560 per month for infants and around $80-$120 less per month for preschoolers. The highest rate for infants in the sample was $800 per month in the eastern United States; the lowest was $240 per month in the South. Hopefully, this gives you some idea of what family day care may cost.

While you want to find the best childcare value for your money, you want to make sure that the rate a provider charges is not so low that the care is compromised. In other words, if you are considering a family day care home that costs a great deal less than all of the other homes you have checked out, you should probably ask yourself what the reason is for the low cost. Chances are the provider is cutting corners somewhere, which may not be such a good thing for the children in her care. She should be able to afford high-quality, nutritious food, as well as art supplies and other activities for the children. If she does not charge enough for these items, you may want to look elsewhere for your child's care.

Unlicensed Family Day Care Homes

You will no doubt find in your search for quality family day care that a great many of these establishments are not licensed. Unlike large day care centers, which would have a difficult time escaping the notice of state childcare facility inspectors, family day care homes are tougher to regu-late. Many care providers simply take in children without bothering to go to the trouble of getting a license. State enforcement of licensing laws is hard because these day care operations are so small.

For some families—especially those with lower incomes—unlicensed care is all they can afford. In some cases, unlicensed day care homes cost less because the provider has not spent the money necessary to comply with state regulations. The point is, as with the issue of low rates, the lack of a license might indicate that the potential family caregiver is not up to minimum standards set for this kind of day care arrangement. That can prove to be a downside for parents seeking good, quality family childcare. (Licensing of family day care homes is discussed in Chapter 6.)

Chapter 6

Evaluating Out-of-Home Care

In both day care centers and family day care, two processes serve to ensure quality in childcare—licensing and accreditation. Licensing is the means by which childcare providers are monitored by each state. All states have licensing and/or registration requirements for day care centers and family day care providers, but the specific circumstances under which a provider must be licensed may differ by state. Accreditation is certification by a nationally-recognized organization that the provider has met a rigorous set of standards of quality in the childcare that is given. Accreditation is voluntary—it is up to the caregiver to apply for the certification. Just because a provider is not accredited does not mean that the childcare is substandard.

Licensing and Accreditation

State governments control the provision of day care, whether by centers or family day care, by enacting regulations that providers are required to follow. Subjects of regulation may include the following:

- the number of children per staff that may be present;
- the manner in which children are transported to and from the child-care facility;
- allowable methods of discipline;
- the care of a child who becomes ill;
- how diaper changes are handled;
- how areas of the facility are sanitized;
- the training required of facility staff and director;

- how field trips may be taken;
- whether and how long children must engage in nap or quiet time; and,
- what information about each child must be recorded.

In most states, all of these areas and many others are regulated. A good source for information about your state's childcare provider regulations is the *National Resource Center for Health and Safety in Child Care* (NRC). This organization is funded by the United States Department of Health and Human Services, and serves the interests of health and safety in childcare settings outside of the home. The NRC's website includes licensing and other childcare-related regulations for each of the fifty states at **http://nrc.uchsc.edu/STATES/states.htm**.

While state license regulations set out the *minimum* requirements that providers must follow, accreditation involves a higher set of standards that usually go above and beyond state mandates. Some states however, have actually adopted accrediting agencies' recommended standards, and made them the law. One example of this is with the maximum ratios of staff to children in day care centers. The National Association for the Education of Young Children (NAEYC) has long advocated for small group sizes per staff member, as studies have shown that this factor can have a great impact on the level of care children receive. A number of states' laws now reflect this recommendation in whole or in part.

Recommended Maximum Group Sizes and Staff-to-Child Ratios

Age of Children	Maximum Group Size	Ratios for Maximum Group
Infants (up to 15 months)	8	1:4
Toddlers (12 to 28 months)	12	1:4
2-year-olds (21 to 36 months)	12	1:6
3-year-olds	20	1:10
4-year-olds	20	1:10
5-year-olds	20	1:10
Kindergartners	24	1:12

(Source: NAEYC)

Family day care programs across the country are accredited by the National Association for Family Child Care (NAFCC), the organization that promotes quality in family day care.

Checking Out Potential Day Care Centers and Family Day Care Homes

Hopefully, you will receive referrals to more than one childcare facility that you feel may work for your family. Once you have a list of providers, you will need to check them out thoroughly so that you can choose the best one for your child. A comprehensive evaluation of a provider should include all of the following:

- an initial conference with the director or owner, either by telephone or in person;
- a check with your state licensing office for any complaints against the provider;
- visits to the center or day care home, on several days and at different times during the day; and,
- teleconferences with at least two other families who have children at the center or home.

Checklist of Points to Consider

The list on page 34 is meant to give you a broad set of topics that you should address either in your interviews with the potential childcare provider or in your inspection of the premises. Of course, not all of these will necessarily apply to the childcare arrangement you are looking at. In fact, as you proceed with your assessment of the provider, you may come up with additional issues that you wish to address. The list will give you a good start in your investigation.

Some of the recommendations mentioned are based on research, either of a specific organization as named, or on general criteria provided by the accreditation agencies for day care centers and family day care (NAEYC and NAFCC). However, a number of the subject areas may be regulated by state law. Your local Child Care Resource and Referral agency may be able to give you specifics for your state. (CCRR information for your area can be found in Appendix B.)

Preliminary Questions

These are questions you should ask right away. Inquire when you first contact the facility, so that you do not waste time visiting centers that clearly will not meet your family's needs.

❏ *Where is the day care center or family day care located?*

Take into account the proximity of the facility to either your work or home. An extra 20-minute commute twice a day may not seem like much until you have made the trip day after day for a period of time. Of course, you do not want to sacrifice quality childcare for a shorter drive, but keep this factor in mind when evaluating your day care options.

❏ *Are there currently any openings at the facility for your child's age group?*

If there are none, ask if there is a waiting list, and how long the facility expects the wait to be for a space.

❏ *Does the facility hold a current state day care license?*

Also, verify this with your state's childcare licensing agency.

❏ *Is the center accredited by the appropriate organization?*

Again, this information is easy to verify.

❏ *What are the facility's hours of operation?*

Be sure that the hours are expansive enough to allow you to time to drop off and pick up your child without stress.

❏ *During what holidays is the facility closed?*

Also, ask if you will be charged for holidays when the facility is not open. Most childcare providers account for holidays in the amount of tuition that is charged.

❏ *What is the tuition?*

Do you pay by the week? Every two weeks? Ask when tuition is payable. Also, find out if there is a grace period for payment. Some facilities will require payment the first week of the month, but will actually accept payment for a week or two afterward without subjecting the parents to a monetary penalty.

❏ *Does the tuition decrease as your child gets older and is more independent?*

❏ *If necessary, does the facility accept part-time clients?*

❏ *How many children is the facility equipped for? How many are enrolled?*
If there is a large number of available spaces, inquire as to why there are not more children enrolled in the facility.

❏ *How are the children separated?*
Where possible, children should be divided into separate areas according to age, for example, so that toddlers are together, apart from school-aged children.

❏ *What is the staff-to-child ratio? How many children per room?*
In general, the fewer children each caregiver has, the better the care each child receives. Be aware of regulations in each state, limiting the number of children per staff member in a particular age group.

Director and Staff

❏ *What is the director's educational and employment background?*
For a day care director, you should look for education and work experience that indicates both the understanding of early childhood education and the ability to administer a childcare facility. The larger the facility, the more formal training the director should have. For a home-based family day care, simply having the experience of operating the business for a certain period of time may be enough of an administrative background. For a large day care center, states are likely to require a certain number of semester hours of college credit in early childhood education.

❏ *Does the director teach in the facility as well, or is she solely an administrator?*
The larger the facility, the more you will want to see a director whose only job is to run the center, rather than to teach as well. Again, your state may have requirements in this area.

❏ *What level of education and childcare experience do the staff members have?*

❏ *How long have the staff members been employed at this particular facility?*
Look for a facility with low turnover in staff. The longer the caregivers have been employed at the facility, the better the quality is likely to be.

❑ *If high turnover, what are the reasons staff members keep leaving?*

Talk to staff as well as the director about this, if possible. Low pay and difficult working conditions can be major determining factors in the quality of care.

❑ *Are director and staff expected to take continuing education courses?*

This may be a state requirement or it may just be a policy of the facility.

❑ *What background checks or other evaluations are performed on potential staff applicants?*

The more evaluation tools the facility uses—references, employment and school history, criminal checks, credit checks, and psychological profiles—the better.

❑ *How are staff members trained?*

The director should have an entire training process that she can explain to you. Better yet, it should be in writing for you to examine. At the least, staff should:

- receive orientation;
- be trained in the basics of childcare, such as diapering, toileting, feeding, and so on; and,
- have knowledge of child development, facility policies, expectations regarding lesson plans and/or daily activities, appropriate discipline, emergency procedures, food handling, biohazards, recognizing and reporting of abuse, and recognizing illness or injury.

❑ *Is staff certified in first aid and CPR?*

All staff members should be certified (and have up-to-date documentation to prove it) as having completed training in infant and pediatric cardiopulmonary resuscitation, as well as in first aid procedures.

Premises

Many of the following items are governed by state day care regulations.

❏ *Is the facility decorated in a welcoming manner?*

Child-oriented décor or artwork and bright or pastel colors create a happy mood for children attending day care.

❏ *Is the furniture comfortable?*

Remember that your child is going to spend a number of hours using the chairs, cribs, and other furniture in the facility each day. Do not underestimate the importance of a comfortable environment to your child's well-being.

❏ *Is the facility clean?*

Look particularly closely at bathrooms, food preparation areas, and diaper-changing areas. Also, inquire as to what chemical compounds are used to clean the premises. Bleach is preferable, so long as there is adequate ventilation.

❏ *Are there any strong odors in the premises?*

Obviously, bad odors indicate a lack of cleanliness. However, even a good scent should raise a red flag if it is very strong—it could simply be an air freshener used to mask a foul aroma.

❏ *What is the temperature in the premises?*

This is another overlooked comfort item. Step into your child's shoes for a moment, and consider how you would like to spend your day in a room that is either too warm or too cold. If the temperature cannot be helped, inquire as to how the staff can make your child more comfortable.

❏ *Are floors and stairs skid-resistant?*

Especially if you have a very young child, you may prefer a facility that does not have stairs. If it does have a stairwell, or if any part of the facility is not carpeted, be sure that the floor is not made up of any sort of slick material that might cause falls.

❏ *Are chemicals such as cleaning compounds or medicine, as well as other dangerous items such as scissors, locked up or placed out of reach of children?*
Any potentially dangerous items should be kept out of reach of children. Especially dangerous drugs and chemicals should be in childproof containers or locked cabinets that children cannot access.

❏ *Is there a sturdy, clean changing table available?*
Diapering areas should be equipped with disposable pads that can be changed with each diaper change, as well as a safety rail and safety belt.

❏ *Is there a covered diaper pail available for discarding soiled diapers? If both cloth and disposable diapers are used, are there separate pails for each type?*
Check to see if the diaper pails are out of reach of infants and toddlers.

❏ *Are hand-washing materials, such as soap and paper towels, readily available?*
Also, inquire whether proper hand washing techniques are taught to new staff and to the children.

❏ *How are the care areas, toys, and so on disinfected, and how often?*
Again, bleach is an effective means of disinfecting. Once toys have been in a child's mouth or on the floor, they should be removed from the reach of children until they can be properly cleaned.

❏ *Is there an adequate number of toilets and sinks to accommodate the number of children enrolled?*
One toilet and sink for every 10-15 children is a reasonable number, but your state may regulate a different number.

❏ *Is there a tub or shower available in case of accidents?*

❏ *Is there adequate space in the premises for the number of children enrolled?*
The American Academy of Pediatrics, for example, recommends 50 square feet of space per child.

❏ *Does each child have a locker, cubby, or other separate area to store his or her own personal belongings?*
This is important if the child wishes to keep a blanket, family picture, or special toy at the facility.

❏ *Are there emergency exits and emergency lighting?*
Older children should be able to point out emergency exits on their own. Emergency lights should be low enough to be easily seen by children.

❏ *Is the lighting bright enough for activity without being glaring?*
Also, ask whether the light can be adjusted for nap or quiet time.

❏ *Is there a playground area?*
Ask to see an inspection report from the local or county building department.

❏ *If playground equipment is available, is it well-constructed and in good repair?*
Be sure that there are no protruding or sharp objects, that swing seats and chains are in good shape, that ladders and climbing apparatus are tightly bolted and steady, and that no rust or splinters are present.

❏ *Is the playground fenced in?*
Fencing needs to be high enough and solid enough to keep children in and intruders out.

❏ *Is the ground beneath the playground covered with a soft material?*
Some recommended materials are wood chips, recycled tires, or sand.

❏ *If there is a sandbox, is it clean?*
Check to see that it is free of debris and excess water.

❏ *If there is pool or other water hazard, such as a koi pond or fountain, is the water inaccessible to the children?*

❏ *Are there areas of sun and shade available in the play area?*

❏ *Are children supervised at all times when on the playground?*

Daily Activities

❏ *What is the schedule of activities for a typical day?*
Ask for a written daily or weekly activity plan, and note whether the activities are play-based, academically-based, or both. The schedule should include indoor as well as outdoor activities—weather permitting—and should give children the opportunity to work with fine, as well as gross, motor skills.

❏ *Is there a written curriculum or lesson plan that is followed?*

❏ *Are the activities appropriate for the ages and abilities of the children?*

❏ *Are the children taken off of the premises for field trips?*

If so, how are they transported? You will want to thoroughly check the driving and criminal records of all drivers employed by the facility, and be certain that the facility has vehicle insurance in appropriate amounts. Also, ask how the facility would handle a situation in which you were not comfortable allowing your child to participate in a particular outing.

❏ *Do third parties or groups come onto the premises to provide recreational activities or educational presentations for the children?*

❏ *How much time do children spend watching television or videos?*

This, of course, should not be a regular activity.

❏ *Is time set aside for children to nap, or to have quiet time?*

Ask also whether children may engage in other activities if they do not feel like napping.

❏ *Are children encouraged to participate in activities, and may they do something else if they do not wish to participate?*

❏ *Do school-aged children have the opportunity to do homework in a quiet setting?*

❏ *Are meals and snacks provided?*

Ask to see a typical menu of food served to the children. Some facilities will ask the parent to send in a snack for the child. Snacks should be nutritious. Also, ask if there is a limit to the number of snacks a child will be given.

❏ *Where are meals prepared?*

Particularly in a family day care home, you will want to know who else in the home has access to the kitchen area.

❏ *Is food properly handled?*

This means that hot food is kept hot, and cold food remains cold. Also, dishes must be properly washed and sanitized.

❏ *Is there fresh food available or is it all processed?*

For example, real cheese is usually preferable to cheese spread, and fresh or dried fruit should be given instead of fruit snacks.

❏ *Is there a variety of food and balanced choices?*

❏ *Are there alternatives for picky eaters?*

❏ *Can special dietary requirements be accommodated?*

❏ *How often is a meal repeated?*

❏ *Are food allergy precautions taken?*

Many facilities are considered *peanut-free zones*. However, there are many common allergies that occur in children, and the facility should have a policy to deal with them. For example, there should be a rule that prohibits children from trading snacks they have brought from home with other children.

❏ *Is the staff willing to give stored breast milk to an infant at the parents' request?*

This should not be an issue in a quality childcare setting.

❏ *If an infant is formula-fed, are the parents required to provide bottles? Prepared formula?*

Some facilities require only that the formula be premixed, while others will insist that the bottles themselves be brought in each day already made up and measured out.

❏ *Is there proper storage equipment for breast milk or formula?*

❏ *Are children supervised at all times, whether inside or outside?*

This means not just that the caregiver is watching the children, but that she is physically present in the same area that they are, in case of emergency.

Policies

❏ *Are policies in writing and available for review by families?*

Ask for a copy to take home and review at your leisure. Write down and return later with any questions you may have after reading the policy.

❏ *What steps does the facility take to ensure confidentiality of information pertaining to each child?*

Personal information, disciplinary actions, and family financial information should never be disclosed to other families with children in the center. Files should be kept in a locked office or cabinet. Staff should be trained not to discuss any child attending the center with anyone other than that child's parents or guardian.

❑ *Are parents welcome to visit at any time?*

There is no reasonable explanation for a childcare provider to discourage parents' visiting the facility at any time, so long as the visits are not disruptive to the staff or children.

❑ *How is discipline handled?*

It is important that you understand exactly what the childcare staff considers acceptable and unacceptable in terms of discipline of children. This item can be stated simply—never allow the caregiver to use physical discipline, threats of physical discipline, verbal belittling or abuse, humiliation, or the withholding of food or water as punishment for misbehavior. No child should be restrained unless he or she is an immediate danger to him- or herself or others, and must stop being restrained as soon as the danger is eradicated. Ideally, discipline should be limited to so-called positive discipline, which encourages and rewards behavior that is courteous and respectful. Time-outs are to be used not as punishment, but as a means of removing a misbehaving or agitated child from a volatile situation, so that he or she can calm down and have a *fresh start* using appropriate behavior. Children who are misbehaving also can be steered toward another activity until they have managed to regain control over their own actions.

❑ *How is toilet training handled by the staff?*

Occasionally, an overworked caregiver may keep a child in diapers or training pants rather than making the effort to put him or her on the toilet. Conversely, a provider might push a child to potty-train when he or she is not ready. Ask for the specific policy of the facility and be sure that it is in accord with your own toilet-training philosophy.

❑ *What is the procedure for a sick child?*

Ask for the policies regarding both a child who is sick before coming to day care and one who becomes sick after arriving. For example, if your child has a fever, some childcare providers require that he or she be fever-free for 24 hours before returning to day care. Again, these procedures may be mandated by state law.

❑ *What is the policy for administering medicine?*

No medicine should be given unless specifically requested by the parents, and only according to the parents' written directions. All medications that are to be given to children must be clearly labeled and stored out of reach of the children.

❑ *Are infants placed on their backs to sleep?*

Most parents are aware that this is the preferred sleep position for children who are not yet able to roll over, unless there is a medical condition that requires another position. All caregivers should be aware of this as well.

❑ *Are infants held or placed in sitting positions when being given bottles? Are bottles hand-held?*

Infants should not be fed in a horizontal position. Moreover, bottles should never be propped for feeding.

❑ *Are staff and children trained in proper hand-washing techniques?*

Facilities should have a written staff policy requiring staff and children to wash hands whenever necessary, but especially after using the restroom, after changing diapers, and before and after handling food or eating. Look for signs near sinks encouraging children to use proper hand-washing techniques. One technique, for example, is to have children rub their hands together with soap and warm water for as long as it takes to sing the Alphabet Song. Only an air-dryer or paper towels should be used to dry hands. Reusable cloth towels are harbors for bacteria and should never be used in a day care setting.

❑ *Is staff trained in handling biohazards, such as blood or fecal material?*

❑ *Is staff trained to recognize signs of illness or injury?*

Day care workers should be able to recognize symptoms of a number of possible illnesses or injuries in children. Asthma, allergic reactions, and insect bites are all examples of ailments that a childcare provider needs be on the alert for. Of course, if there is a child in the facility with a specific condition, such as epilepsy, the entire staff should be made aware of what to look for and how to handle a seizure.

❏ *Is staff trained to recognize signs of physical or sexual abuse in children?*
Ask the director what specific training the staff has received in recognizing and reporting abuse of children. (Abuse indicators are discussed in Chapter 22.)

❏ *Are children provided with sunscreen when going outdoors in warm-weather months?*

❏ *What steps does the facility take to prevent lice infestation?*
Children should never share hats, pillows, dress-up headgear, combs, or brushes. If a child gets head lice, he or she should be required to stay home until the infestation has been completely eradicated.

❏ *How much notice is given if there is a fee increase? How often can an increase be expected?*

❏ *How are disputes between parents and staff handled?*
Ask if there is an appeal process if you are unhappy with the resolution to a dispute that is offered by the facility. This may not be a possibility with a smaller center or family day care home, but there may be an appeals board with a larger, franchised day care provider. Ask to see the policy on dispute resolution before placing your child with the caregiver.

❏ *Under what circumstances can a family be requested to remove their child from the day care facility?*
There should be a policy specifically stating when the child can be expelled from the program. It will likely be allowed when a child presents a danger to him- or herself or others, or when the parents' account with the facility has become delinquent. (Termination of the caregiver relationship is discussed further in Chapter 23.)

Interactions with the Staff

If you are evaluating a new childcare situation, you may not be able to answer some of the following questions by an inspection of the premises. Ask the director for references from other families with children who are enrolled. Better yet, also ask for references from families who no longer have children in the facility, and inquire as to why the families left.

❏ *How do the children in the facility appear? Do they seem happy and relaxed for the most part, or are many of them anxious or crying?*

Although anyone can have a bad day, if repeated visits show that the children tend to be more unhappy than happy in the facility, this should raise a red flag for you.

❏ *Is the childcare staff responsive to the children?*

Do the caregivers bend down to talk to the children at the children's level, or do they tower over the children? Does it take them a long time to answer a child's question or request for assistance? Do not base an opinion on a five-minute visit. Any parent knows that there are moments during the day that can be overwhelming when caring for several children at one time. Visit more than once, and make sure that nonresponsive conduct on the part of the staff is not a pattern at the facility.

❏ *Does the staff provide parents with written daily reports of the child's activities?*

If not, there should at least be a written report on a weekly basis or more often as needed.

❏ *Does the staff respond to parents' concerns about their child's progress?*

If the staff or director seems to be dismissive to your concerns about either the facility or your child's experience in the center, you may want to consider whether this is the best day care environment for your child.

Safety and Security Concerns

❏ *Are working smoke and carbon monoxide detectors in place in the facility?*

❏ *Are there emergency exits in the facility?*

❏ *Is there a security alarm on doors and windows in the facility?*

There should be some method by which the staff can monitor who comes in and out of the facility to be sure that only authorized persons have access to the children. Also, the facility needs to have a means of keeping children from wandering off. If there is not a receptionist at the main entrance at all times, there should be an alarm that indicates the door is being opened.

❏ *In the case of a day care center, is there a locked interior door and intercom or other system by which a visitor can be identified before entrance to the facility is allowed?*

❏ *Are toys, games, and other supplies used by the children safe and in good working order?*

❏ *Are crayons, play dough, paint, and markers nontoxic?*

❏ *Are electrical outlets covered when not in use?*

Similarly, are electrical cords out of reach of toddlers? What about appliances, such as a coffeepot or hot plate, in the break room?

❏ *Are steps protected by child safety gates?*

❏ *Are cribs designed to conform to federal guidelines?*

According to the federal Consumer Product Safety Commission, the slats on cribs must be no more than $2\frac{3}{8}$ inches apart.

❏ *Does staff ensure that none of the children are wearing clothing with draw-strings on them?*

Drawstrings on shirts and jackets pose a strangulation hazard to young children.

❏ *If the premises was built before 1978, does the facility provide documenta-tion of lead and asbestos screening, showing that neither material is pres-ent on the premises?*

Many states have regulations concerning the presence of lead and asbestos in day care facilities.

Emergencies

❏ *Does the facility have an emergency plan for disasters?*

The facility's disaster plan should be written and available for inspection. Natural disaster plans will differ according to the part of the country in which you are located. For instance, midwestern day care centers do not need a plan for hurricanes, but will have to have a plan for tornadoes. Other nonweather related emergencies, such as natural gas leaks or fires, should have separate written action plans. Whatever the plan involves, there must be a procedure for contacting parents should such an emergency occur. The director should have a system for keeping contact information, such as cell phone and emergency contact numbers for working parents, updated at all times.

❏ *Does the facility conduct emergency drills with staff and children?*

❏ *What is the facility's written policy regarding medical emergencies, such as injury to a child during the course of the day?*

Inquire as to which hospital the child would be taken to, and whether there is a physician and dentist that the facility uses in case of emergency.

Miscellaneous Concerns

❏ *What documents are required to register?*

Often, you will be required to present your child's birth certificate, photo identification of yourself, and immunization records for your child in order to register for day care. Some public programs may require proof of residency to show that you are entitled to taxpayer-supported benefits. Also, if your child is enrolled in a program geared toward low-income families, you may have to show proof of your income and perhaps proof of your monthly living expenses as well.

❏ *What supplies are included with the cost?*

Some facilities provide lunches for the children in the tuition costs, others may charge extra for meals. Diapers and wipes may also have to be provided by parents or may be available for a charge. Field trips or other outings may also be charged to parents over and above the basic day care fees. Inquire up front as to what specifically is included in the cost of childcare to avoid surprises later on.

Section III

Childcare Inside the Home

Many working parents prefer that their children be cared for within their own homes. The following are just a few of the numerous reasons.

- It is not necessary to get children ready to go out to a center or family day care.
- There is less chance of illness because there are no other children around to pass on germs.
- It is less disruptive to the child's lifestyle because he or she can still play with neighborhood friends.

There are a few downsides as well. One is that there is little oversight of the childcare giver. In some cases, the cost of in-home care is greater than that of a center or family day care. Another consideration is that some children in the in-home care setting may actually be less able to socialize with other children, leading to possible feelings of isolation. On the other hand, depending on the number of children that you need to find childcare for, care in the home may be the most cost-effective way to go.

Chapter 7

Locating Nannies

So, how does one begin a search for a nanny? There are generally two ways to go about it. You could go through a nanny agency or you could seek out nanny candidates on your own. The advantage to using an agency is that they do the recruiting and screening legwork for you, although you will still want to check the candidate's references yourself rather than leaving this to the agency.

The disadvantage with an agency is the expense. Some agencies charge a flat fee, which may start at $1,000 or more. Other agencies may charge a percentage of the nanny's salary, in some cases up to 25%. Usually, the fee is payable upon the signing of an employment agreement, or sometimes after the nanny has been employed for a certain period of time, such as ninety days.

There are a number of ways to locate a nanny on your own and save all those fees. Finding your own in-home caregiver, however, can be a great deal of work. You may have to advertise for help or search advertisements of nannies looking for positions. If you find a candidate who appears to be suitable, you will have to research her background thoroughly.

Agencies

If you are not familiar with any reputable nanny agencies, you should be able to locate some in the Yellow Pages of your telephone directory. Look under "Nanny Services." The Internet is another good resource for agencies. Some agencies will be local, and the nannies they place already live in your area. Other agencies operate nationwide, and can connect you with nannies from out of state as well as close to home. This will give you a greater pool of candidates from which to choose, but you probably will be required to pay an out-of-state nanny's relocation costs.

As already mentioned, agencies can make the screening process much easier for you. Aside from the background checks the agencies perform, they also can take into account your preferences regarding the personality and other attributes of your nanny. For example, if you prefer a caregiver who is an outgoing person to someone with a quiet, introverted disposition, an agency can provide you with a pool of candidates with the desired quality. This will save you the effort of weeding out incompatible applicants on your own.

Having a nanny whose personality fits in with your family is important under any circumstances, but it is especially important if you are looking for a live-in caregiver. Not only do your children have to spend a great deal of time with the nanny, but if she is living under your roof, so will you. It is difficult having a nonfamily member residing in your household day in and day out, even a conscientious and agreeable one. If the nanny's demeanor does not match your preferences, it could make for a difficult living situation.

Aside from the day-to-day routine your family will share with the nanny, you may want to take her along on family outings and vacations so that she can provide childcare for you while you are on the road. For that reason, it is not just a personality match you will want to look for. You will want your nanny to share some of the same interests as well. If your family is an outdoorsy bunch, a nanny that prefers needlepoint to hiking and biking might not be the best candidate. Again, a good agency will have profiles of its nannies and will keep you from wasting your valuable time interviewing unsuitable candidates.

Finding a Nanny on Your Own

If you choose to forgo the agency and do your own nanny search, you will have to be resourceful in order to assemble a good-sized pool of candidates. Classified ads, whether yours or those placed by people looking for nanny positions, can provide you with some leads. Nanny ads can be found not only in large city newspapers, but in local papers and specialty classified publications such as the *Penny Saver*. If you live in an urban area, your prospects will be more numerous than if you are in a suburban or rural area.

Want ads can be an extremely hit or miss method of finding worthy applicants. The more ads you have, the tougher your job will be, because you will have to sift through them all to decide which candidates you will make initial contact with. A better process for finding potential nannies is to conduct a more focused search, if possible. To do this, you should direct your efforts toward several good sources of candidates.

> **From the Expert**
>
> One of the most effective ways of locating a nanny is simply by chatting with others who already are working as in-home caregivers.

Often, nannies have friends or acquaintances who are also nannies. They may know other nannies from spending time in the park, at preschool, or at other activities with their employers' children. If you have friends or coworkers who are employing in-home caregivers, ask them if their nannies can refer you to others who are looking for childcare work.

Another way to obtain nanny leads is by asking around at the type of establishments that typically cater to people who might be able to connect you with potential caregivers. Examples would be your local park district, YMCA, or other organization where you might find families with young children participating in activities. Talking with the director or even the receptionist might lead you to a family who uses a nanny, which may in turn get you in contact with the nanny's friend, who also works as a child-care provider, but is between jobs. If you have a community center, church, or coffeehouse that has a designated area for posting ads, staple up a few flyers stating that you are looking for in-home childcare. Include your phone number and the ages of your children, but no other personal information.

An even better place to contact and to post ads would be a college in your area, if possible. Call the employment placement office at the school and ask if you may place a job posting. Some colleges that grant degrees in early childhood education even have services that match early childhood students who want to earn extra money and gain childcare experience with local families looking for nannies or babysitters.

Nanny schools themselves may be one of the best places to look for an in-home caregiver on your own. There, you have a pool of prospective nannies, presumably eager to work. Of course, the downside to nanny students and recent graduates would be their lack of experience. If that is not a problem for you, however, your family can give a new or aspiring nanny that all-important first job.

What follows here are some nanny training programs around the country. This list is not inclusive. Some of the training programs listed are part of a community college or university's curriculum. The website link may be just to the school, where you can contact them for further information. You should conduct your own search for programs located in your area.

Nanny Training Programs
(noninclusive)

American College of Early Childhood Education
760 Market Street
Suite 1009
San Francisco, CA 94102
415-677-9717
www.nannycollege.com

Calibar Training Institute
Nanny and Childcare Program
500 7th Avenue
2nd Floor
New York, NY 10018
212-564-0500
www.caliberny.com/prog_child.html

Domestic Workers United
c/o CAAAV
Nanny Training Course
2473 Valentine Avenue
Bronx, NY 10458
718-220-7391 ext. 11
www.domesticworkersunited.org/samplenanny.htm

English Nanny and Governess School
37 South Franklin Street
Chagrin Falls, OH 44022
800-733-1984
www.nanny-governess.com

Middlesex Community College
Childcare Specialist/Nanny Certificate
Bedford House
Room 105
Bedford, MA 01730
781-280-3563
www.middlesex.mass.edu/AcademicCatalog/PDF/
Certificate/CSNC.pdf

Northwest Nannies Institute
11830 S.W. Kerr Parkway
Suite 100
Lake Oswego, OR 97035
503-245-5288
www.nwnanny.com

Southeast Community College
Early Childhood Education
8800 O Street
Lincoln, NE 68520
800-642-4075 ext. 2603
www.southeast.edu/Programs/Curriculum/ECED.htm

Sullivan University
Professional Nanny Diploma
3101 Bardstown Road
Louisville, KY 40205
502-456-6504
www.sullivan.edu/louisville/programs/education_nanny_d.htm

Vincennes University
Professional Nanny Certificate
1002 North First Street
Vincennes, IN 47591
800-742-9198
http://216.37.53.162/factsheets.asp?cid=25&ctid=153

Chapter 8

The Hiring Process

Before you leave your children with an in-home care provider, you first must go through the process of interviewing your applicant and checking her background. Once you find a provider you wish to hire, you would be wise to formalize your employment relationship with a written agreement to cut down on the possibility of future misunderstandings with the provider. (See Chapter 9.)

It is entirely possible that you will have to go through the various steps in the hiring process a number of times before you find a suitable nanny. Even if you receive many responses to your advertising for in-home childcare, you may not come up with any candidates that you are interested in pursuing further. You may find a prospective nanny who is willing to fill out a formal application, but that does not mean that she will actually come in for her scheduled interview. Sometimes, the nanny can be hired, with her background check completed and all of the necessary employment forms filled out, and she might simply fail to show up for work the first day.

The point is to be prepared for the possibility that you will not find the perfect childcare provider on the first attempt. Try not to be discouraged if this is the case. Keep in mind that the goal is to find the best, most reliable care for your child that you possibly can.

Application

Whether your initial contact with a nanny candidate is a referral from an agency, a telephone call in response to a newspaper ad, or a chance meeting at your child's school, you should ask for a written application, followed by a formal interview.

The application does not need to be a computer-generated form or a long, involved document. It should, however, ask for the following information.

❏ The candidate's full name, and any other names she has used.
❏ The candidate's address, and addresses of places she has lived during the last ten years.
❏ An explanation of the candidate's childcare experience.
❏ The candidate's complete employment history, including contact information for all former employers.
❏ The candidate's educational history, with a list of all high schools and colleges attended.
❏ The candidate's driver's license number.
❏ The candidate's Social Security number.
❏ The candidate's citizenship status (if not a citizen but a legal resident, ask for a copy of her Green Card or work visa).
❏ Contact information for at least two employment references and two personal references (nonrelatives).

The preliminary information you obtain through the application can help you decide whether to proceed further with the hiring process. If you decide to invite the candidate for an interview, you can ask questions of her that expand on the information that she filled in on the application.

Unlike evaluating a day care facility or home, where you can actually visit and assess the conditions, you probably will not have as much to go on when trying to determine if a nanny candidate will work out for your family before extending an employment offer. For that reason, you will really want to make your interview with a potential caregiver count. Be sure to thoroughly explain what you expect from the nanny you hire, not just in terms of the tasks you want her to perform, but also her childrearing style, the house rules you want her to follow, and the like. You should ask anything you want to know about her in deciding whether to hire her during the interview.

Interview Discussion

The interview of prospective nannies is the most important part of the hiring process. This is your chance not only to get information about each candidate by asking questions, but also to observe the demeanor of each interviewee, which will give you some insight into her personality. In fact, it is a good idea to pose some hypothetical scenarios to her, to see how she responds.

The truth is, most nanny candidates will know the *right* answers to give to your questions regarding how to care for your child. The manner in which the questions are answered, however, may speak volumes as to the nanny's true beliefs in a particular area. For instance, you should be reluctant to make an offer to a candidate who has trouble looking you in the eye when you ask if she has used physical punishment as a method of discipline, even if she denies ever doing so.

In your earlier contact with the nanny, you should already have established that she is legally authorized to work in this country. Even if she has already provided copies of documents indicating proof of citizenship, legal residence, or a work permit, request that she bring the actual documents with her to the interview for you to examine.

The interview itself should be a dialogue, not simply you asking questions and waiting to hear her answers. It should be an *interview discussion*, with emphasize on the importance of the conversation. You should review your expectations of the nanny along with her expectations of your family. Ask questions in a way that makes her have to explain her answers, rather than simply using "yes" or "no" questions that only require her to say what you want to hear.

In addition to the actual interview discussion, you should introduce the candidate to your children. Keep it brief, but use this meeting to observe her manner with the children. Do not be alarmed if the children do not automatically warm to this new person, but do ask them later what they thought of her. Once you decide on a candidate, you should ask for a trial period of one or two weeks. During this time, be present and see how the nanny relates to the children. For now, you are just trying to see if she seems comfortable around your children, if she seems to like them, and so on.

The following is a checklist of items that you may want to cover during your interview discussion. Perhaps not all of them are applicable to your situation. For instance, some questions will be pertinent only if you are looking for a live-in nanny. Depending on your family's circumstances, there may be other questions or topics not listed here that you will find necessary to talk about.

Children
❏ Names, ages, and grade levels
❏ Interests and extracurricular activities
❏ Academic strengths and weaknesses
❏ Special abilities or talents to be encouraged
❏ Developmental milestones, particularly in preverbal children
❏ Personalities and dispositions
❏ Any medical, emotional, or other developmental conditions

Parents
❏ Marital status (if divorced and remarried, for example)
❏ Where employed
❏ Work hours
❏ Additional hours that childcare would be needed
❏ Parenting style
❏ Past caregivers used and reason employment ended

Household and Neighborhood
❏ Any other relatives living in the home
❏ Pets
❏ Children's school

❏ Location of libraries and parks in the area
❏ Location of hospital and pediatrician's office

Nanny's Background

❏ Where she grew up
❏ Size and make-up of her family
❏ Schools attended
❏ Highest educational level achieved
❏ Specific schoolwork in childcare field
❏ Work history, particularly past childcare positions
❏ Reason for choosing childcare profession
❏ Professional association or other memberships
❏ First aid or CPR training

Nanny's Personality

❏ Personality traits: outgoing/introspective; optimistic/pessimistic; calm and collected/nervous and high strung; and so on (her perception of her personality)
❏ Interests and hobbies (look for a match with your family's interests)
❏ Comfort level caring for different types of children (preferences for girls or boys, infants or school-aged)

Nanny's Philosophy

❏ Discipline methods used
❏ Handling of various situations, such as child refusing to get on school bus, weaning toddler from a pacifier, and so on
❏ Learning activities provided for the children
❏ Other activities for children (*e.g.*, crafts, outings, sports)
❏ Whether she allows children to help with household tasks
❏ Moral beliefs held

Nanny's Responsibilities

❏ Childcare duties (be specific—for example, bathing children, supervising daily piano practice)
❏ Housekeeping duties (again, be specific—for example, preparing two meals per day, making beds, tidying up children's play area)
❏ Activities to be done with children
❏ Transporting children to school or activities (ask to see driver's license and proof of automobile insurance)
❏ Caring for pets
❏ Recognizing signs of illness or injury

Terms of Employment

❏ Work hours
❏ Compensation (how much and when paid)
❏ Vacation and paid holidays
❏ How taxes are to be handled
❏ Later-born children
❏ Insurance or other benefits
❏ Use of family vehicle
❏ Written consent for background check before offer is extended

House Rules or Policies

❏ To whom the children may be released (relatives, friends' parents)
❏ Nanny's and children's use of telephone, computer, television, electronic games, and so on
❏ Smoking (whether permitted or not; if so, where and at what times)
❏ Dietary requirements of family (for example, vegetarian, lactose-free)

References and Background Checks

If you find your nanny through an agency or service, be sure to ask what screening process is used for the nanny candidates. A good agency will have some sort of screening process for nannies that are sent out on interviews. However, do not take that agency's word for it. Get the name of every screening company or investigator the agency uses, and double check directly with them to be sure that they have, in fact, performed the background checks that the agency claims. Even if you use an agency, be sure to obtain and check at least three references, at least one of which comes from someone else that used the candidate as a nanny or sitter. Other references should come from other former employers, teachers, or members of the candidate's church.

Those parents who find a nanny on their own have the burden of doing their own criminal and background checks as well. If you will be doing this, you will want to obtain a written consent from your nanny candidate to perform the check. (A sample consent form authorizing a background check is included in Appendix D.) You also need to get the following information from her (if you do not already have it in her application):

• Social Security number;
• driver's license number;
• addresses of places she has lived for the last ten years; and,
• complete work history, including contact information for all former employers.

You will probably not have the resources to conduct a thorough background check on your own. There are record-checking services that will perform the work, for a fee. The problem is knowing whether the service you use is reputable. One way to help ensure that you have a trustworthy service doing the background checks for you is to hire a private investigator to do the work. States usually require private investigators to be licensed, which may afford some measure of reliability. Internet outfits that offer background checks abound, but generally are subject to little or no regulation. Keep that in mind if you are not interested in doing your own legwork.

In general, a complete background search will consist of a trace of the applicant's Social Security number, usually going back about seven years, to ensure that the applicant is who she says she is. The trace should be able to tell you where the applicant has lived during that period of time, which will allow the background check service to narrow down which states it will focus on for criminal and driving record checks. Credit reports can be obtained by contacting one of the following three major credit reporting agencies in the country.

Equifax Credit Information Services, Inc.
P.O. Box 740241
Atlanta, GA 30374
800-685-1111
www.equifax.com

Experian
475 Anton Boulevard
Costa Mesa, CA 92626
888-397-3742
www.experian.com

TransUnion
P.O. Box 2000
Chester, PA 19022
800-916-8800
www.transunion.com

Finally, contact former employers listed on the nanny's application. Verify that she did in fact work where she has claimed, and ascertain why she left the previous employment.

Chapter 9

Employment Issues

A childcare provider who looks after your child in her home rather than yours is usually not considered to be your *employee*, but is instead known as an *independent contractor*. If you, rather than the nanny or the nanny agency, control the nanny's work, you are an employer. You want to have a written employment agreement in place. Having a written employment agreement helps make the relationship run more smoothly and provides a method to address problems before they come up.

Also as an employer, you have various legal responsibilities of which you need to be aware. You may be required to withhold certain payroll taxes, sometimes called *nanny taxes*, from the nanny's paycheck, and pay them over to the Internal Revenue Service. You may be liable for state taxes as well. There also are state and federal statutes that apply to the business relationship between you and the nanny, perhaps in much the same way that your own workplace may be regulated.

Please keep in mind that this chapter is meant only as an overview of your potential tax and legal liabilities. Consult a tax expert or lawyer for specific advice on what you are or are not required to file or pay if you hire an in-home childcare provider.

The Employment Agreement

Once you have settled on your preferred nanny candidate, it is advisable to formalize your professional relationship with an *employment agreement*. Unlike the application, this should be a comprehensive document, with as many terms of your agreement memorialized in writing as possible. (A sample employment agreement is included in Appendix D.) The main reason to have a contract with specific terms is to help prevent your nanny from accusing you of breach of contract if you decide to terminate the employment relationship. A discussion of some of the more important parts of the agreement follows.

Parties
Be sure to specify the people who are to be bound by the agreement. This means the nanny, you, and your spouse (if applicable). Include the addresses of all parties.

Responsibilities of the Childcare Provider/Job Description
Describe what tasks you want the nanny to perform relative to the job of providing childcare. (Additional housework is discussed in a later section.) Be thorough in including the general categories of activities you wish the nanny to undertake, but leave flexibility in the particulars. For instance, require that the nanny facilitate learning, but do not limit the methods by which she can accomplish this. Provide examples of educational activities, but state that the list is not limited to those that are specified.

Start Date/Contract Term
Differentiate between the date the contract is entered and the date that employment is to start. If they are two separate dates, both should be included in the contract. The agreement date is the date that the employment relationship is entered. The start date indicates when the nanny's care-giving responsibilities and the parents' duty to pay the nanny begin. Also, provide either an end date or a specific time period for the life of the agreement. A one- or two-year term is fairly typical.

Pay Rate/Overtime
Wages should be very specific. The pay rate should be expressed in hourly, daily, or weekly terms. If the nanny may be expected to provide

babysitting services above and beyond her normal work hours, overtime pay should be designated in writing. If possible, explain in the contract the circumstances under which overtime work would be requested—for example, the amount of advance notice that the nanny could expect before being called upon to stay late at work.

Taxes

Employment taxes in the nanny situation are discussed in Chapter 9. For purposes of the nanny agreement, you will want to set out which party is responsible for remitting the necessary taxes from the nanny's pay to the proper state or federal agency. Certain taxes must be withheld by the employer while others may be paid by either party on behalf of the nanny. The latter type of tax can be withheld and paid over by the employer only if the nanny agrees.

Work Hours

It is necessary to state exactly what hours and days of the week the nanny is responsible for working. If your work schedule varies from week to week, you should include language declaring that that is the case, and that the nanny will be given her work schedule within 24 hours of you receiving it yourself. If you expect that your hours will change at some point in the future, leave room for change in the contract, by providing that you can change the nanny's work hours with a certain amount of advance notice (if possible, at least two weeks notice would be preferable).

Additional Children

Even if you do not plan on having more children, it would be a good idea to include a provision covering extra pay for extra kids. If your plans do end up changing for some reason, you will have one less issue to worry about. If you discuss such a possibility in advance, you can determine how your nanny feels about taking on the care of another child—particularly a newborn.

Vacation, Holidays, and Sick Days

Paid days off for the nanny need to be explicit in the agreement. State the paid holidays by name. If a holiday falls on a weekend and you wish to give the nanny another day off as a make-up holiday, specify which day it will be. If you want the days off to correspond to your own work schedule, and you do not know which days will be holidays for you from year to year, state that you will give notice of the paid holidays by a certain date — for example, by December 1 of the year before the year in which the holidays are to be given.

Insurance

Insurance in a nanny situation generally refers to two different types of policies — automobile and health. If you want the nanny to drive your children to activities in your car, you will want to add her to your insurance as a covered driver. If you expect her to use her own vehicle, you can handle it in one of a couple of ways. You can purchase auto insurance for her, but that may be on the expensive side. You could agree to pay for part of her insurance premium, but then you will want to include in the contract a requirement that she present you with proof, probably every six months, that she has sufficient automobile insurance.

At the very least, you should require that the nanny have the following kinds of insurance:

- *medical payments insurance*, which covers medical expenses incurred by a driver or her passengers as a result of an accident;
- *personal injury liability insurance*, which covers claims by others for bodily injury;
- *property damage liability*, to pay claims for damage to the personal property of another, resulting from an auto accident caused by the nanny; and,
- *uninsured/underinsured motorist liability insurance*, which pays for expenses incurred in an accident either with another driver who has insufficient insurance coverage, or with a hit-and-run driver.

Some states have statutory requirements for the minimum amount of liability insurance a driver must have; however, state law mandates often do not go far enough. For liability insurance, the policy should include personal injury expense limits in the minimum amount of $100,000 per person or $300,000 per accident.

Be aware, however, that some insurance policies will not cover an accident that occurs while your nanny is performing job duties for you. Under a legal doctrine called *respondeat superior*, an employer can be held legally responsible for the actions of an employee that are committed during the course of the employment. One example would be an auto accident that occurs while the nanny is taking the children to school. Whether the nanny will be covered by her own policy or by yours, check thoroughly to be sure that you will not be personally liable for damages that she may cause.

The primary reason some families offer health insurance to their nannies is to attract the best candidates for the position. Unfortunately, health insurance for a nonfamily member can be extremely expensive to purchase. For that reason, if you are considering providing her with insurance, you should discuss with your potential nanny whether she wants health coverage, and if so, whether she would accept a lower salary in exchange for it. She already may be covered by her own or her spouse's policy. Whatever you both decide, include the terms in your written agreement.

Expenses

Depending on the number and ages of children in your household, there may be a variety of extracurricular activities that your nanny will have to drive to. In addition, you may want her to take your children on outings, such as a trip to the movies, to the ice cream parlor, or to the bowling alley. You can either provide the nanny with cash in advance, or you can simply reimburse her after she submits receipts for her expenses. In any event, you should require her to get your prior approval before taking the children on an excursion, so that you are not caught off guard with an unplanned bill for activities.

If the nanny is using the family car for transportation, you will not need to worry about mileage expenses. When the nanny uses her own car, however, you may wish to offer reimbursement on a per-mile basis. The amount, of course, is open to agreement. One guideline is the Internal Revenue Service standard mileage expense deduction, which is 40.5 cents per mile (in 2005).

House Rules
Providing a list of house rules gives the nanny a guide to the rules that she and the children are required to follow. Any policy that you expect to be enforced should be included in this section. The following are just a few possibilities for you to consider:
- rules regarding the children's friends coming into the house;
- rules limiting the amount of television the children may watch;
- rules setting limits on computer or hand-held electronic games;
- rules prohibiting unhealthy snacks;
- requirements for chores to be performed by the children; and,
- limits on telephone use by the nanny and the children.

Acceptable Methods of Discipline
Describe both acceptable and unacceptable approaches to discipline. You should already be familiar with your nanny's philosophy regarding discipline from your initial interview, but putting it in writing emphasizes your own philosophy further. Spanking or other forms of corporal (physical) punishment should not be allowed, according to the vast majority of experts. Time-outs and redirection are good forms of discipline for younger children; older ones may be responsive to grounding or taking away some other privilege or prized item. Obviously, your own preferred method of correction is the one you should require of your nanny.

Additional Duties/Housework
You want to be as thorough as possible with your list of additional duties you expect. List not only the tasks that you expect the nanny to perform,

but also the jobs for which she is not responsible. Be very clear, so there are no misunderstandings. If you want the nanny to take on housekeeping duties, be sure to discuss this in advance, then outline the duties in the agreement. If possible, also state how often you expect the tasks to be done. Some housework must be performed on a daily basis, while other jobs need to be done only once a week.

At the same time, you should anticipate that there might be some duties that you will want the nanny to handle that you have not thought to set out in the agreement. For that reason, you may want to include a statement that other, nonspecific tasks may be required of the nanny from time to time.

Annual Review/Pay Raises

If you have found a good nanny, you will want to keep her by offering her pay increases on a regular—usually yearly—basis. You may put right in the contract that she will receive a certain percentage increase every year. However, it may be better not to commit yourself to a set amount, but rather to make the increase contingent on an annual review. At the review, give the nanny an evaluation of her job performance for the past year. Based on how happy you are with the childcare your nanny is providing, you can decide what kind of a raise to give her.

Emergencies

Be very clear on the procedure you wish the nanny to follow in case of an emergency—especially a medical emergency. Of course, if a serious injury, fire, or crime occurs, the nanny first should summon emergency personnel, most likely by calling 911. Otherwise, the nanny should get in touch with you immediately. Keep all work and cell phone numbers listed in a conspicuous place near the telephone, and be sure the nanny is aware of the list's location.

Consent/Authorization Forms

In the case of a medical emergency, especially if the nanny cannot reach the parents, it is crucial that the nanny has written authority to seek treatment for the children. The parents should complete and sign a consent form for each one of their children that specifically names the nanny and authorizes her to obtain emergency services, such as paramedic assistance or hospital care, as necessary.

Release of Children

There may be occasions when a member of your extended family will want to take your children out for a treat. Perhaps your child's friend will call wanting to invite your child for a playdate. You may wish to treat each of these requests on a case-by-case basis and have the nanny contact you at work to see if you approve of her releasing your child to the relative or neighbor. On the other hand, you may feel that anytime your mother wants to take your child to the park, it is perfectly fine with you, and the nanny should let your child go.

You should clarify whatever policy you are comfortable with, and if there is anyone you want the nanny to release the children to without having to contact you first, you should list them specifically in the agreement. You should be sure to introduce them to the nanny as soon as possible once her employment begins, so she is familiar with them. Anytime you allow your child to leave the house with a person the nanny does not know, such as the parent of your child's friend, you should require that the nanny verify the identity of the person by requesting identification. Of course, you will want to let the other parent know your nanny will be asking for identification, so the parent will not be caught off guard and possibly become offended.

Relocation Expenses

If you have a nanny who has relocated from out of town specifically for this position, you may wish to specify whether or not you are paying any of the costs of relocation. Be clear about expenses both for the move to your town and for her return home at the end of the caregiver relation-ship. Some families agree to pay some or all of these costs in order to recruit the best possible nanny. If you are not willing to contribute to these expenses, include a provision in the agreement that the nanny is responsible for her own moving costs. This is more likely to come up in a live-in nanny situation.

Termination/Notices

The contract should set out the proper method for ending the employment relationship by either party. Unless there are issues involving imminent harm to the children or to your household property, it is courteous and pro-fessional to give the other party notice of the intent to terminate the agree-ment. If you are the one ending the contract, you should give the nanny time—with pay—to find other employ-ment. If the nanny decides to end the relationship, she should continue to work for a period of at least several weeks to allow you to make other childcare arrangements. Put your notice require-ments in writing in the agreement.

Even if you have all the necessary pro-visions concerning the separation with your nanny in writing, signed by both parties, the actual process of terminating the employment of the nanny can trigger unforeseen reactions, including her refusal to vacate your home voluntarily. This is not to say your written employ-ment agreement is meaningless, but that you should take care to address as many contingencies as possible in the agreement. A thorough contract will help to put you on firm legal ground, should it be necessary to take any action to conclude your association with

> ### From the Expert
> In the case of a harmful sit-uation, however, such as an incident of abuse or neglect, or if you have rea-son to believe the nanny is stealing, obviously you want her to leave the household right away. You can include a provision in your contract stating that a dismissal for cause due to harmful or dishonest con-duct will be immediate and without pay for the notice period.

the nanny or au pair. (Termination of the relationship between the parents and the childcare provider are discussed generally in Chapter 23.)

Nanny Taxes

The following is a general summary of your obligation for so-called *nanny taxes*.

Income Tax Withholding

You do not have to withhold federal income tax from your nanny's wages, because she is the one who is responsible for paying the tax. If she chooses, she can wait until she files her yearly federal income tax return to pay whatever tax she owes. If the nanny does want you to withhold income tax, and you agree to do it, then you will need to pay the withheld amounts over to the IRS. Also, she will have to provide you with a completed IRS Form W-4, the *Employee's Withholding Allowance Certificate*. This form tells you how many allowances your employee is claiming, based on various deductions, credits, and other income adjustments. You need to know the number of allowances in order to calculate the proper withholding.

Regardless of whether you actually withhold the income tax for your nanny, if any income or nanny taxes are owed, you will be required to report the nanny's wages. To do this, file a *Schedule H* (Form 1040) along with your own tax return, which is due April 15th. You also will report the nanny's wages to the Social Security Administration (SSA) by filing Copy A of IRS Form W-2, *Wage and Tax Statement*, along with IRS Form W-3, *Transmittal of Wage and Tax Statements*.

Before January 31st of the year after the year in which you paid wages to your nanny, you must provide her with Copies B, C, and 2 of the W-2 form. In order to properly file the W-2 and other necessary documents with the SSA or IRS, you will need to apply for an *Employer Identification Number* (EIN) from the IRS. To apply for an EIN, you must complete and file an IRS Form SS-4, *Application for Employer Identification Number*.

Some lower-income wage earners are eligible for a federal tax credit called the *Earned Income Credit* (EIC). As an employer, you also need to be aware of the EIC, because you may have certain obligations as a result of the credit.

If you agree to withhold income tax for your nanny, but when you attempt to calculate the amount of withholding, the tax tables indicate that nothing is required to be withheld (because her income is below a certain level), you must give your nanny notice of the EIC.

> **From the Expert**
>
> Copies of Schedule H, Form W-2, Form W-3, Form SS-4 and other IRS instructions and publications can be viewed online at **www.irs.gov**, or can be obtained in hard copy by contacting the IRS at 800-TAX-FORM (829-3676).

There are several ways you can do this. The most common way is to provide her with Copy B of the W-2 form. Proper notice must be given by January 31st of the year following the year in which the nanny could claim the credit. The IRS suggests that the employer of household help give the employee notice of the EIC if her wages are not up to the EIC maximum eligible level ($31,030 in 2005).

Some employees who are able to claim the EIC also are entitled to have the EIC paid to them in advance. If your nanny provides you with a completed IRS Form W-5, the *Earned Income Credit Advance Payment Certificate*, you will have to calculate how much to pay. Because this is a tax credit, you also will reduce the amount of federal income tax and FICA withholding by the amount of the advance EIC payment. If you find yourself in the position of having to make an EIC payment in advance, consult IRS Publication 15, *Employer's Tax Guide*, for help in calculating the amount to pay.

> **From the Expert**
>
> For more information about tax liability for employers of household help, such as nannies, you may wish to consult a copy of Internal Revenue Service Publication 926, *Household Employer's Tax Guide*.

Social Security and Medicare (FICA) Taxes

FICA stands for *Federal Insurance Contributions Act* and refers to Social Security and Medicare taxes that are withheld from an employee's wages in addition to federal and state income tax. You do not have to pay FICA taxes on your nanny's wages unless you pay her $1,400 or more in cash wages each year (for tax year 2005). Moreover, you do not have to pay these taxes at all if the wages are being paid to your spouse, minor child, or parent. However, there is an exception when it comes to your parent. If you are divorced and not remarried, widowed, or your spouse is disabled and cannot care for your children, *and* your children are under the age of 18, you do have to count the wages you pay a grandparent to watch the kids. If the total wages exceed $1,400, you will be required to withhold FICA taxes.

From the Expert

If the tax requirements are confusing, it may be wise to consult a local accountant about your tax liabilities when hiring a nanny.

FICA liability is 15.3% of the employee's cash wages, which means you do not count the value of the employment benefits you give your nanny. Of the 15.3%, you and your nanny are each liable for one-half of the amount, or 7.65%. However, the employer will often simply pay the entire amount rather than withholding it, providing an extra benefit to the nanny.

Unemployment Taxes

If you pay wages of $1,000 or more in a calendar quarter of 2005, you also are required to pay *federal unemployment tax* (FUTA), which is generally .8% of the wages paid until wages exceed $7,000. After that, there is no liability for *federal* unemployment tax, although you may be required to pay state unemployment tax.

State Taxes

In addition to federal withholding and FICA liability, you may have to withhold or report state income tax on the nanny's wages as well. Also, states may require employers to pay for workers' compensation insurance. States' laws vary in these areas, so be sure to get competent tax advice when hiring a nanny.

Employment Eligibility Verification

Once you hire a nanny and become an employer, both you and the nanny are required to complete a United States Citizenship and Immigration Services (USCIS—formerly the Immigration and Naturalization Service (INS)) Form I-9, also known as the *Employment Eligibility Verification*.

You are not required to file the completed form with the federal government. Keep it for your records, because the law does mandate that you have it available for inspection by the proper federal authorities if necessary. You must keep the I-9 for the longer of three years after you hire your nanny or one year after the employment relationship ends.

For you to complete your portion of the I-9, you are required to review certain documents proving that your nanny is legally eligible to work in the United States. She needs to provide you with documents that show (1) her identity and (2) employment eligibility. Some documents are adequate to show both, but some only show one or the other. For example, a United States passport will serve as proof of both identity and eligibility. A driver's license, however, will show only identity, and the nanny also will have to give you proof of eligibility, such as a Social Security card. A complete listing of appropriate documents is included with the Form I-9. A copy can be obtained online at **www.uscis.gov**.

Minimum Wage and Overtime Laws

As an employer, you have to abide by other state and federal labor laws. The federal *Fair Labor Standards Act* (FLSA) governs minimum wage and overtime pay for covered employees. Although casual babysitting arrangements are not subject to the FLSA, domestic workers, such as full-time nannies, must be paid minimum wage. Overtime pay in the amount of one and a half times the employee's regular wage must be paid for hours worked in excess of forty per week. (However, this part of the law does not apply to live-in nannies.)

Where the state minimum wage law differs from the federal law, the higher of the two is the wage you must pay. The federal minimum wage is currently $5.15 per hour. Most of the states that have their own minimum wage laws mandate the same amount as the federal government. A handful of states require a higher minimum wage.

States with Higher Minimum Wage Amounts

Alaska	$7.15
California	$6.75
Connecticut	$7.10
Delaware	$6.15
District of Columbia	$6.60
Hawaii	$6.25
Illinois	$6.50
Maine	$6.35
Massachusetts	$6.75
New York	$6.00
Oregon	$7.25
Rhode Island	$6.75
Vermont	$7.00
Washington	$7.35

NOTE: *Workers who are under the age of 20 only need be paid $4.25 per hour for the first 90 consecutive calendar days of employment or until the worker turns age 20, whichever comes first. After that, the minimum wage goes up to the regular amount.*

Chapter 10

Au Pairs

Au pairs may be a more cost-effective option for families with two or more children than paying for each child to attend outside childcare. An au pair is a young person from another country who comes to the United States to absorb American culture by living with a family. Sometimes, the au pair attends school while in this country. In return, the au pair agrees to help with childcare, and may even take on some light housekeeping. Au pairs, however, are not employees of the working parents, but are meant to be considered houseguests, or one of the family. In fact, au pair means *on a par*.

The fact that au pairs are not workers hired by families is an important difference from nannies; unfortunately, this is not the only difference. Au pairs are young, and they often are inexperienced with caring for children. They are also far from home, which could lead to a number of problems. Some au pairs will suffer from homesickness. Others may like America a little too much, and may be more interested in carousing or clubbing than in learning what family life is like in our country.

One possible advantage is that your children may be more at ease with a young au pair than with an older caregiver. On the flip side, however, your children may not see the au pair as an authority figure, which may make her less than useful as a childcare provider.

Locating an Au Pair

The United States Department of State—through the Bureau of Educational and Cultural Affairs—has designated several au pair organizations to administer the Exchange Visitor visas (known as J-1 visas) that some au pairs use to enter the United States. These programs are reputable sources of au pairs, as they are the direct connection to au pairs with the J-1 visa.

Exchange Visitor Visa Providers

(J-1 Visa)

Agent Au Pair
1450 Sutter Street
#526
San Francisco, CA 94109
415-462-1906
www.agentaupair.com

American Institute for Foreign Study
River Plaza
9 West Broad Street
Stamford, CT 06902
800-928-7247 (toll-free)
203-399-5025
www.aupairinamerica.org

AuPairCare
600 California Street
Floor 10
San Francisco, CA 94108
800-4AU-PAIR
www.aupaircare.com

Cultural Care Au Pair
One Education Street
Cambridge, MA 02141
800-333-6056
www.efaupair.org

**Cultural Homestay International
Au Pair USA**
104 Butterfield Road
San Anselmo, CA 94960
800-432-4643 (toll-free)
415-459-5397
www.chiaupairusa.org

EurAuPair Intercultural Child Care Programs
www.euraupair.com
(Contact information varies by region.
Check the website for your regional office.)

goAUPAIR
111 East 12300 South
Draper, UT 84020
888-287-2471
www.goaupair.com

Au Pair Foundation
1010 B Street
Suite 200
San Rafael, CA 94910
866-428-7274 (toll-free)
415-257-4783
www.aupairfoundation.org

InterExchange, Inc.
161 Sixth Avenue
New York, NY 10013
212-924-0446
www.interexchange.org

USAuPair, Inc.
P.O. Box 2126
Lake Oswego, OR 97035
503-697-6872
www.usaupair.com

The State Department's au pair program provides a uniform set of requirements for both au pairs and the families that host them. Au pairs placed through this program can remain with the family for up to one year, although under some circumstances, this can be extended an extra year. The au pairs are expected to provide up to 45 hours of childcare per week (up to ten hours per day), and must also be enrolled in at least six hours of post-secondary coursework at an accredited school, which includes a community college. Au pairs in this program are not allowed to care for infants less than three months of age, unless there is a responsible adult present. In addition to a weekly payment and an educational stipend, families are expected to provide the au pair with a separate bedroom, use of a vehicle, and all meals. Au pairs are also entitled to two weeks of paid vacation and at least one weekend off every month.

Some of the agencies can put you in touch with foreign youths holding J-1 visas. More often than not, however, the prospective au pairs you will find through these agencies will hold some other type of temporary visa, and will not be subject to the State Department standards.

> ### From the Expert
> There are plenty of au pair agencies out there. The Internet is full of online agencies that put families in touch with young adults looking to come to the United States under the sponsorship of a family.

Cost of an Au Pair

The typical bottom line *cash* cost for an au pair is in the area of $13,000. The family pays a placement fee to the sponsoring agency, which usually runs about $5,000. There may be an application fee of several hundred dollars as well. Of course, the cost of meals is not factored into that total amount, so your cost will be more, in actuality. The weekly payment you give the au pair is meant to cover her expenses beyond room and board, and most au pair agencies recommend that families require the au pair to purchase a phone card rather than letting her use the household phone at will. If you have two or more children, an au pair may end up being a bargain in comparison to full-time day care.

Chapter 11

Using Relatives as Childcare Givers

Even as recent as a couple of decades ago, members of extended families were likely to live in fairly close proximity to one another, making it easy to share the burden of caring for each other's children when necessary. As modern society becomes more and more transient, however, many families find themselves in unfamiliar cities with no relatives around to help out with childcare needs.

Working parents who are fortunate enough to be surrounded with relatives willing to care for their children during the parents' work hours have yet another option for childcare, but they need to consider all angles before jumping into such an arrangement. It is crucial to the child's safety that the parents objectively evaluate a care-by-relatives arrangement. While it may seem to be a perfect solution at first glance, the reality of relying on a grandparent or other family member for day care may not be as favorable as it seems. The following factors are a starting point for appraising such a situation:

- the availability and reliability of the relative to provide care according to the parents' schedules;
- the ability of the relative to provide adequate care;
- the safety of the relative's home (if care is to be provided there);
- the relative's philosophy concerning discipline; and,
- whether the relative can provide safe transportation to and from school or activities.

Availability and Reliability of the Relative

Availability and reliability are actually separate—but related—concerns. *Availability* refers to whether the relative is able to care for the child when the parents need her to, while *reliability* is whether the relative *actually does* care for the child when she is supposed to. A relative who often has other obligations in her life that cause her to cancel on days she is supposed to provide care is not reliable. Even if she is providing care for free or for much less than a professional childcare provider, it is no bargain if the parents often find themselves having to find backup care because the relative has other demands on her time. In such cases, the parents may feel that they cannot complain because of the *deal* they are getting on childcare. They may feel resentful toward the relative, placing strain on the extended family relationship.

Ability of the Relative

The *ability* of the relative to provide the childcare is the most important consideration in a care-by-relatives scenario. The relative who is to provide care must be physically and emotionally fit to look after one or more children on a regular basis, often for many hours at a time. In the case of a grandparent, this may be the greatest obstacle to retaining a relative as the care provider. With parents waiting longer and longer to have children these days, the pool of grandparents caring for children is aging as well. Advanced age brings on issues of both physical and mental health that must be addressed if a grandparent is to care for young, energetic children.

Even younger relatives (aunts, uncles, and so on) need to be evaluated before entrusting them with the care of children. Sit down with your relative and honestly discuss the demands of the job. Consider not only the physical work involved, for example, in caring for infants and toddlers. Also discuss the emotional toll that may result from watching older children who are getting to the *tween* years of 8-12, when the problems of peer pressure and the onset of puberty present challenges for kids and parents alike.

Do not only look at the emotional stability of your relative. Her personality is important to assess as well. Will she provide a nurturing environment for your child? Will she be patient with him or her? Just as significant is her ability to accept suggestions from you. Will she take offense if you ask her to handle a parenting issue in a different way from what she is used to? Take a hard look at these considerations before leaving your child with the relative.

Another requirement you might have is that the relative be able to transport your child to his or her activities. For this reason, you will want to ascertain that your relative has a valid driver's license, current automobile insurance, and the ability to operate a motor vehicle in a safe manner. If you have an infant or small child, you also should make sure that the relative knows how to install a child safety seat and knows how to secure your child properly in the seat.

> ### From the Expert
> If the caregiver relationship fails in a care-by-relative situation, more than the childcare arrangement is at stake. You can find yourself in awkward circumstances with your relative, and possibly even with the rest of your extended family, for a long time.

All of these issues will require you to ask your relative questions that may make one or both of you uncomfortable. Always keep in mind, however, that your child's safety is the primary consideration. Because of that, you should be prepared to ask whatever questions are necessary to establish that your child is in good hands.

Family Issues

Another potential sticking point that you may not have thought of is the possibility of family conflicts boiling over with the childcare arrangement. The discord may result directly from the relative care situation, such as a disagreement over a parenting issue. A different possibility, however, is that some other prior source of strife between you and the care-giving relative becomes aggravated because of the new relationship the two of you share. For example, if you feel that your mother was always less than responsive to your worries and problems when you were a child, you may become upset with her if you perceive her as distant toward your own children. If you feel that your mother-in-law is overbearing or bossy to you and your spouse, it may make you bristle to hear her dole out orders to your children, even if it would be perfectly acceptable to you if a babysitter did exactly the same thing.

Compensation

The issue of compensation for the relative's care-giving services can be another obstacle in this type of childcare arrangement. Some relatives (such as grandparents) will insist upon watching the children for no charge. Unless you truly are not in a position to pay anything for childcare, insist that your relative take some sort of compensation. This may help avoid the relative obtaining real or imaginary *leverage* over you in some later family situation.

> **Example:** Your in-laws care for your children full-time in your home at no charge. As a result, they now expect you and your family to spend every holiday with them, rather than splitting time with your own parents, because they feel as if you *owe* them.

Discuss payment for services rendered before you actually start the caregiver arrangement with your relative. Try not to be embarrassed or feel awkward bringing up the subject. The more you are able to keep this a business relationship, the better the chance of the arrangement being successful. If your relative is offended by the offer of money, phrase it in terms of her doing you a favor—if she will accept money for the services, it will make you (or your spouse) more comfortable with the arrangement.

If you are unable to pay in cash, you might attempt to work out a barter system. For example, in exchange for childcare, you spend one weekend day per month running errands for your relative or doing odd jobs for her. If your caregiver is a relative with young children of her own, offer to watch her children during some of your time off so that she can attend to her own business.

In the end, the key to having a successful childcare partnership with a family member is good communication. This means you need the ability to discuss issues with your relative/potential caregiver in an honest and open manner. All of you, including yourself, your significant other, and your relative must have this capability. If you are not comfortable addressing possible problems with your family member ahead of time, your child (and perhaps your entire family) probably will be better off if you make an alternative day care arrangement.

Section IV

Occasional or Part-Time Childcare

Day care centers and family day care are typically geared toward families with *regular* — 9-to-5, Monday-to-Friday — work schedules. Evening and weekend childcare is usually tougher to find. Some day care facilities will not accept families with part-time or occasional childcare needs, because they have no trouble filling available spaces with full-time children.

The most difficult situation is the case of working parents who do not have fixed hours. Even childcare providers who do take part-time children often require families to adhere to a fixed schedule. Parents who learn of their assigned work hours only on very short notice (for instance, in the case of substitute teachers) may find themselves with a tough job in the search for quality childcare.

With erratic work hours, family day care homes are likely to be more flexible than centers. Because the caregiver is working in her own home, she may be more willing to take children on a drop-in basis at odd hours, such as in the evening. Because most large centers close by 6:00 or 7:00 p.m., they probably will not be an option.

One idea is to begin compiling a list of possible sitters, so that you have several reliable people to call if you need to find childcare on short notice or at a late hour. One place to find short-notice sitters might be a local senior citizens center. Retirees make good occasional sitters because they often have free time on their hands, and because many of them have years of childcare experience. Of course, you will have to take into account the physical condition of a potential sitter who happens to be a senior citizen. Be sure that she will have the stamina to meet the demands of caring for your children.

Chapter 12

After-School Care

For most people, the need for quality childcare does not end when the children go off to school full-time. Even working parents with the most reliable, 9-to-5 schedules have to fill in that gap in the late afternoon. Many childcare providers who take children on a full-time basis may also be willing to provide after-school care for older children. For this reason, you should check with the same childcare providers in your area that others use for their younger children.

The importance of quality after-school care cannot be overstated. Children with working parents may spend three, four, or five hours every weekday in these programs, so it is crucial that their experience is a positive one. Just as important as quality is the availability of after-school programs. According to the federal resource website **www.after-school.gov**, the hours between 3:00 and 6:00 p.m. is the time period in which young people without supervision are most likely to commit violent crimes, experiment with drugs and alcohol, and engage in sexual behavior. Providing these children with after-school activities is a proven method of cutting down on juvenile criminal behavior. Unfortunately, there are many more children without activities after school is out each day than there are available spaces in after-school programs.

Evaluating after-school care raises the same concerns as assessing any other childcare provider. You will want to look at ratios of staff to children; the cleanliness and safety of the premises; the activities, facilities, and equipment that are available to the children; and, the background and training of the staff and the director. Ask for and check references from others who have children in the program, and if possible, from those who have had their children in the program in the past but no longer do. Try to find out their reasons for withdrawing their children from the program.

Day Care Centers and Family Day Care

Some day care centers do provide after-school care if they have the space to take on additional children late in the afternoon. Because the state-required staff-to-children ratios are lower for school-age children, it is easier to staff a room for older children for a shorter period of time. It can be more difficult for family day care providers to do this, because they often are limited in their ability to accept children after school due to space and staff restrictions.

Sitters

Even if you are unable to find a drop-in spot at a center or family day care, potential sitters may be more abundant in the hours after school. A local college student might make a good after-school caregiver—not just because of the money she is able to earn, but also because she is trying to build up a pool of references she can call upon to give her good reviews when she goes out to get her first job after graduation. You may even be able to find a high school student, although with homework and extracurricular activities of their own, younger teenagers just might not be able to fit in a baby-sitting job every single day.

A great source for after-school care can be found among *stay-at-home moms* (SAHMs). Many SAHMs are former career women themselves. They often have gone through some of the issues of giving up the independence of earning their own income. Sometimes, SAHMs decide to piece together odd jobs or part-time work around their children's school schedules in order to earn extra cash. After-school hours are a good time for many of these women to take on a job for some spending money.

To tap into this group of potential childcare providers, ask someone in authority in your child's school or district if you can do a distribution of flyers among the student body, advertising for after-school care. If the school or district will not allow you to circulate a flyer, ask if you can post a notice in a conspicuous place near the school office, where a mom would be likely to pass while there on school business. The other, usual sources of networking apply here as well—try your church, library, park district, dance school, ice rink, and so on for places to post ads seeking after-school childcare.

After-School Programs

Organized after-school programs are another option for some families. These are especially attractive for families with older children, sometimes called *tweens*. Tweens generally fall between the ages of 8 and 12 years old. Tweens might feel that they are too old to have a baby-sitter, and yet they simply may not be mature enough to look after themselves in the hours between the end of school and their parents' return from work. Moreover, in the case of older tweens, parents may be reluctant to leave the children to their own devices after school, even if they are able to take care of themselves.

After-school programs are starting to take off in many parts of the country for just this reason. It is a simple concept—if children have a supervised activity after school to keep them busy, they will be less inclined to find something illegal or destructive to do for entertainment. Unfortunately, at this point in time, demand far outpaces supply.

To locate an after-school program in your area, check first with the office at your child's school—some offer these programs right at the school. Then, if necessary, branch out from there. Park districts, the local YMCA, your church, or another religious establishment in your area are all good resources for after-school care or for tips leading to other care-givers. Depending on your geographic location, other regional groups may be able to give assistance. Particularly in urban areas, Boys and Girls Clubs may be available with programs or suggestions. In rural areas, you may have more luck with a local 4-H chapter. Junior Achievement is another possible resource.

From the Expert

On the Internet, you might want to check out the National AfterSchool Association at:

www.naaweb.org

Child Care Aware at:

www.childcareaware.org

or the Federal Government Clearinghouse at:

www.afterschool.gov

These sites do not provide links directly to after-school programs, but are useful sources of information to help you in your search.

Do not limit yourself to considering only national associations or local charitable organizations. While doing an online search for after-school programs, you may find offerings in more unorthodox locations, such as a martial arts academy, a fitness center, a museum, or a computer learning center. As with any program to which you are thinking of entrusting your children, be sure to research the program and the staff, ask questions, and check references.

Chapter 13

Childcare During Summer Vacation

The perennially sticky problem of summer break childcare can throw the most unflappable working parent into a panic. Many families end up patching together a network of summer camps, temporary sitters, and vacation time in order to make sure that their children are looked after for those twelve weeks off school. Year-round childcare providers are often unwilling or unable to make room for a temporary charge, although if there is a surplus of childcare providers in your area, it might not be such a problem.

Sitters

The good news is that although your child is out of school, so are all the local high schoolers or older students who may be looking for extra cash for college or a car. Not to advocate ignoring employment tax filing requirements, the reality of the situation is that many working parents hire sitters for cash. This may make a babysitting job more attractive to a teenager than a minimum wage job, where income taxes are taken out before she even sees her paycheck. The main potential problem with hiring a teenager is the age factor — teenagers are inexperienced and some can be undependable.

Another possibility for parents is to find a teacher who is looking for extra money over summer vacation. Do not limit yourself to your own child's school. Stop in at the offices of the elementary, middle, and high schools of your own school districts, as well as surrounding districts. The market for baby-sitting teachers may be limited, at least if it is 40+ hours a week of childcare that you want. Unless they really need the money, teachers may prefer to follow their own pursuits on their hard-earned summer vacations.

Summer Camp

Camps can be another great way to secure summer childcare. Many different types of organizations offer full-day programs, or even overnight camps, during summer vacation. Churches, park districts, the YMCA and other charitable organizations, private schools, and private for-profit operations (such as health clubs) may all be sources of vacation day care. Camps may be directed to a particular age group or might be geared toward a particular interest. For example, a budding equestrian might find a horseback riding camp. The possibilities for specialized activities are almost limitless. Some programs run for the entire or almost the entire vacation period, while others might only operate for several weeks at a time or require enrollment in more than one session to cover the whole summer.

Parents may wish their children to attend a camp that is affiliated with a particular religious, cultural, or charitable organization. There are camps that are geared toward children of certain ethnicities, such as Hispanic-American programs. There are also camps for special needs children and for children who have—or had—various health conditions. Examples are camps catering to diabetic children or to children with cancer.

Before deciding to send your child off to camp, assess his or her readiness to be on his or her own in a new situation. Even a child who seems to be well-adjusted to the daily grind of school may be intimidated by summer camp, especially if he or she has not been to this particular camp before. When you are visiting camps that you are considering, bring your child with so that he or she can give you his or her thoughts on each one. If your child feels he or she has some control over where he or she spends summer vacation, he or she may feel more comfortable with the arrangement. If your child has a friend or two who are able to attend the same camp, that might also help to smooth the adjustment.

In some areas, you might find camp guides or special advertising sections in the local newspaper. Usually, these begin to appear in the spring, or even as early as midwinter. If you do not know where to find a camp guide, contact the office staff of your local newspaper and see if they publish one. If they do not, ask if they would be willing to compile one for their readers.

Sometimes, local colleges operate summer camps for children. This allows the college students—often those who are majoring in the education field—practical experience and the opportunity to earn college credit for working with children. If there is a college or university in your area, a call to the education department might provide you with a lead.

The Internet can be of great assistance in providing leads for summer camp programs. Some of the more popular nationwide Web directories for summer camps include the following.

- www.kidscamps.com
- www.gocamps.com
- www.camppage.com
- www.campchannel.com
- www.summer-daycamps.com

Please remember, however, that these websites are merely listings of camp programs that choose to advertise with the site. It is up to you to thoroughly research any camp you are considering

From the Expert

The *American Camp Association* (ACA) has an accreditation program for summer camps throughout the United States. More than 2,300 programs are accredited. This means the ACA has reviewed the camp program and inspected the camp location, and the program meets the ACA's standards for things such as activities, safety, cleanliness, child development, health care, management, and staffing. You can contact the ACA at 765-342-8456 or online at **www.acacamps.org**.

From the Expert

There are many sites available that have listings for a particular region. A search engine such as Google or Yahoo can help. Try entering the search term "summer camp guide" along with your county or geographical area.

to determine if the program is right for your child. It should go without saying that a check of references is in order with any camp in which you might enroll your child. Obtain as many references as you can, and contact all of them. Ask the people to whom you are referred if they know of anyone who was not happy with the program, and then ask the camp to put you in touch with any of those people. If your state allows it (not all do), ask the camp director and staff to give written consent for a criminal background check.

The American Camp Association (ACA) website has a useful section on questions to ask when evaluating a camp program. The organization suggests that you ask for information such as: the ages of the camp counselors, what percentage of counselors return to work at the camp each year, and the background and training of the counselors and the director. The ACA also recommends asking specific questions about operating and other policies, particularly how issues such as discipline and homesickness are handled.

Overnight camps, of course, present the possibility of a whole other set of adjustment issues for children. You should consider the potential problems with overnight camp very carefully before enrolling a child, especially a young child who has not had much experience staying overnight away from his or her family.

Costs

Costs for camp will vary widely depending upon the length of the session, whether the program is day or overnight, the activities that are offered, and the facilities that are available to the campers. Some specialty camps are subsidized by large organizations. For example, the American Cancer Society sponsors a number of camps for cancer patients and survivors that are free to qualified campers. On the other end of the scale are exclusive camp programs, geared toward wealthy clientele, that can cost hundreds of dollars per week.

Chapter 14

Childcare Options for the Night Shift

More and more working parents are facing the challenge of finding supervision for their children while the parents work evening or overnight hours. Some businesses, by their nature, need to operate on a 24-hour-a-day basis. Hotels, hospitals, and transportation centers are examples of such businesses. For many couples who have trouble affording full-time childcare, service industries are one possible solution. Because these types of businesses are open much later than the 9-to-5 operation, they offer many families the opportunity to have a double income without the expense of day care. One parent can work a typical daytime shift, and can care for the children in the evening, while the other parent earns the second income or the evening shift.

Many night shift workers, however, do not have the option of relying on their spouses or significant others to watch the kids while at work in the evening. Perhaps both parents are required to work the night shift. It could be that the worker is a single parent. One of the trickiest situations for a working parent is finding quality, reliable childcare for the third shift. Not only are providers hard to find, they often are more expensive because they are supplying an unusual service and thus can charge a premium. As always, your local Child Care Resource and Referral agency (CCRR) may be able to help.

Having relatives who are willing to spend the evening or night with your child, or who allow your child to stay at their house while you work, may be the simplest way to fill a need for nighttime care. The problem is when the only available relatives have children of their own, or when they have already spent an entire day working and wish to have the evening free. For that reason, an older, retired relative may be more likely to want to help. (Chapter 11 discusses in general the pros and cons of having a relative care for your children.)

If there is a college in your area, you may have another source of night-time childcare. Try advertising for help by placing signs in the student union or another place on campus where students congregate and postings are allowed. Nighttime care can be a very attractive way for a college student to make money, especially if the children's bedtime schedule allows the student to get in some homework while she is earning the cash.

Another possibility for night shift workers is trying to trade childcare services with someone working daytime hours. This may work especially well for two people who work for the same employer, or at least in the same field. One example is the nursing profession, where third-shift assignments are routine and shift hours are typically similar from hospital to hospital. A nurse who works the 11 p.m. to 7 a.m. shift might be able to find a 7 a.m. to 3 p.m. worker to swap childcare. Of course, the logistics of switching off the children during a shift change would have to be addressed. Also, trading childcare duties leaves little downtime for either working parent.

In some parts of the country—particularly in areas that rely heavily on tourism for their economic well-being—day care centers are more likely to offer evening hours. The number of hotels and late night entertainment establishments in some of these areas means a greater number of night-shift workers. Thus, there is a high demand for nighttime childcare in these regions. If you do not live in such an area, you may have

> ### From the Expert
>
> You may be able to find nighttime childcare, as with other types of care, by searching online. You could do a Google search using the terms "nighttime," "evening," "childcare" (or "child care"), or some other similar wording. There are Web directories out there as well, such as **www.daycarehotline.com**, with listings of all types of childcare (not necessarily limited to nighttime).

better luck with a family day care home than with a center. Some care-givers may welcome the opportunity to earn money by providing care to a child who will spend the majority of his or her time sleeping.

Certain issues may arise in a nighttime care situation that are different from what comes up in traditional childcare settings. Your child could have trouble falling asleep, or may have a bedwetting problem. Any issues that you are aware of should be brought to the attention of the provider and discussed so that you are both satisfied with how the situation is to be handled if it occurs. Of course, if you are looking for childcare for an infant, you will want to make sure the childcare provider knows to place the baby on his or her back to sleep.

Chapter 15

Backup Childcare

What if your child attends a family day care and the day care provider's own children develop a contagious illness? What if the day care provider becomes sick? Suppose your child is in a day care center, but comes down with a stomach flu the same day that you have a presentation you cannot miss at work? Sometimes, a nanny or sitter simply fails to show up. What do you do? No matter what your childcare situation, you want to have a backup plan for childcare in place for the inevitable day when something goes wrong.

One good way to ensure a backup plan is to ask the childcare provider to have one for you, especially if your child is in a family day care or you have a nanny. When you first interview potential care-givers, find out what they will do if they are unable to care for your child due to their own illness or personal emergency. If your nanny comes from an agency, see if the agency will send a substitute. (Make sure you can check the credentials of the backup caregiver well before you need her help.) If you use a family day care, ask what the contingency plan is when one becomes necessary.

Even if the childcare provider tells you that there is a plan in place for these contingencies, have your own plan as well. If your child is in a day care center, you have to be prepared for the time he or she comes down with pinkeye (possibly picked up from the center), and is prohibited from coming back to the center until he or she has been on antibiotics for 24 hours. Unfortunately for many parents, if they have not planned ahead, the backup plan is that mom or dad misses work.

Sources for Backup Childcare

Drop-in care is a good option if your child's caregiver is unavailable. Some day care centers and family day care homes allow parents to bring children in on an as-needed basis. You should locate such facilities well before you need them. Most will require you to register your child ahead of time, and some may require payment of an application fee. Drop-in care tends to be more expensive per hour or per day than regular full-time care. In an emergency, however, it could be well worth the price if you can avoid having to take an unplanned day off work.

Relatives, neighbors, and friends all can be sources of backup care in a pinch. If there is someone you know with children of her own who is available during your work hours, you may be able to work out a child-care swap. This is where you repay the backup caregiver in kind for helping you out in a childcare emergency. For example, if you have to leave your child with the next door neighbor for six hours when your nanny develops a bronchial infection, you pay the neighbor back by giving her six hours of baby-sitting services for her children, at her convenience. Of course, you can always work out an arrangement by which you simply give her a cash payment for her services. Whatever you both prefer is fine, just be sure to have a deal worked out before you need her help.

Retirees living in your area could also make great backup childcare providers. They typically have more free time than those working or raising children, or at least they often have more ability to be flexible with their time. You do, however, need to be satisfied that the retiree is physically able to take care of one or more children for the amount of time that you need.

If you do not know anyone who might be interested in being an as-needed caregiver, you might try adver-

From the Expert

Being grandparents themselves in many cases, retirees can be exceptionally qualified to take care of children if you are stuck without childcare.

tising at your local senior center or community center. As with any other potential caregiver, unless you know the person well that you are thinking of using for your backup childcare, obtain consent to perform a criminal background check.

Sick Child Day Care

As demand for quality childcare grows, so does the movement toward day care programs that are specifically set up to provide care for sick children. A few companies are even beginning to implement sick care programs—some of which are in-house—for their employees. Additionally, some day care centers now include a separate area of the facility as a sort of *quarantine area*. Regularly enrolled children who happen to have fallen ill on a particular day can come to day care, yet remain segregated from the healthy children.

These types of programs are far from being the norm, however. Until employers learn to see the economic benefits of helping their employees secure backup childcare, most working parents will be on their own in these circumstances. More often than not, they will have no choice but to call in *sick* themselves when their children are ill.

Section V

Paying for Childcare

Childcare costs vary widely according to the age of your child, where you live, and which care option you choose. Nannies hired through agencies can command fees running upward of $35,000 per year. For a kinder-garten-age child living in a smaller city and attending a day care center, $7,000 for full-time care might be more typical. For minimum wage earners, particularly in single-parent households, childcare costs may easily take up more than half of the family income.

Even under financial circumstances that are not so dire, there may be assistance available from government agencies, private organizations, or employers. Help may come in the form of direct cash payments, either to the parents or to the caregiver. It may take the form of a subsidy or a dis-counted childcare rate. You may be eligible for a tax break—either a credit or a deduction. An employer might even provide a childcare facility located right on the company premises.

Chapter 16

Government Assistance

For families that qualify, state and federal agencies may provide help with the cost of childcare. Assistance generally comes in two forms — tax relief and subsidized childcare. Most government help requires a family to meet a certain level of need. Just about all public assistance programs mandate that the parents seeking help are either working, attending school, job training, or are actively looking for work.

Tax Credits

The Internal Revenue Code grants several child- and childcare-related income tax credits, which serve to leave more money in the pockets of working parents that can be used for childcare expenses. A tax credit is an amount of money deducted directly from the total tax amount for which the taxpayer is liable. Therefore, if you owe the IRS $1,300 in income taxes and you are eligible for a $1,000 tax credit, you are now responsible for paying only $300 to the IRS. That other $1,000 remains yours to apply to your other expenses, such as childcare costs. The most common credits that working families can take advantage of are discussed in the following sections.

Child Tax Credit

The *Child Tax Credit* may be up to $1,000 per qualified child. A qualified child is a taxpayer's child, stepchild, foster child, or grandchild who is under the age of 17, and whom the taxpayer (and no one else) claimed as a dependent on the taxpayer's tax return for that year. Even the taxpayer's sibling, niece, or nephew qualify, if he or she was under the age of 17, lived as a member of the taxpayer's household, and was cared for by the taxpayer in the same way as the taxpayer's own children.

This credit is not limited to low-income families. However, it is reduced once your modified *adjusted gross income* (AGI) exceeds a certain level, which in turn depends upon the type of return you are filing:

- $110,000 if you are married and filing jointly;
- $75,000 if you are unmarried; and,
- $55,000 if you are married and filing separately.

The credit you are entitled to receive decreases $50 per $1,000 of modified AGI in excess of the above amounts. If your modified AGI is high enough that you do not qualify for any child tax credit, your credit simply amounts to $0. The reduction in credit cannot result in a negative amount.

To figure out whether you are eligible for the Child Tax Credit, you can complete the worksheet found in the instruction booklet that accompanies your IRS Form 1040. You should receive the form and booklet in the mail near the beginning of each calendar year so you can file your income tax return before the April 15th deadline. If you do not receive the form and booklet by mail, you can obtain a copy from your local post office or by contacting the IRS at 800-829-3676. You can also browse instruction publications and forms online at **www.irs.gov/formspubs/index.html**.

Child and Dependent Care Expenses

The *Child and Dependent Care Expenses Credit* allows a taxpayer to deduct, directly from the amount of tax he or she owes, up to 35% of the annual expenses for the care of qualifying dependent children. (Other dependent family members' care expenses may also qualify, but this discussion will focus only on childcare expenses.) You may receive a credit of up to $3,000 for one qualifying child, and $6,000 for two or more such children.

In order to qualify for the credit, your childcare expenses must be for your child under the age of 13, whom you claim as a dependent for income tax purposes. If you are not married to your child's other parent, only one of you are able to claim the credit. In addition, you must maintain a household in which you live with the child. It is also a requirement that your childcare expenses were incurred so that you could work or look for work. The payments you make for childcare cannot be made to someone else that you claim as a dependent (for example, another, older child of yours who baby-sits the qualifying child). In fact, you are required to identify your childcare provider on your return. Finally, if you are married, your return must be jointly filed in order to claim the credit.

The percentage of expenses for which you may claim a credit decreases as your adjusted gross income increases. In the event you receive childcare benefits from your employer, you still may be eligible for a tax credit. However, the dollar limit of $3,000 for one child and $6,000 for more than one child is reduced by the amount of the benefit you receive. For example, if your company provides you with a dependent care benefit of $500 per year and you only have one child, you still may be entitled to a Child and Dependent Care Expenses Credit. The maximum credit you will be eligible to claim, however, will be $2,500 ($3,000 less $500).

For 2004, the allowed percentages of expenses that may be taken as a credit were as follows.

$15,000 or less	35%
$15,001–$17,000	34%
$17,001–$19,000	33%
$19,001–$21,000	32%
$21,001–$23,000	31%
$23,001–$25,000	30%
$25,001–$27,000	29%
$27,001–$29,000	28%
$29,001–$31,000	27%
$31,001–$33,000	26%
$33,001–$35,000	25%
$35,001–$37,000	24%

$37,001–$39,000	23%
$39,001–$41,000	22%
$41,001–$43,000	21%
$43,001 or more	20%

To claim the Child and Dependent Care Expenses Credit, you must attach either an IRS Form 2441 (if you are filing a Form 1040) or a Schedule 2 (if you are filing a Form 1040A) to your federal income tax return. Find them at **www.irs.gov**.

If you have additional questions about the Child and Dependent Care Expenses credit, IRS Publication 503, *Child and Dependent Care Expenses*, can probably provide you with some answers. This booklet also can be obtained by contacting the IRS or through the IRS website.

Earned Income Credit

The *Earned Income Credit* also directly reduces the income tax owed and is designed to help certain lower income families. A qualifying taxpayer can even receive the credit in advance as part of his or her paycheck during the year.

The taxpayer must meet the following requirements in order to be eligible for this credit.

- The taxpayer's adjusted gross income (for 2004) must be less than:
    - $34,458 if the taxpayer has more than one qualifying child ($35,458 if married, filing jointly);
    - $30,338 if the taxpayer has just one qualifying child ($31,338 if married, filing jointly); and,
    - $11,490 if the taxpayer has no qualifying child ($12,490 if married, filing jointly).
- The taxpayer's earned income must also be less than these amounts, but he or she must have some earned income.
- The taxpayer must have a Social Security number.
- The taxpayer may not file his or her return as *married, filing separately*.
- The taxpayer must be a citizen or resident alien of the United States during the entire tax year.

- The taxpayer's investment income must be $2,650 or less.
- The taxpayer may not exclude income earned in a foreign country from his or her gross income.

A qualifying child must be a child, stepchild, or descendent of the taxpayer, or may be a sibling, niece, nephew, or foster child of the taxpayer if the taxpayer has cared for the child as if he or she were the taxpayer's own child. The child also must be under the age of 19, a full-time student under the age of 24, or permanently disabled. He or she must have lived with the taxpayer during at least half of the tax year. Only one taxpayer is allowed to claim the Earned Income Credit using a particular qualifying child, even if more than one person is eligible. Finally, the taxpayer claiming the credit may not be the qualifying child of another person who is claiming their own Earned Income Credit. There is a separate set of rules for taxpayers who do not have a qualifying child.

You claim the Earned Income Credit by filing an IRS Schedule EIC with your federal income tax return. If you wish to receive the credit throughout the tax year, you must file an IRS Form W-5. Copies of the Schedule EIC form and the W-5 form can be obtained from the IRS.

IRS Publication 596, *Earned Income Credit*, contains a great deal of useful information for those seeking to claim the Earned Income Credit. As with other IRS forms and publications, it is available through the IRS website or by calling the IRS and requesting a copy.

State Tax Benefits

Some states provide income tax credits for dependent and child care expenses. According to the *National Association of Child Care Resource and Referral Agencies* (NACCRRA), the following states currently offer some sort of dependent and child care tax credits.

Arkansas	Massachusetts
California	Minnesota
Colorado	Missouri
Delaware	Nebraska

District of Columbia	New Mexico
Hawaii	New York
Idaho	North Carolina
Iowa	Ohio
Kansas	Oklahoma
Kentucky	Oregon
Louisiana	Rhode Island
Maine	South Carolina
Maryland	Vermont
	Virginia

Temporary Assistance for Needy Families

The government program that was commonly referred to as *welfare* until about a decade ago, underwent reform and now is known as *Temporary Assistance to Needy Families* (TANF). Help is given to low-income or otherwise needy families by way of state services that are funded by both state funds and federal block grants. The services must promote one of the four stated purposes of the federal TANF statute.

1. To assist needy families.
2. To promote job preparation, work, and marriage, in order to end dependence by needy parents.
3. To prevent the occurrence of out-of-wedlock pregnancies.
4. To promote the formation and maintenance of two-parent families.

The provision of childcare to low-income families falls under one of these purposes. The main difference between the old system and the present one can be summarized in the word "temporary." Under most circumstances, TANF assistance to adult members of one family lasts a maximum of five years.

The requirements for TANF eligibility differ from state to state. If you have reason to believe your family might be eligible for temporary assistance, you should contact your state Department of Human Services. State Departments of Human Services and telephone numbers can be found starting on page 120.

Child Care and Development Funds

In order to promote state-administered programs to assist low-income families with their childcare needs, the federal government provides funds to the states via the *Child Care and Development Block Grant*. Receipt of the funds is contingent upon the states following various federal regulations and other requirements related to families who are either receiving or transitioning away from welfare dependence.

Some state programs provide funds to childcare providers, so the providers are able to offer subsidized care to families at a discounted rate. Other programs give the money directly to the families, usually in the form of vouchers that can be applied to the cost of day care.

For additional information about child care and development programs in your area, you might try getting in touch with the agency in your state that is in charge of administering local child care and development organizations. Contact information for each state agency appears on page 124.

Head Start

Head Start is a jointly-sponsored state and federal program geared toward children from birth up to age five who are from low-income families. The federal *Administration for Children and Families* (ACF), part of the Department of Health and Human Services, grants funds to school districts and other public and private organizations to be used for programs to help ensure that these children are developmentally prepared to enter school.

Head Start is not a childcare provider per se, but is an educational program. Hours vary from program to program, but typically last somewhere between three and six hours a day, several days a week. In some areas, traditional childcare operations work with Head Start programs to allow children a full day or full week of care. Because Head Start is a comprehensive approach to improving the chances of low-income families, childcare programs may receive grants to help subsidize care.

To obtain information about any Head Start programs in your area, contact your regional ACF office. You can do this online at **www.acf.hhs.gov/ programs/acfdps/index.htm#Regional_Office_Locations** or by telephone through the regional ACF office for your area.

Region I
(Connecticut, Maine, Massachusetts, New Hampshire, Rhode Island, Vermont)
617-565-1020

Region II
(New Jersey, New York, Puerto Rico, Virgin Islands)
212-264-2890

Region III
(Delaware, District of Columbia, Maryland, Pennsylvania, Virginia, West Virginia)
215-861-4000

Region IV
(Alabama, Florida, Georgia, Kentucky, Mississippi, North Carolina, South Carolina, Tennessee)
404-562-2900

Region V
(Illinois, Indiana, Michigan, Minnesota, Ohio, Wisconsin)
312-353-4237

Region VI
(Arkansas, Louisiana, New Mexico, Oklahoma, Texas)
214-767-9648

Region VII
  (Iowa, Kansas, Missouri, Nebraska)
  816-426-3981

Region VIII
  (Colorado, Montana, North Dakota, South Dakota, Utah, Wyoming)
  303-844-3100

Region IX
  (Arizona, California, Hawaii, Nevada)
  415-437-8400

Region X
  (Alaska, Idaho, Oregon, Washington)
  206-615-2547

You also can contact the *Head Start Information and Publication Center* at:
1133 15ᵗʰ Street, NW
Suite 450
Washington, DC 20005
866-763-6481

The Childcare Answer Book

State Departments of Human Services and Telephone Numbers

Alabama
Alabama Department of Human
  Resources
334-242-1850

Alaska
Alaska Department of Health and
  Social Services
907-465-3030

Arizona
Arizona Department of
  Economic Security
602-542-4296

Arkansas
Arkansas Department of
  Human Services
501-682-8650

California
California Health and Human
  Services Agency
916-654-3454

Colorado
Colorado Department of
  Human Services
303-866-5169 (TANF Eligibility Verification)
303-866-5822 (Public Information)

Connecticut
Connecticut Department of
  Social Services
860-424-5008

Delaware
Delaware Health and Social
  Services
302-255-9037

District of Columbia
D.C. Department of Human Services
202-279-6127

Florida
Florida Department of
  Children and Families
850-488-4855

Georgia
Georgia Department of
  Human Resources
404-656-4937

Hawaii
Hawaii Department of
  Human Services
808-586-4888

Idaho
Idaho Department of Health and
  Welfare
208-334-0668

Illinois
Illinois Department of
  Human Services
217-557-1564

Indiana
Indiana Family and Social Services
  Administration
317-233-4453

Iowa
Iowa Department of
  Human Services
515-281-4848

Kansas
Kansas Department of Social and
  Rehabilitation Services
785-296-3271

Kentucky
Kentucky Cabinet for Health and
  Family Services
502-564-6786

Louisiana
Louisiana Department of
  Social Services
225-342-7475

Maine
Maine Department of Health and
  Human Services
207-287-3707

Maryland
Maryland Department of Human
  Resources
410-767-7758

Massachusetts
Massachusetts Executive Office of
  Health and Human Services
  (EOHHS)—Department of Social
  Services
617-748-2353

Michigan
Michigan Department of Human
  Services
517-373-7394

Minnesota
Minnesota Department of Human
  Services
651-297-3933

Mississippi
Mississippi Department of Human
  Services
601-359-9662

Missouri
Missouri Department of Social
  Services
573-751-3770

Montana
Montana Department of Public
  Health and Human Services
406-444-2596

Nebraska
Nebraska Health and Human
  Services System
402-471-9108

(continued)

Nevada
Nevada Department of Human
  Resources
775-684-0505

New Hampshire
New Hampshire Department of
  Health and Human Services
603-271-4957

New Jersey
New Jersey Department of Human
  Services
609-292-3703

New Mexico
New Mexico Human Services
  Department
505-827-6345

New York
Office of Children and Family
  Services
518-473-7793

North Carolina
North Carolina Department of
  Health and Human Services
919-733-9190

North Dakota
North Dakota Department of
  Human Services
701-328-4933

Ohio
Ohio Department of Job and
  Family Services
614-466-6650

Oklahoma
Oklahoma Department of Human
  Services
405-521-3027

Oregon
Oregon Department of Human
  Services
503-945-5922

Pennsylvania
Pennsylvania Department of Public
  Welfare
717-787-4592

Rhode Island
Rhode Island Department of Human
  Services
401-462-6260

South Carolina
South Carolina Department of
  Health and Human Services
803-898-2865

South Dakota
South Dakota Department of
  Social Services
605-773-3165

Tennessee
Tennessee Department of Human
  Services
615-311-4287

Texas
Texas Health and Human Services
  Commission
877-787-8999 (Program Eligibility Verification)

Utah
Utah Department of Human Services
801-538-3991

Vermont
Vermont Agency of Human Services
802-241-2220

Virginia
Virginia Department of Social
  Services
804-726-7105

Washington
Washington Department of Social
  and Health Services
360-902-7800

West Virginia
West Virginia Department of
  Health and Human Resources
304-558-7899

Wisconsin
Wisconsin Department of Health
  and Family Services
608-266-1683

Wyoming
Wyoming Department of Family
  Services
307-777-7561

(Source: American Public Human Services Association)

State Child Care and Development Programs

Alabama

Child Care Subsidy Program
Alabama Department of
    Human Resources
Child Care Services Division
50 Ripley Street
Montgomery, AL 36130
334-242-9513

Alaska

**Alaska Department of Health
    and Social Services**
Division of Public Assistance
Child Care Program Office
619 East Ship Creek
Suite 230
Anchorage, AK 99501
907-269-4500

Arizona

**Arizona Department of
    Economic Security**
Child Care Administration
1789 West Jefferson
Suite 801A
Phoenix, AZ 85007
602-542-4248

Arkansas

Division of Child Care
Arkansas Department of
    Human Services
P.O. Box 1437
Slot S145
Little Rock, AR 72203
800-445-3316

California

**California State Department of
    Education**
Child Development Office
Policy, Program, and
    Legislation Unit
1430 N Street
Sacramento, CA 95814
916-322-6233

Colorado

**Colorado Department of
    Human Services**
Division of Child Care
1575 Sherman Street
Denver, CO 80203-1714
303-866-5958

Connecticut

**Connecticut Department of
    Social Services**
Child Care Team
25 Sigourney Street
Hartford, CT 06106-5033
860-424-5006

Delaware

**Delaware Department of
 Health & Social Services**
Lewis Building B
Herman Halloway Campus
1901 North DuPont Highway
New Castle, DE 19720-1100
302-255-9500

District of Columbia

**D.C. Department of Human
 Services**
Office of Early Childhood
 Development
717 14th Street NW
Suite 1200 #730
Washington, DC 20005
202-727-1839

Florida

**Florida Partnership for School
 Readiness**
600 South Calhoun Street
P.O Box 7416
Suite 251
Tallahassee, FL 32314-7416
850-922-4200

Georgia

**Georgia Department of
 Human Resources**
Child Care and Parent Services
 Section
Two Peachtree Street, N.W.
Suite 29-213
Atlanta, GA 30303-3142
404-657-3489

Hawaii

**Hawaii Department of
 Human Services**
Benefit, Employment, and
 Support Services Division
820 Mililani Street
Suite 606
Honolulu, HI 96813-2936
808-586-7050

Idaho

**Idaho Department of Health
 and Welfare**
Division of Welfare
P.O. Box 83720
Boise, ID 83720-0036
208-334-5818

(continued)

Illinois

**Illinois Department of
Human Services**
Office of Child Care and
Family Services
400 West Lawrence Street
Springfield, IL 62762
217-785-2559

Indiana

**Indiana Family and Social
Services Administration**
Division of Family and Children
Bureau of Child Development
402 West Washington Street
Room W386
Indianapolis, IN 46204
317-232-1144

Iowa

**Iowa Department of
Human Services**
Division of Adult, Children, and
Family Services
Hoover State Office Building
5th Floor
Des Moines, IA 50319-0114
515-281-5688

Kansas

Child Care Subsidy Agency
Kansas Department of Social
and Rehabilitation Services
Docking State Office Building
Room 681W
915 S.W. Harrison
Topeka, KS 66612
785-296-0159

Kentucky

**Kentucky Cabinet for Families
and Children**
Department of Community
Based Services
Division of Child Care
275 East Main Street
3C-F
Frankfort, KY 40621
502-564-2524

Louisiana

Child Care Assistance Program
Louisiana Department of
Social Services
Office of Family Support
Program Policy Section
438 Main Street
P.O. Box 94065
Baton Rouge, LA 70804-9065
225-342-4055

Maine

Maine Department of
Human Services
Office of Child Care and
Head Start
11 State House Station
221 State Street
Augusta, ME 04333-0011
207-287-5060

Maryland

Maryland Department of
Human Resources
Child Care Administration
311 West Saratoga Street
1st Floor
Baltimore, MD 21201
410-767-7128

Massachusetts

Massachusetts Office of
Child Care Services
600 Washington Street
Suite 6100
Boston, MA 02111
617-988-6600

Michigan

Michigan Family Independence
Agency
Child Development and
Care Division
235 South Grand Avenue
Suite 1302
P.O. Box 30037
Lansing, MI 48909-7537
517-373-2035

Minnesota

Minnesota Department of
Human Services
Transition to Economic Stability
444 Lafayette Road
Roseville, MN 55155-3834
651-284-4203

Mississippi

Mississippi Department of
Human Services
Office for Children and Youth
750 North State Street
Jackson, MS 39205-0352
601-359-4555

Missouri

Children's Division, Early
Childhood and
Prevention Services
P.O. Box 88
Jefferson City, MO 65103-0088
573-522-1385

(continued)

Montana

Montana Department of Public
Health and Human
Services
Human and Community
Services Division
Early Childhood Services
Bureau
P.O. Box 202952
Helena, MT 59620-2952
406-444-1828

Nebraska

Nebraska Department of
Health and Human
Services
Child Care
P.O. Box 95044
Lincoln, NE 68509-5044
402-471-9434

Nevada

Nevada Department of Human
Resources
Welfare Division
1470 East College Parkway
Carson City, NV 89706
775-684-0630

New Hampshire

New Hampshire Department of
Health and Human
Services
Division for Children, Youth,
and Families
Child Development Bureau
129 Pleasant Street
Concord, NH 03301-3857
603-271-8153

New Jersey

New Jersey Department of
Human Services
Division of Family Development
Child Care Operations
P.O. Box 716
Trenton, NJ 08625-0716
609-588-2163

New Mexico

New Mexico Department of
Children, Youth, and
Families
Child Care Services Bureau
P.O. Drawer 5160
PERA Building
Room 111
Santa Fe, NM 87502-5160
505-827-7499

New York
New York State Department of Family Assistance
Office of Children and
Family Services
Bureau of Early Childhood
Services
Capital View Office Park
52 Washington Street
Rensslaer, NY 12144-2796
518-474-9324

North Carolina
North Carolina Department of Health and Human Services
Division of Child Development
2201 Mail Service Center
Raleigh, NC 27699-2201
919-662-4543

North Dakota
North Dakota Department of Human Services
Economic Assistance Policy
Division
600 East Boulevard Avenue
Department 325
Bismarck, ND 58505-0250
701-328-2310

Ohio
Ohio Department of Job and Family Services
Bureau of Child Care and
Development
30 East Main Street
3rd Floor
Columbus, OH 43215-3414
614-466-1043

Oklahoma
Oklahoma Department of Human Services
Division of Child Care
Sequoyah Memorial Office
Building
2400 North Lincoln Boulevard
P.O. Box 25352
Oklahoma City, OK 73125
405-521-3931

Oregon
Oregon Department of Human Services
Child Care Division
500 Summer Street N.E. E62
Salem, OR 97301-1067
503-945-5651

(continued)

Pennsylvania

Pennsylvania Department of Public Welfare

Bureau of Child Day Care Services

Office of Children, Youth, and Families

Health and Welfare Building

Room 131

P.O. Box 2675

Harrisburg, PA 17105-2675

717-787-8691

Rhode Island

Rhode Island Department of Human Services

Office of Child Care

Louis Pasteur Building #57

600 New London Avenue

Cranston, RI 02920

401-462-3415

South Carolina

South Carolina Department of Health and Human Services

Bureau of Community Services

P.O. Box 8206

Columbia, SC 29202-8206

803-898-2570

South Dakota

South Dakota Department of Social Services

Child Care Services

700 Governors Drive

Pierre, SD 57501-2291

605-773-4766

Tennessee

Tennessee Department of Human Services

Citizens Plaza

14th Floor

400 Deaderick Street

Nashville, TN 37248-9600

615-313-4770

Texas

Texas Workforce Commission

Child Care Services

101 East 15th Street

Room 440-T

Austin, TX 78778-0001

512-936-0474

Utah

Utah Department of Workforce Services

Office of Child Care

140 East 300 South

Salt Lake City, UT 84111

801-526-4340

Vermont

Vermont Department for Children and Families
Child Developmental Division
103 South Main Street
2 North
Waterbury, VT 05671-2901
802-241-3110

Virginia

Virginia Department of Social Services
Child Day Care
7 North 8th Street
Richmond, VA 23219
804-726-7632

Washington

Washington Department of Social and Health Services
Economic Services Administration
Division of Child Care and Early Learning
P.O. Box 45480
Olympia, WA 98504-5480
360-725-4665

West Virginia

West Virginia Department of Health and Human Resources
Bureau for Children and Families
Office of Children and Family Policy
Division of Early Care and Education
350 Capital Street
B18
Charleston, WV 25301-3700
304-558-1885

Wisconsin

Wisconsin Department of Workforce Development
Child Care Section
201 East Washington Avenue
Room G-100
P.O. Box 7972
Madison, WI 53707-7972
888-713-KIDS

Wyoming

Wyoming Department of Family Services
Hathaway Building
Room 344
2300 Capitol Avenue
Cheyenne, WY 82002-0490
307-777-6848

(Source: United States Department of Health and Human Services, Administration for Children and Families)

Chapter 17

Employer Assistance

Depending on the size of the company you work for, your employer may provide assistance in your quest for childcare. Start with your employer's human resources department, if there is one; otherwise, try talking to your office manager. If your company does not offer childcare-related benefits to its employees, you might be able to convince your employer that it is in the best interests of the company to do so.

Childcare benefits offered by employers serve as an excellent recruitment tool for qualified employees. Moreover, once hired, employees who are able to take advantage of employer childcare benefits are less likely to miss work and are more likely to remain with the company. If you make a request for childcare assistance to your office manager or human resources director, pitch it in terms of how it will actually increase profits for the company. The company will gain by reducing the costs of having to recruit new employees and retain current ones, as well as the costs of lower productivity from employees with outside childcare issues that must be tended to.

Employer assistance may take one of several different forms. Some types of assistance are more direct than others. Some companies might offer cash to defray childcare expenses. In other cases, a company may have an arrangement with an area day care provider to give discounted rates to company employees. The provider benefits by having a steady source of clients. Still others might set up a flexible spending account program, also known as a *Dependent Care Assistance Plan* (DCAP), which allows employees to use pretax income to pay for childcare costs. This means that the money that goes to pay the day care provider does not have income taxes taken out first. This can result in a substantial savings to working parents.

If you receive a subsidy from your employer or if your employer offers flexible spending accounts to its employees, there may be certain tax consequences for you. In particular, your ability to claim the federal Child and Dependent Care Expenses Credit may be affected. If subsidies or DCAPs are options at your workplace, you will have to consider carefully whether the financial benefits to you are greater than the tax benefits to which you may be entitled.

On-Site Day Care

Even if your company historically has not been helpful with employees' childcare issues, you may be in a position to convince the powers-that-be that it is in their interest to make day care assistance a priority. Employee productivity is likely to increase when a company offers on-site or near-site childcare. This is due to great reductions in sick leave or vacation days taken by employees who have day care issues, such as a sitter not showing up for work.

After pointing out the benefits to the company's employees from having on-site childcare, you could try bringing the *Employer-Provided Child Care Credit* to your employer's attention. This is a tax credit recently passed by Congress. It allows the employer a credit of 25% of the employer's qualified childcare expenses. If applicable, the employer is also entitled to a credit of 10% of the employer's qualified childcare referral costs. *Qualified costs* include expenses of building or operating a childcare facility, training childcare employees, and contracting with an outside day care facility to provide childcare to the company's employees. The total credit for the employer may not exceed $150,000 per year.

From the Expert

Research has shown that employee turnover can be reduced by as much as 500% if employer-sponsored childcare is available.

Dependent Care Assistance Plans

Dependent Care Assistance Plans (DCAP), also known as *flexible spending accounts*, provide an indirect way for employers to help working parents with childcare costs. With a DCAP, the employee may elect to have a certain amount of pretax income taken out of the employee's pay to pay childcare expenses. The employer deducts the money from the employee's wages and sets it aside in the flexible spending account. Periodically, the employee submits proof of payments made to the childcare provider and is reimbursed from the account. Because the DCAP funds are deducted from the employee's wages before taxes, the savings to the employee may be substantial. The employee may set aside up to $5,000 per year in a flexible spending account.

The downside to flexible spending accounts is that if you do not use all the money in the account each year, you will forfeit the funds and they are returned to your employer. For example, if you overestimate the amount you actually will require for childcare during the plan year, or if you cut back your hours and no longer need to pay full-time rates for day care, you could find yourself out of a good deal of money.

There is another consideration for those who have the option of paying into a flexible spending account—you may not claim a federal Child and Dependent Care Expenses Credit for childcare expenses that you have paid for out of a flexible spending account. In other words, if you have the full $5,000 invested in a DCAP and you spend $6,500 for childcare during the year, you can claim only the $1,500 over the amount that came from your DCAP for the tax credit. This is the case even if you would be eligible for the full $3,000 credit if you did not have the option of a flexible spending account.

Subsidies

Subsidies are payments made by the company to help defray the employee's childcare costs. The payments might be made to the employee, or the company could make the payments directly to the childcare facility. As with an employer-provided DCAP, the difference is in the amount of the Child and Dependent Care Expenses Credit that the employee is entitled to claim on his or her income tax return. The Child and Dependent Care Expenses credit may be taken only for the childcare costs you actually paid. If your employer paid the caregiver on your behalf, those payments are not eligible for a credit against *your* tax liability. Your employer, however, can deduct payments made to a childcare provider for the benefit of the company's employees as a business expense. Whatever subsidy your employer may offer for childcare, be aware that it is considered a benefit that is taxable as income under the Internal Revenue Code.

You may claim a credit of as much as 35% of your childcare expenses. This means that the amount of the credit, whatever it may be, is applied against your tax liability dollar for dollar. In other words, the credit reduces the actual amount of tax owed. For example, if you owe $10,000 in income tax, and then claim a $2,000 Child and Dependent Care Expenses credit, your tax liability is reduced by that amount (to $8,000). (The Child and Dependent Care Expenses Credit is discussed in greater detail in Chapter 16.)

Section VI

Your Child's Well-Being in the Childcare Setting

You have analyzed the pros and cons of childcare, made the decision to place your child in a day care situation, done your research, located and evaluated a caregiver, and figured out how to cover the costs. Now it is time to help your child become acclimated to this new environment, and more importantly, to ensure that he or she feels secure when away from you.

Once your child is comfortable with the childcare arrangement, you will want to make sure he or she continues to grow socially and emotionally while in the care of the provider. Developing a good rapport with the caregiver will benefit your child. By keeping lines of communication open, you can team up with the caregiver to exchange information about and deal with any issues that may arise regarding your child's development.

Chapter 18

Helping Your Child Adjust

Depending upon your family situation, your child may have no trouble at all getting used to a new childcare situation. On the other hand—particularly if he or she is a certain age and has been home with you as the primary caregiver for the past few years—going to a new location or having a new caregiver in the home all day may prove to be a difficult transition. The good news is that most children do eventually make peace with the new order. If you did not ask the childcare provider during your interview how she handles children with separation anxiety, be sure to do so before the first day your child is in day care. In addition, there are steps that you can take to facilitate the change in routine and ensure your child is comfortable with the different setting.

Out-of-Home Care

Enrolling a child in a day care center or family day care presents a whole set of potential adjustment problems. Not only is the child with a new caregiver, he or she is in an entirely new environment. The more time he or she has to get used to the idea *before* going to day care for the first time, the smoother the transition is likely to be.

One of the best ways to put your child at ease prior to starting day care is to have him or her visit the facility or family day care home, preferably more than once, for short visits. He or she can interact with the primary caregiver at the facility, as well as with the other children that will be in his or her room, or not interact at all. It may take some time before your child is ready to participate with his or her classmates, and that is all right. Your job is to be supportive of your child and not push him or her into playing with or talking to others if he or she is not yet comfortable doing so.

Some experts suggest reading books with your child about going to day care before the first day arrives. One children's book dealing with separation anxiety is *Benjamin Comes Back*, by Amy Brandt and Janice Lee Porter (Redleaf Press, 1999). Both before and after reading together, talk about your child's feelings. Always be reassuring, explain why this arrangement is going to be good for him or her (he or she will make friends, get to play, etc.), and above all, remain positive. Your child is likely to adopt your outlook. If you have a bad attitude about the child-care situation or your return to work, chances are good that he or she will feel the same.

Another way to ease this big change in your child's life is to get him or her on an adequate sleep schedule at least several days, if not weeks, before the first time at day care, if he or she is not already on one. Grade-school-aged children typically need at least 10 or 11 hours of sleep every night; toddlers and preschoolers need even more. Determine how much time you and your child will need to unhurriedly prepare to leave each morning, and make that your child's wake-up time. Then count back-wards from that time, 10, 11, or 12 hours, depending on your child's age and sleep pattern, and make that bedtime. Then keep to that schedule. A regular bedtime every night will help give a sense of security to a child in transition.

Try to spend a few minutes with your child when putting him or her to bed. Sing to him or her, read a book, or just talk (or let him or her talk). Not only will these become cherished moments for both of you, but the dependability of the routine will help him or her deal with feelings of uncertainty about going to day care.

When packing up for day care either the night before or the morning of the first day, you could try having him or her pick out a special item to bring. Be sure to check with the day care director first, to see if there are items they will not allow. A good facility will have space to store this belonging, and should not have a problem with him or her bringing a blanket or a toy that does not pose a hazard to others. If there is a good reason for not letting him or her bring an item, let him or her pick out a picture — or better yet, help him or her make a small photo album or scrapbook — that he or she can look at during the day. Your child may even come up with his or her own ideas for making the first day more enjoyable.

The transition to the new childcare setting may go more smoothly if you can take it in small steps. If possible, consider bringing your child in for an hour or two the first time. Of course, if you are beginning a new job and cannot take time off, staying in the day care center or home with your child will not be an option. One way around this would be to go into the facility or home an hour earlier than you normally would for the first several days, to give your child time to become accustomed to the surroundings. If you do this, however, you will want to move bedtime up an hour as well, so that your child still gets the necessary amount of sleep.

On the big day, when it is time to leave your child with the caregiver and make your way to work, reassure him or her that you will return at a specific time (such as after lunch, after naptime, or some other time that your child will understand). Try, with the caregiver's help, to get him or her interested in an activity. Then you should leave. He or she may show some distress, and it is perfectly all right to give your child a big hug, but it also may be necessary to be firm in explaining that you have to leave. If he or she remains resistant to your leaving, the caregiver should take over and allow you to go. Of course, you can and should contact the childcare provider at least once during the course of the day to see how your child is progressing.

A pattern of separation anxiety may repeat for more than a week or two. It is important not to react strongly to your child's anxiety by becoming impatient with him or her, or by showing that his or her behavior is upsetting you. Keep communicating with the childcare provider to see if your child remains agitated for a good part of the day or if the tears dry up shortly after you leave. If the situation does not seem to resolve itself quickly, and the pattern continues for more than a couple of weeks, it will be necessary to examine the childcare setting to see if there is more than just separation anxiety.

> **From the Expert**
>
> If a pattern of separation anxiety repeats for more than a week or two, it could be that there is something about this particular day care that simply is not working for your child, and perhaps it might be time to reconsider the arrangement.

In some cases, it is not your leaving the day care facility that is traumatic for your child, but simply arriving at the center or home with your child triggers the distress. Once a tantrum becomes a regular morning activity, it may be a difficult habit to break. If your child acts out in your presence but calms down once you leave, one possible answer might be to have someone else take your child to day care for several days. Most parents are familiar with the phenomenon of the child who is a little angel for everyone but his or her own mom or dad. Having an third party drop your child off (if you have a close friend or relative who can do this for you) may help to cut off the custom of throwing a fit at the day care door.

Even if your child is adjusting fantastically to the new childcare situation, your continued involvement in his or her day, whenever possible, will help to keep him or her happy and secure at the center or family care home. If your childcare is close to work, perhaps you can have lunch with him or her on the same day or days during the week. Even if it is hard to visit on a regular basis, visiting periodically to bring a special snack to your child or read a book to the class will reinforce that you have not forgotten about him or her just because you are apart.

In-Home Care

The advantage in-home childcare has over day care centers and family day care is the familiarity of the surroundings for your child. He or she will be able to play in his or her own backyard during the day and will have his or her own toys around. Still, there may be some adjustment problems even if the childcare provider comes to your own house. There is bound to be a change in routine, or differences between your parenting style and your nanny's manner of childrearing, that might unsettle your child.

The best way to avoid these kinds of issues is to be sure that the nanny is thoroughly apprised of the customs and procedures your child knows. If possible, have the nanny come to your house for several days while you are still available to guide her thorough a typical day with your child. Show her the locations of first aid materials, toys and games, cleaning supplies, cooking utensils, and other items that she may need during the course of the day. Explain to her when you would like meals to be served and when children should be put down for naps. Go over limits that you would like enforced with regard to the use of televisions, telephones, and computer games. The better the nanny's understanding of your rules and expectations, the less confusion your child will have with a new caregiver.

As with out-of-home care, easing into the new situation slowly and having your child spend time with you and the nanny before leaving him or her alone in her care are both good ways to make the new childcare arrangement go smoothly. Take the nanny to your child's activities or school and introduce her to your child's teachers. Try some fun outings with the nanny and your child, such as a trip to the park or out to lunch, so your child will know that his or her life will not be disrupted too much by this new state of affairs.

Again, if you work near your home, lunch visits are a good way to keep in touch with your child throughout the day. If you are not close to home, it is easier to speak to your child by phone when he or she is at home than if he or she is at a large day care center. Depending on your agreement with the nanny, you may want to have her bring your child to your workplace from time to time during your lunch break. That is another advantage to in-home care.

If you have a live-in nanny or an au pair, the transition may be easier yet. With live-in help, your children literally have all day and night to become accustomed to having the caregiver around. Because an au pair is not an employee but a guest of the family and is likely to be young as well, your child may not see her as a caregiver or authority figure, but more of a playmate. As has been discussed already, however, this could end up being a positive or a negative.

Chapter 19

Maintaining a Good Relationship with the Childcare Provider

No matter if you have outside or in-home childcare, one of the best things you can do for your child is to keep up a good association with the childcare provider. The most crucial element of a good relationship is communication. It goes without saying that you should feel comfortable bringing any of your concerns relating to your child's care to the day care provider. Remember, however, that it is just as important that the caregiver be at ease bringing up her childcare-related issues to you.

The best way to make your childcare provider comfortable with you is to treat her with respect. Always speak politely to her, not only for her benefit, but for your child's as well. You are the example that your child is most likely to follow as he or she grows up. Similarly, you should not condescend the caregiver. Even a nanny—who is technically an employee of yours—should be treated as an important helper in your job of raising your child.

You also should show a great deal of interest in your child's progress in the day care setting. If the day care center or family day care provider does not give you a regular, written report on your child's day or week in the facility, ask for one.

Out-of-Home Caregivers

One advantage of an outside caregiver over a nanny is that you will not have to worry about the caregiver leaving for another family. Still, when you leave your child with someone else for a large part of the day, you do want to be sure that you have a good rapport with her. Your child's interests are best served when all of those who have responsibility for his or her well-being can speak freely about his or her care and development.

Day care center staff are typically overworked and underpaid. Like many teachers, early childhood workers often purchase supplies for their classrooms out of their own pockets. Family day care is almost always a small-budget operation. Donating gently used toys or other items that your family no longer needs and that can be used in your child's day care is a great way to earn you the appreciation of the caregiver. If you do not have the means to donate anything, see if you can spend some time volunteering in the facility. Perhaps you can offer to lead a craft or play a game with some of the children. If the only time you have available is at the end of the day when you come to pick up your own child, offer to help straighten up your child's classroom. Taking some of the work off the hands of the caregivers is likely to win you undying gratitude. Even if you have no extra time to spend in the room, you could ask if they have any work that you can bring home to help out, such as typing up the day care center's newsletter or repairing broken toys.

In-Home Caregivers

It may be necessary to treat the in-home caregiver more delicately than it would be for the day care center or family day care staff. If the nanny or au pair becomes unhappy with her situation as the childcare provider in your home, she may simply leave. A good nanny or au pair is tough to find. If you have a good one, you will want to do all you can to hang on to her.

Some childcare experts suggest that a weekly or other regular parent/nanny conference be held from the beginning of the employment or au pair relationship, so that it is a habit right away rather than something you do not bother with until there is an actual problem.

Do not look at these conferences as merely a way for you to air your grievances or correct what you may see as flaws in your nanny's handling of various situations. They are also an invaluable way for you to get another perspective on your child's development. Not only might your nanny have good parenting ideas that you may not have thought of, but she just might observe things about your child that either you have never noticed or your child has never shown you. For example, your nanny might bring out a talent or interest in your child that you would not have otherwise ever discovered. Weekly conferences should serve as a dialogue that assists you in your parenting duties by giving you a fresh perspective of your child.

In the same way that many out-of-home caregivers provide written reports on the progress of the children in their care, the nanny should be willing to give you a summary of your child's day or week while you were at work. One nanny organization recommends having the nanny keep a journal of your child's activities for you to review. It does not have to be lengthy—just a short journal entry each day or so to keep you up-to-date on what your child is doing. This would be a good topic to discuss with potential nannies during the hiring process, so they are not taken by surprise when you add this task to their duties after they have been hired.

Sticking to the terms of your employment contract with the nanny is one of the best ways to avoid disagreements with her as time goes on. If you have an agreement to employ the nanny for 45 hours of childcare per week, with overtime on an as-needed basis, do not take advantage of the nanny by regularly asking her to work overtime (unless she asked for additional work hours). Even if you are paying her time-and-a-half for the extra work, at some point her time will be worth more to her than the additional pay. She may become resentful if you repeatedly come in later than expected.

Another point of difficulty can be raised when the nanny gives you a bad report about your child's behavior. If you do not follow through by giving your child a consequence for the misbehavior, your child may come to understand that the nanny's reports to you have no undesirable result for him or her. Not only will this teach your child that he or she can act as he or she pleases when in the nanny's care, it will undermine the nanny's position in your household. This may offend the nanny as well as render her ineffectual.

> **From the Expert**
>
> If your nanny feels that she is respected, and that her opinions and input are valuable, she is more likely to respond in a positive manner when you bring differences of opinion to her attention.

If you are not certain that your nanny's version of events is accurate, by all means, investigate further. However, if you simply fail to follow up on her report with a repercussion for your child, you may be sowing the seeds for a failed relationship with your nanny.

Using common sense in dealing with your nanny will go a long way toward keeping you both happy with the caregiver relationship. There are bound to be differences of opinion with her from time to time. It is not crucial that you are in agreement at all times. What is most important for the stability of your childcare arrangement over the long term is the manner in which you deal with potential conflicts when they arise. Your tone and the attitude that you take when discussing problems with your nanny will be what determines how your family's relationship with her continues in the future.

Handling Difficulties in the Childcare Relationship

Hopefully, all of your hard work and research will lead you to a beneficial childcare arrangement in which your child thrives. From time to time, though, problems can arise with the childcare provider. Whether the issue is the caregiver, another child, or your own child's behavior, a satisfactory resolution depends on the seriousness of the problem and the willingness of both the caregiver and the parents to work together for the best interest of your child. Of course, if his or her well-being is at stake, it will be necessary to end the relationship with the provider and make another arrangement for your child's care. Moreover, depending upon the severity of the situation, you may even want to get the proper authorities involved.

If you do decide to end your family's relationship with the caregiver, for whatever reason, you should know how to deal with the situation in a manner that makes the transition as easy as possible for your family. If you have live-in help, there will be extra considerations involved because the caregiver will have to actually pack up and move out of your household.

You also need to be especially sensitive to the effect the end of the childcare relationship has on your child. He or she may have become attached to the caregiver and will have to adjust to a new situation. There are steps you can take to help your child during this time of change.

Chapter 20

Monitoring the Childcare Situation

Whether or not your child seems comfortable with your childcare arrangement, it is necessary to keep tabs on the situation to ensure that it continues to be satisfactory. If your child is old enough to express him- or herself and relate things that have happened during the course of the day, talking to him or her usually is the best way to keep track of his or her progress in day care. However, if your child is too young to speak, or if you are not confident that he or she would be forthcoming about a problem, there are other ways to monitor the quality of the care he or she is receiving.

Visits to the Childcare Facility

A very effective way to oversee how your child is doing in day care is to maintain a presence there by making frequent visits. While scheduled visits are useful, unexpected drop-ins may give you a more realistic view of how your child's day care situation is working on a day-to-day basis. This is true whether you use in-home or outside childcare.

For some, this will not be such an easy proposition, because the day care facility may be located close to home but far from work.

You do not need to make each visit as though you are looking for a potential problem in the day care setting. Come in on a scheduled visit with a craft for your child's class or a book to read. If you are making a surprise visit, use the opportunity to give your child a big hug and let him or her know that you just wanted to see how he or she was doing. If your child is having problems adjusting to a new setting, you may wish to size things up from afar. If possible, observe your child through a classroom door or from down the hall.

A surprise visit to a family day care home may be a bit more difficult. Generally, there will not be any reception area—you will be trying to gain entrance into a private home. Of course, if you are discouraged by the day care provider from visiting at any time, you should consider whether this is the best situation for your child. Even if the caregiver has a reason for limiting visits by parents, such as avoiding disruption to the children's routine, such a policy is questionable.

Networking with Other Families

Particularly if you work far from the childcare, it makes good sense to get to know other families who may be able to take a look at your childcare arrangement while you are not available. If your child has a nanny or au pair, you might enlist the help of neighbors, or perhaps the families of your child's playmates, to occasionally check in at your house to see how things are going. If you are using a family day care or center, getting to know the parents of other children at the facility may be helpful.

To meet other day care families, be on the alert for things you might have in common with another family. If you are dropping off an infant around the same time another parent is leaving a baby of about the same age, try striking up a conversation with the parent about what your children may have in common—age, milestones, and so on.

Nanny Cams

Video surveillance systems have become more popular in the last decade as a means to keep tabs on children in in-home childcare settings. Hidden cameras can now be made that fit into any number of everyday household items.

Although the name suggests otherwise, the nanny cam can be used for more than simply spying on your in-home caregiver. In fact, some day care centers now have their own secure surveillance systems, which can be accessed by parents during the day via the Internet. Using their computers at work, parents can view their child's room, activity rooms, or other areas.

The downside to surveillance in a day care center is the possibility that the video stream may be seen by unauthorized people. It is possible that video may be intercepted by third parties who have specialized electronic equipment for that purpose, or another parent may

> **From the Expert**
>
> To gain entry to the website, parents must have a password that the center provides. Otherwise, the video signal is scrambled, so not just anyone can observe your child.

hand out the security password to a nonapproved person. To try to cut down on this potential problem, day care centers usually change and redistribute the password fairly often. In addition, these systems are typically set up so they do not record the goings-on at the center, but merely transmit for at-the-moment viewing. This way, there is no permanent image of the children.

Surveillance systems are an especially useful tool for parents whose work takes them far from the day care site. They also benefit the childcare provider, because they make the day care facility more attractive to potential clients. Surveillance can assist the parent/childcare provider relationship in general by helping to clear up any misunderstandings over the events of a particular day. For example, a child may be telling his or her parents that other children are bullying him or her at day care, when it is actually the child him- or herself who is the aggressor. Parents who are reluctant to assign any blame to their own children may be more likely to accept the reality of the situation if they can see it for themselves.

If you do have in-home childcare, nanny cams can help you track your child's daily routine with the caregiver. A miniature camera by itself can cost less than $100; however, the cost can rise fairly rapidly if you add accessories. If the camera comes hidden in another object, it is more likely to start in the $200 range. The price goes up if you add wireless technology, monitors, recording equipment, and so on. If you wish to have the video transmitted by way of the Internet, you probably will have a nominal monthly charge for the service. Otherwise, you may need to purchase recording equipment so you can tape the activity for later viewing.

One thing you will need to decide is whether you will let your nanny or au pair know that she is being watched. If you choose not to tell her that you have a surveillance system and she finds out on her own, she will probably see the situation as a lack of trust on your part. This may seriously affect her relationship with your family. Of course, if you actually do not trust her, she probably should not be your childcare provider in the first place. Perhaps a reasonable solution might be to tell her that you have a camera in place, but it is for the purpose of staying connected with your child while you are at work.

If you do decide to secretly record, you need to check the laws of your state regarding the extent to which taping is legal. As a general rule, videotaping by hidden camera, without audio, is allowed in all states. Some states prohibit recording of sound. Be sure to seek legal advice in this area before purchasing recording equipment.

Chapter 21

Resolving Problems with the Caregiver

It is rare indeed for a parent/caregiver relationship to go so smoothly that there never is a difference of opinion or other difficulty between the parties. If there is an issue involving actual harm to your child, *working things out* is not an option you will want to pursue. On the other hand, less serious problems might be able to be resolved. This would avoid having to go through the process of finding childcare all over again. If you wish to continue the association with your childcare provider, you will want to approach the problem in a firm and direct—yet diplomatic—way. (Situations of child abuse or other harmful circumstances involving your caregiver are discussed in Chapter 22.)

Philosophical Differences

Hopefully you have found a provider who sees eye-to-eye with you in most areas of childcare. However, very few people have identical ideas about how children should be raised. When a difference in opinion as to your child's care arises, the first thing you should do is decide how significant the disagreement is. If the issue is, for example, that the caregiver allows your child to watch too much television, simply requesting a cutback may be all you need to do. On the other hand, if you feel she is placing your child in timeouts inappropriately too often, or for too long, more work may be required to resolve the problem.

If you have a complaint with the care that your child is receiving, the most important thing to remember is to remain calm and bring your concerns to the attention of the caregiver in a considerate manner. This means speaking in a courteous tone and relating your concerns without being accusatory. Listen to what the caregiver has to say. She may have a good reason for what she is doing, or there may be circumstances of which you are not aware. If possible, speak with the caregiver when there are no other parents or children around. If she is busy caring for children, she may not be able to have a productive discussion with you. If you try to talk to her when other parents are present, she may become defensive.

Even though you are the final decision-maker when it comes to your child, try to take into account the training and background your caregiver has. Some childcare workers have years of education and experience to help them in their profession. They may be trying to use techniques in caring for your child that have worked with many other children in the past. Try to keep an open mind. If you approach the situation as a partner with the caregiver, you both will be more likely to reach a solution that is in the best interest of your child.

When the Childcare Provider is Unreasonable or Unreliable

Another kind of problem can occur when the childcare provider is not willing to see your point of view, to respect your wishes with respect to the care of your child, or to show up for work in a timely fashion. These are tough situations that may prove less likely to be resolved.

When a childcare provider flatly refuses to do things your way, you need to examine the reasons why. First of all, ask her. You cannot make an informed decision about the future of your family's relationship with this caregiver if you do not know why she is taking a certain position. Then, consider your own reasons for disagreeing with her position. It is possible that this is an honest disagreement. If so, it is up to you whether it is a deal-breaker for your day care arrangement. On the other hand, it could be that your own rationale for taking a stand is not entirely defensible.

Example: Your family day care provider has begun screening off your child's crib at naptime because he has been having trouble settling down and is causing disruption for the older children. You believe that the child should not be placed in a separate area for naps. You feel that being isolated from the caregiver and the rest of the children causes him anxiety and keeps him from napping. The day care provider refuses to keep him in the main room because of the effect on the other children. She feels it will do him no harm to become used to sleeping alone, and she takes steps to comfort him while he is in the crib in order to help him fall asleep.

It is not unreasonable of the caregiver to handle this situation in this way, in light of the interests of the other children involved and her attempts to help the toddler adjust to the change in his napping environment. The parent may not like how the caregiver resolves issues, but should recognize the limitations a family day care provider may have in a case such as this. If the parents feel strongly enough about their position, they may end up having to make new childcare arrangements.

In the case of a day care center, issues may be easier to resolve. There will be a director on staff who can assist in mediating disagreements between parents and caregivers. Also, there is more day care staff who may have other problem-solving suggestions. It may be possible to move a child to another area of the facility where another staff member can be the primary caregiver for the child.

Unreliability is a particularly difficult problem to overcome. It is disruptive to you and your family when the caregiver does not show up, or in the case of a family day care, the caregiver is unable or unwilling to take your child for that day. Obviously, this problem is much less likely to occur in a day care center

> ### From the Expert
> Should unreasonableness or unreliability of your childcare provider become a problem that you do not believe you can resolve, you may wish to dissolve the relationship with the caregiver. (Termination of a day care provider is covered in Chapter 23.)

where there are many day care workers to cover for a sick or otherwise absent coworker, or with a live-in nanny or au pair.

If you have a live-out nanny, you should have a written agreement detailing how missed days are to be handled. (Nanny employment agreements are discussed in Chapter 9.) Typically, an agreement will give the nanny a certain number of sick days and vacation days, and any missed work beyond those limits are without pay. Unfortunately, the money is only part of the problem. Far worse for many parents is that they themselves often have to miss work when the nanny or family day care provider is unavailable.

If you have gone through a nanny agency to find your caregiver, it may be able to help you secure backup childcare. If you have found a nanny on your own or use a family day care provider, hopefully you have discussed backup care before placing your child with that provider. Otherwise, you should always have a plan in place for the unfortunate event that your childcare arrangement falls through. (Chapter 15 discusses backup childcare.)

Chapter 22

Harmful or Abusive Situations

Because you have done your homework before leaving your child with a caregiver for the first time, the chances of your child being placed in a dangerous childcare setting are minimal. At the same time, you do need to be continually aware of your child's day care environment in case circumstances change. Harmful situations are not limited to outright cases of child abuse. Neglect by a caregiver can prove to be just as dangerous to children as can allowing a hazardous condition to occur in the child's environment.

The best way to keep your child safe is to prevent a dangerous situation before it happens. This requires you to be vigilant by watching for signs of potential problems, communicating with the caregiver as well as your child, and being prepared to address immediately any issues about which you may be worried. This seems obvious, but oftentimes parents are hesitant to voice concerns over things they observe at the facility or new behaviors in their child they find disturbing. They do not want to be perceived as troublemakers, and they may fear their questioning of the caregiver will cause her to resent the entire family, with a negative effect being felt by their child. It is of the utmost importance, however, that you do not ignore signs of trouble in the childcare setting, even if the indications are little more than your own gut instincts. When you have a little voice in your head telling you that there is a problem, you need to investigate further.

If you are reluctant to speak with the caregiver about a problem situation, try first to phrase your concern in the form of a question. Present the situation using facts, not opinions (if possible), then ask the childcare provider why she thinks this problem exists. For example, you could say, "My child seems to be agitated in the mornings when we are in the car coming to day care. He never acted this way in the past. I am stumped— do you have any idea why he might be acting like this?" Gauge the caregiver's reaction. If she becomes defensive or is dismissive of your concerns, that does not by itself mean that there is a problem. It might, however, give you a reason to reconsider whether this is the best care arrangement for your child.

Preventing the Harmful Environment

Preventing a harmful environment can be summed up with one word— attention. Pay attention to your child; pay attention to the childcare provider; and, pay attention to the facility. You took a close look at the childcare environment before you decided to enroll your child, but your responsibility does not end there. Continued mindfulness of the conditions at your child's day care is crucial to keeping him or her safe.

Observing the facility on a daily basis at drop-off and pickup times is one way to monitor conditions there. If you and your spouse do not normally bring your child to day care yourselves, try to come in from time to time during the course of the day. Making periodic unscheduled visits can give you an idea of how the facility is run when the day care providers are not expecting company. If this is not possible because of the distance from the facility to your workplace, you can talk to other families with children at the facility to see that safety and care standards remain consistently high.

When your childcare provider is a nanny or au pair, asking a neighbor or relative to drop by on occasion can help you keep tabs on the situation. Installing a video surveillance system (*nanny cam*) in your home is another option. (The pros and cons of nanny cams are discussed in greater detail in Chapter 20.)

If childcare is provided in your home, you clearly have more control over the environment than if your child is cared for outside of the home.

There are a number of resources to help you ensure that your home is safe even when you are not there to supervise. The United States *Consumer Product Safety Commission* (CPSC), for example, provides information about household products that have been recalled due to safety hazards they may present. The CPSC may be reached at 301-504-7923 or online at **www.cpsc.gov**. *The National Resource Center for Health and Safety in Child Care* is another information source for parents and caregivers alike, with tips on subjects such as various child illnesses and conditions, administering medications, and health and dental check-ups. You can contact the National Resource Center at 800-598-5437, or view its website at **http://nrc.uchsc.edu**.

Avoiding Child Abuse in Childcare

It goes without saying that if you suspected that a potential childcare provider was a child abuser, you would not ever have allowed that person to care for your child. So how would you know if your child was a victim of abuse or neglect at the hands of a caregiver? It is important to recognize warning signs of neglect or abuse, in case any of them are manifesting themselves in your child. Of course, if your child is willing and able to tell you about any incidents that have occurred in the childcare setting, that will be the best evidence of an abusive or neglectful situation. Sometimes, however, children either are too young to comprehend or explain what has happened to them, or may actually have been intimidated by an abuser into silence. In these cases, it is up to the parents to investigate the possibility of mistreatment by the childcare provider.

Although any child abuse indicators may have another, perfectly innocuous explanation, be alert if any of the following occur or appear.

- The caregiver attempts to deter you from visiting whenever you wish.
- Your child, even after having time for adjustment to the childcare setting, is nervous, unhappy, or frightened when it comes time to leave for day care (or, if you use in-home care, when the caregiver arrives at your home).
- The caregiver does not greet your child in a warm or friendly manner (on a regular basis, that is—anyone can have an off day).

- The caregiver becomes defensive if you question her or raise issues to her about your child's care.
- The caregiver is hesitant to give you a recap of your child's activities during the day.
- Unexplained injuries appear on your child, especially if they occur more than once or if they appear near the buttocks or genital area.
- Your child is suddenly exhibiting changes in behavior or mood swings.
- Your child is acting out in inappropriate ways, such as exhibiting aggression where he or she never did before.
- Your child makes inappropriate statements, such as expressing a desire to kill people or talking about sexual topics or genitalia in an age-inappropriate manner.
- Your child is suddenly complaining of physical ailments.
- Your child has begun wetting the bed or having accidents during the day.
- Your child has begun showing fear during routine activities, such as taking a bath or undressing at bedtime.
- Your child is dirty or has a full diaper when you come to pick him up (again, this is bound to happen once in a while—it becomes a problem when it happens on a regular basis).

Not only should you be familiar with signs of abuse, you should be sure that your childcare provider recognizes them as well. If you did not do so before enrolling your child in day care, ask what child abuse prevention training the childcare provider has received and request a copy of the provider's written policies—particularly those relating to discipline. If your child is in a day care center, all staff should be alert to the possibility that other staff members may commit abusive acts. The staff should be visible to other staff members at all times while caring for the children for whom they are responsible.

If your child has suffered an injury in day care that is not readily explainable, or if repeat injuries have occurred, you should take your child to his pediatrician for a thorough examination. The physician is trained to recognize old injuries, and she may pick up on signs of additional injury that you have not noticed.

Addressing Abuse or Neglect

If you believe you have an abuse or neglect situation on your hands, whether it involves your own child or another child in the facility, you should report the incident immediately to the proper authorities. Child abuse hotline numbers for each state are listed starting on page 164. If the abuse concerns someone else's child, you will want to speak with those parents as soon as you possibly can, so they can take whatever action they see fit, including finding another childcare provider.

As soon as possible after compiling the evidence of abuse, document the incident to the best of your ability. Do not add commentary or fill in facts that you have not seen or heard yourself. Write down what is within your own personal knowledge. If you are basing your conclusion of abuse on something that somebody else told you, whether it was your child or another parent, have them make notes, if possible. Obviously, you will have to do the writing for a very young child, and sometimes another parent will decline to get involved. In those cases, note that you are reporting information that you have received on a second-hand basis.

Once you have made a report to the appropriate state agency, make a follow-up call to the agency after several days to be sure that someone is working on the case. Document each contact you have with the agency, including dates of calls and names of agency staff to whom you have spoken. Keep this information in your records, because you may need to refer to it at a later date, particularly if you decide to seek legal recourse against the childcare provider.

Child Abuse Hotline Telephone Numbers
(Listed by State)

Alabama
334-242-9500

Alaska
800-478-4444

Arizona
888-767-2445

Arkansas
800-482-5964

California
916-445-2771

Colorado
800-422-4453

Connecticut
800-842-2288

Delaware
800-292-9582

District of Columbia
877-671-7233

Florida
800-962-2873

Georgia
800-422-4453

Hawaii
800-422-4453

Idaho
800-926-2588

Illinois
800-252-2873

Indiana
800-800-5556

Iowa
800-362-2178

Kansas
800-922-5330

Kentucky
800-752-6200

Louisiana
225-342-6832

Maine
800-452-1999

Maryland
800-332-6347

Massachusetts
800-792-5200

Michigan
800-942-4357

Minnesota
651-291-0211

Mississippi
800-222-8000

Missouri
800-392-3738

Montana
866-820-5437

Nebraska
800-652-1999

Nevada
800-992-5757

New Hampshire
800-894-5533

New Jersey
800-792-8610

New Mexico
800-797-3260

New York
800-342-3720

North Carolina
800-422-4453

North Dakota
701-328-2316

Ohio
800-422-4453

Oklahoma
800-522-3511

Oregon
800-854-3508 ext. 2402

Pennsylvania
800-932-0313

Rhode Island
800-742-4453

South Carolina
803-898-7318

South Dakota
605-773-3227

Tennessee
877-237-0004

Texas
800-252-5400

Utah
800-678-9399

Vermont
800-649-5285

Virginia
800-552-7096

Washington
866-363-4276

West Virginia
800-352-6513

Wisconsin
608-266-3036

Wyoming
800-422-4453

*(Source: United States Department of Health and Human Services,
Administration for Children and Families)*

Whether an incident of abuse or neglect involves your own or another child, you will want to remove your child from the childcare facility immediately. If you have in-home care, the nanny will have to leave the premises at once. After you notify the proper office for reporting child abuse, you will want to contact the nanny's agency (if there is one), and tell the director what has happened and what steps you have taken. Document all contact between you and the nanny agency as well. Make notes of any conversations you have. Depending upon the severity of the abuse, you will want to keep records in case you decide to pursue legal action against the nanny or her agency.

Chapter 23

Terminating the Childcare Relationship

Any number of circumstances may cause a family to decide to end its relationship with the childcare provider. The decision may not be because of a problem with the relationship. The family may decide to relocate, or one of the parents may wish to quit the corporate rat race in order to stay home with the kids. Maybe the caregiver is moving home, getting married, or graduating from school. Whether the relationship with the caregiver ends on good terms or bad, the family should take steps to make the transition to life without the caregiver as smooth as possible for everyone.

Put It in Writing

Regardless of the type of childcare, when the parents wish to terminate the services of the provider, they should put the termination in writing. The form of the writing may depend upon the particular childcare arrangement and the circumstances surrounding the decision to terminate. Childcare arrangements that end on a positive note require less detail than relationships that are terminated for cause. If you are terminating the relationship due to misconduct, abuse, or negligence by the caregiver, you should state that in your notice.

If it is a matter of leaving a day care center due to a move to a new city, a simple paragraph giving notice of your child's last day at the center should suffice. However, be aware of notice policies that your childcare provider may have. Typically, centers require two to four weeks' advance notice of terminating a child's enrollment. The center may ask you to pay tuition up front (upon enrollment) to cover that notice period. If you remove your child from the facility before the expiration of the enrollment period, you will forfeit the payment.

Even if you have hired a nanny who never bothers to show up for her first day of work, you should send a written termination notice stating it is effective immediately. This will avoid the possibility of the nanny later claiming that any sort of payment or benefits are owed to her as your employee.

In-Home Care Terminations

Ending in-home care arrangements can prove to be a bit trickier, especially if the split is not amicable. With outside care, all you have to do is remove your child from the facility. An in-home caregiver is, to some degree, entrenched in your household, especially when the caregiver is a live-in one. Not only do you have to end the relationship, you have to be sure that the caregiver packs up and leaves. If you have relocated a nanny from out of state, or if you have an au pair from another country, you may even be obligated to contribute to the costs she incurs in returning home, such as airfare. If you go through an agency for your in-home childcare, be sure to find out exactly what your liability is regarding termination before the caregiver arrives.

When ending a live-in caregiver situation, you may not want to leave the nanny alone in your home once you have told her you are terminating her employment. For that reason, you should try to time the termination so that you are able to be home for several days to supervise her departure. If that is not possible, you could arrange for another person that you trust to be present in your home while the nanny gathers her belongings.

It is possible that your childcare provider will not have the means to return home or even to secure lodging right away. In such a case, you might make the departure go more smoothly if you offer to put her up in a local hotel for a night or two. Even if you do not feel the nanny deserves that consideration, it might prevent her causing a scene or other trouble. This will make your life easier, but more than anything, it will benefit your children if you can avoid conflict as much as possible.

Problems the In-Home Caregiver Can Create

There have been cases where disgruntled nannies have retaliated for being fired by notifying the state department of children's services or labor board—falsely—that the former employer either harassed the nanny or abused the children. One of the best ways to avoid the nightmare scenario of a child abuse accusation is to keep complete records. You will want to keep a log containing not only the nanny's job performance during the course of her employment, but also of any injuries that your child may have suffered during her employment. Include dates and names of anyone else who would have personal knowledge of any incidents, either of injury to your child or misconduct by the nanny. Put any complaint you may have about the nanny's performance in writing. If the nature of the complaint is serious enough that a repeat occurrence would cause you to fire the nanny, be sure to put the complaint in the form of a disciplinary warning. Give a copy of the warning to your nanny. Also, have her sign another copy with an acknowledgement that she has received the written warning.

Claims of Sexual Harassment

To keep safe from a charge of sexual harassment by the nanny, take great care to maintain your relationship with her on a professional level. Sometimes, especially with a live-in nanny or a working relationship in which the nanny is considered one of the family, the line between familiarity and impropriety can be a bit blurry.

In general, the federal laws that prohibit sexual harassment apply only to employers with at least 15 employees; therefore, they will not apply to a nanny situation. However, some states have human rights laws of their own that make essentially all employers liable for harassing conduct of a sexual nature. Examples of conduct that may amount to sexual harassment include: overt sexual advances; obscene comments; language or jokes (verbal or written); unwanted physical contact, such as grabbing, rubbing against, or other touching; personal questions of a sexual nature; and, the display of obscene or pornographic material in the work area of the employee.

State laws against sexual harassment usually also prohibit retaliation by an employer if the employee reports harassment to the proper state agency. Typical penalties for a finding of liability for sexual harassment are fines, restitution for lost wages or benefits, reinstatement if the employee has been wrongfully terminated, and punitive damages. The safe course of action, if you have any doubt, is to completely avoid the above types of behavior around the nanny.

Giving References

At some point after ending your professional relationship with the childcare provider, another family that is considering hiring her to care for their children may contact you. Even if your parting with the nanny was on good terms, it is possible that you had complaints with her job performance that you never addressed with her, or that you did bring to her attention but she never corrected. This situation might make it uncomfortable for you to give a glowing recommendation of her to another potential employer, even though you do not wish to speak poorly of her.

There is nothing wrong with stating your opinion of her abilities as a nanny. In fact, consider the situation from the other family's point of view. They are in the same boat that you were in when you were deciding who should care for your children. If there was an issue with her childcare capabilities, surely a family thinking about offering her a job would appreciate hearing about it. It is not necessary to present a laundry list of faults that you believe your nanny has. Simply make a general statement of what her professional shortcomings were and note that this is simply your opinion. Of course, if there were actual instances of misconduct on her part, then it would be most helpful to the potential employer if you related the circumstances surrounding the event.

Termination by the Childcare Provider

Sometimes it will be the caregiver who will end the relationship with the family. A nanny may decide to leave for a more desirable position. A family day care home may close because the owner decides to pursue a different business. Day care centers typically have a procedure for terminating a child's enrollment if the family's account is overdue for more than a certain period of time, such as fifteen or thirty days. Typically, they also will be able to expel a child who chronically misbehaves, or who poses a danger to other children or staff. Most day care providers will ask you at the outset to sign an agreement that you will abide by their policies. Usually, the policies will give them a wide-ranging ability to end the business relationship with your family upon giving sufficient notice.

The real issue if the childcare provider terminates you, therefore, is not whether they can do it, but whether you have a remedy if they do. Legally, of course, you cannot force a nanny or au pair to continue working for you. As for a day care facility, you could try to argue a cause of action for breach of contract, but unless you have suffered some real financial damages from the termination, you are likely to be out of luck. Most families whose childcare arrangement is terminated suffer inconvenience, at the very most.

Your Child's Reaction

Whatever your own feelings about the ending of your business relationship with the childcare provider, do not ignore the effect the termination may have on your child. Even if you dislike the nanny or day care worker, be careful not to underestimate how much she means to your child. In some cases, such as with an au pair, the length of the caregiver relationship is determined before employment even begins. You can help your child, from the beginning of the childcare relationship, to adjust to the eventual end of the caregiver's tenure. In other cases, the association may end abruptly. Either way, you should prepare your child for the day when your family and the caregiver part ways.

Of course, if the reason you are terminating the childcare provider is that your child does not like her, he or she likely will be happy to see her go, and you will have no adjustment issues. However, a child can become fond of a caregiver fairly quickly, and if this is the case in your family, you need to be sensitive to your child's attitude toward the termination. Not only could your child be saddened to see the nanny leave (or to be removed from the

> **From the Expert**
>
> Email, regular mail, and telephone communication with a past caregiver can help your child make peace with the end of the caregiver relationship.

outside day care setting, as the case may be), but he or she may actually come to feel insecure by the upheaval. He or she may believe that, since this person—a person he or she cared about—was taken from him or her so easily, other loved ones could be sent away as well.

Depending on your child's age and the circumstances of the caregiver's departure, you should try to explain to your child your reasons for ending the relationship. If your separation from the caregiver is friendly, see if she would be willing to keep up communication with your family. If she will remain in the area, perhaps you and your child can get together with her on occasion, at least until your child adapts to the new situation.

Set Up a Replacement

However you decide to end the caregiver relationship, make sure that you have a reliable replacement provider for your child ahead of time, if at all possible. Do not be surprised if your child is resistant to the idea of a new caregiver at first. If it took him or her some time to become comfortable with the former caregiver, expect it to take even longer to warm up to the new one. Even an infant can easily show displeasure with a new caregiver and routine. With older children, it is important to allow them to voice their feelings about the situation. This will give them some sense of control over their lives, which in turn will help them along in the process of readjustment.

Section VIII

Additional Childcare Issues

Sometimes, traditional childcare arrangements will not work. This might be because of an unconventional work situation, or because a special consideration regarding the child must be taken into account. For some families, it is not childcare itself that is the issue, but the logistics of getting the child there and back that presents the problem for working parents.

What should you do if your child has a special need? You will want to find a caregiver, whether it be a nanny or a day care center, that is qualified to handle the particular condition or disability that your child is contending with. At the same time, you may prefer to see your child integrated in a childcare environment with children who are not disabled. Experts indicate this is a very beneficial type of childcare setting for special needs children.

What if your workplace is in your home? Is there a way to accomplish any work with children underfoot? It certainly would help the bottom line of your household expenses if you could avoid paying for childcare while you were working.

No *one size fits all* answer exists to the question of how to best provide care for your child while you are working. Nontraditional families, as well as atypical work situations and childcare needs abound. With some determination and investigation, it may be possible to find a reasonable answer to your unique childcare requirements.

Chapter 24

The Special Needs Child

Parents of children with disabilities or other special needs often have plenty of stress built into their lives already. Finding specialized childcare or a suitable facility for these children can be a real obstacle for working parents.

Locating Specialized Childcare

For preschool and school-aged children, federal legislation may provide some assistance in the search for special needs childcare. The federal *Individuals with Disabilities Education Act* (IDEA) mandates that public schools provide special needs children, free of charge, with education in the most inclusive program possible. Public school administrations are required to fashion, and review on an annual basis, a so-called *individualized education program* (IEP) for each special needs child. Teachers, parents, and even the child in some cases, are charged as a team with the duty of forming the IEP.

The stated purposes of the IDEA are as follows.

- To ensure that all children with disabilities have available to them a free, appropriate public education that emphasizes special education and related services designed to meet their unique needs and prepare them for employment and independent living.
- To ensure that the rights of children with disabilities and parents of such children are protected.

- To assist states, localities, educational service agencies, and federal agencies to provide for the education of all children with disabilities.
- To assist states in the implementation of a statewide, comprehensive, coordinated, multidisciplinary, interagency system of early intervention services for infants and toddlers with disabilities and their families.
- To ensure that educators and parents have the necessary tools to improve educational results for children with disabilities by supporting systemic-change activities; coordinated research and personnel preparation; coordinated technical assistance, dissemination, and support; and, technology development and media services.
- To assess—and ensure the effectiveness of—efforts to educate children with disabilities.

The Individuals with Disabilities Education Act does not by itself provide for childcare. Rather, it requires states to develop and maintain early intervention services for children under the age of three. The purpose of these early intervention programs is to ensure that special needs children are adequately prepared for school in an inclusive environment when they get older. You should check with the IDEA early childhood administrator in your state to see what types of programs are available. The administrator also may be able to help you locate appropriate and affordable childcare for a special needs infant or toddler.

The National Early Childhood Education Technical Assistance Center (NECTAC) can provide you with contact information for the program administrators in your state. Contact them at:

From the Expert

To determine if your child is eligible for benefits under the IDEA, contact the United States Department of Education at:

Office of Special Education and Rehabilitative Services
U.S. Department of Education
400 Maryland Avenue, S.W.
Washington, DC 20202-7100
202-245-7468

NECTAC
Campus Box 8040, UNC-CH
Chapel Hill, NC 27599-8040
919-962-2001
www.nectac.org

Deciding on the Type of Childcare

When evaluating potential childcare providers, whether in-home or outside care givers, most of the questions you should ask are the same ones you would ask if you did not have the extra considerations associated with a special needs child. Look for a safe and nurturing environment, well-trained and plentiful staff, attentiveness to the children, and good communication between staff and parents. Depending on your particular circumstances, however, there may be other issues you should be concerned with as well.

The first question you should ask is whether you want a childcare setting that is geared specifically toward children with special needs. Many parents wish their children to be integrated into a so-called *inclusive day care situation*, one that caters to children of all different levels of ability. In fact, inclusive childcare is to be preferred, according to a number of experts such as the American Academy of Pediatrics.

Whether inclusive childcare will be an option for your family, of course, depends upon the nature of your child's needs. If all your child requires is that the facility itself be accessible to those with physical disabilities, integrating him or her in a inclusive day care center is likely to be simpler than if he or she has a complex developmental or psychological disability that requires specially-trained staff.

Without a doubt, the next issue is whether the caregivers are qualified to attend to your child. This will be the case whether you are looking for in-home or out-of-home care. You will have to research this area thoroughly. Inquire about the staff or the individual caregiver's experience with the particular need that your child has. You might even want to discuss potential caregivers with your child's pediatrician or specialist, who may have additional suggestions for questions to ask and things to look for when inspecting the facility.

Another consideration will arise if you have other children who are not considered to have special needs. If one child has specialized care requirements, it will be necessary to decide whether all of your children will be able to attend the same day care. In such a case, a nanny or a family day care provider with special training might be a more practicable solution. Of course, in a truly integrated family day care or day care center, the varying abilities among different children should not pose a problem.

Evaluating Special Needs Childcare Options

In many ways, searching for quality childcare for a special needs child is no different than trying to find day care for a nondisabled child. If you are considering day care centers, you have the same concerns—safety, cleanliness, a nurturing environment, stimulating activities, and so on. The most important factor is that the potential caregiver is qualified to care for children in general. If you answer that affirmatively, *then* you can move on to her ability to care for someone with a special need.

Just as in the case of a nondisabled child, you will want to perform thorough background checks on all potential caregivers—check references, education and employment history, and criminal and driving records. Do this whether you are looking at a day care center, family day care, or in-home care. In some states, day care workers are required to submit to background checks before being allowed to work as childcare providers in that state. Potential employers, as well as the general public, can have access to the background information for a fee.

What is different about the evaluation of a potential childcare provider for a special needs child, however, is that you also have to assess her ability to care for someone with your child's particular condition. As a result, you will

From the Expert

If you decide to utilize one of the many services that will perform background checks for a fee, be aware of what you are getting for your money. Some of these services will conduct criminal checks on the actual staff members, and some will merely review the facility's record, which you can do yourself through your state's licensing agency.

need to question her extensively about her prior experience with this particular special need. Find out if she has had training related to the condition, and be sure to ask what hands-on experience she has with children who have this need or disability.

You may want to go a step further, however, especially if you are thinking of hiring a nanny or placing your child in a family day care where there is only one caregiver present. There are firms that will perform psychological assessments on potential childcare providers—you might consider requiring one for your childcare candidate. Even the most loving and experienced caregiver can be put to the test caring for a special needs child. If the caregiver has no helper while she is caring for the special needs child, she may find herself overwhelmed. It is possible that an overburdened caregiver could take her frustration out on the children in her care. A psychological assessment might indicate whether a potential nanny or family day care provider has any tendencies in this direction. Seeing the red flags early is better than placing a special needs child in a possibly harmful situation.

Americans with Disabilities Act

If you are considering day care centers or family day care, your other concern with special needs care will be whether the childcare premises are appropriate for your child. The federal *Americans with Disabilities Act* (ADA) governs both the treatment of the special needs child by the day care program, and the physical accessibility of the actual premises of the facility. Under the ADA, a day care center or family day care home, unless it is operated by a religious organization, may not discriminate against a child on the basis of the child's disability. The day care provider may not deny enrollment to a child because the child has a special need. Moreover, if a day care provider does accept a special needs child for enrollment, the provider must provide care that is equal to that given to all other enrolled children.

Furthermore, the day care provider is legally required to make reasonable accommodations to make the day care program, activities, and physical locations available to the child. These requirements do not apply, however, if the child's attendance would cause a direct threat of harm to others. Also, if the program cannot be modified without being fundamentally altered, the provider will not be required to make an accommodation. Finally, the day care premises must be made accessible to the special needs child, if the premises can be readily modified.

What all this means in practical terms is that an outside childcare provider cannot simply refuse to accept your child just because he or she has a special need. This is true even if the facility had negative experiences with other children in the past who had the same need. The provider must conduct an individualized assessment of your child's case, taking into account his or her condition, the possible effect of his or her presence on the health or safety of others at the facility, and what steps may be taken to integrate him or her into the program and provide inclusive, equal care.

If you have specific questions regarding a particular situation relating to special needs childcare and the ADA, the United States Department of Justice administers an ADA Information Line at 800-514-0301. Live assistance is available to answer questions during weekday hours. There also is a 24-hour automated service that you can use to order ADA publications. Finally, the Justice Department website contains an ADA Home Page, which contains numerous publications covering many aspects of disability rights law, along with links to other federal agencies responsible for administering the ADA. This website is available at **www.usdoj.gov/crt/ada/adahom1.htm**.

Cost Considerations

As previously discussed, in-home care tends to be expensive, and specialized in-home care can be cost prohibitive for the average family. The higher the level of skill that is required to care for your child, the more expensive the care is likely to be. At the point that you are seeking nursing care for your child, you are no longer talking about a day care situation *per se*. While insurance might cover such care in some circumstances, families with more than one child still will have to locate care for their child without special needs.

Chapter 25

The Work-at-Home Parent

A popular misconception among those who earn a paycheck at a job away from their own house is that a home office would be an ideal employment situation. The truth of the matter is that, for many, working at home with young children around is almost impossible—without help.

If you earn a decent salary and can afford a formal childcare arrangement for your child, you have plenty of options available. Many people who work at home, however, do so for the advantage of having an income without the expense of childcare. For example, a person who is starting a business may work from home until the enterprise is up, running, and capable of supporting the cost of a separate worksite. In another case, an independent contractor may have sporadic work, so regular childcare is not cost effective. The objective in situations such as these, therefore, is to find safe, reliable childcare that will not eat up all of your profits.

Finding Childcare so You Can Work

Chapter 12 included a brief discussion of stay-at-home moms (SAHMs). This chapter talks about their peers, the *work-at-home moms* (WAHMs). (The jargon associated with work-at-home arrangements discriminates in favor of women, but this discussion applies to males as well as females, because there certainly are plenty of stay-at-home and work-at-home dads out there with childcare needs.)

The childcare providers of choice for WAHMs are often family members, because they are inexpensive to hire and a background check on them is unnecessary. (Issues that may be of concern to you if you have relative-provided childcare are discussed in Chapter 11.) However, childcare by relatives is a luxury not available to many WAHMs. Creative solutions may be the order of the day if family is not nearby, available, and willing to help out.

One of the advantages of working at home can be the flexibility of your work schedule. When it comes to childcare, however, this may prove to be one of the problems as well. If you do not work regular hours, you might have trouble settling on an arrangement with a caregiver who expects to work certain hours each day or certain days each week. You may end up being limited to baby-sitters for your childcare requirements. During the regular work/school week, it might be even tougher to find help, because the middle- and high-schoolers that you might call upon to sit during the weekend are not available.

Another advantage of being at home with your children while working is that you can keep tabs on your child's caregiver. As such, she does not necessarily have to be a top-flight nanny in order to provide suitable childcare. For example, a younger girl who does not have much baby-sitting experience, can serve as a *mother's helper*. Even if you would not be willing to leave your child alone in the care of a 12- or 13-year-old for more than a few hours, you certainly would be more at ease with the arrangement if you were in the next room and available to troubleshoot, if necessary. Similarly, if you had an elderly family member who would make a great sitter, except for the fact that she could not lift your child into a highchair or crib, your presence in the house for such situations would overcome that particular obstacle.

> **From the Expert**
> Keep in mind the possibility of hiring a retiree. (See Chapter 15.)

Using Other WAHMs for Childcare

A great way to solve the WAHM childcare dilemma, if you can manage it, is to trade baby-sitting services with others who are in the same boat. How do you find other WAHMs who might be interested in a childcare swap? The answer is networking. It is more than just locating other WAHMs; it means making a connection—maybe it is friendship, perhaps simply a business arrangement. It has to be a secure enough relationship that you would feel your child is safe in the care of this other person. It can be much dicier than locating traditional childcare, because there may be no references to check (although a background search may be in order if this is not someone you have known for a long while). Seeking out another parent who can care for your child on your schedule, whose child you can care for on your schedule, and above all, who is trustworthy and reliable, is a hit-or-miss proposition.

Networking is a good idea for parents in all types of situations, not only those who are working at home and looking for a childcare swap arrangement. Working parents who want to know what is going on with their children in day care should network with others whose children attend the same facility.

To get your network up and running, start close to home and work your way out from there. Network in your neighborhood—your friends, your child's school, the community pool, or your child's soccer practice. Set a goal to introduce yourself to someone new in your community every week. If you are new to the neighborhood, see if there is a newcomers' club. Some communities have mothers' clubs, geared toward parents with children who are school-aged and younger. Local churches also may have mothers' groups for members of the congregation or the community at large.

Networking in the neighborhood can be more difficult for those in urban areas, where connections sometimes are hard to establish, and in rural areas, where networking resources may be scarce. If you need to branch out in your search for WAHMs in your area, try one of a number of national parenting-related organizations. They may prove to be good sources for those connections that you want to make.

National Parenting-Related Organizations

International MOMS Club
1464 Madera Road
#N 191
Simi Valley, CA 93065
www.momsclub.org

Mothers & More National Office
P.O. Box 31
Elmhurst, IL 60126
630-941-3553
www.MothersandMore.com

MUMS: National Parent to Parent Network
(for parents of children with a health condition or disability)
150 Custer Court
Green Bay, Wisconsin 54301-1243
877-336-5333
www.netnet.net/mums

National Organization of Mothers of Twins Clubs
(for parents of multiples)
NOMOTC Executive Office
P.O. Box 700860
Plymouth, MI 48170-0955
877-540-2200
www.nomotc.org

Chapter 26

The Single Parent

The term "single parent," in present-day lexicon, usually refers to a parent who is not married to or otherwise cohabiting with the other parent. Here the discussion is limited to those parents who are unable, for whatever reason, to depend upon their child's other parent for any childcare assistance. Many parents who are not together do work out the logistics and the costs of childcare between them. Some of these arrangements are agreed upon by both parents, while others are ordered by family court judges. The dilemma is for the single parent who is entirely on his or her own, either by choice or by circumstance.

Several unique issues face the single parent who must secure childcare. Couples generally have a ready-made backup plan, so that if one is unable to care for the children because of illness or travel, the other parent can often manage, even if it is inconvenient. Single parents may not be able or willing to rely on the other parent to pick up that slack.

Another potential problem for the single parent is a financial one. As the sole source of income for the family, the single parent sometimes has fewer childcare options than a typical double income family, because of the cost involved.

Finding Support

At the same time, the possible solutions to day care dilemmas are not all that different for single parents than they are for couples. Single parents have to locate and evaluate quality care for their children, just as couples do. They have to figure out which childcare situation is best for their family, and they have to determine whether they can afford to pay for the childcare they choose, the same as couples. The difference is that each member of a couple has a sort of built-in support system—the other parent. The single parent may have to come up with that extra support—whether it is moral, financial, logistical, or otherwise—on his or her own.

If this is the situation in which you find yourself, consider first whether your extended family is in a position to help you out. Grandparents, aunts, and so on can form a great web of support for working parents who are without partners. Of course, family issues are always a possible obstacle to a good childcare arrangement, so be sure to evaluate that likelihood when deciding whether to ask a relative to take on caregiving duties for your child. (Some of the pros and cons of relying on extended family for childcare are discussed in Chapter 11.)

Networking

Networking can be another excellent source of support for single parents, especially those who do not have extended family nearby to help out. Many churches now have ministries that serve the needs of single parents in general, or divorced or widowed parents in particular. Local and national organizations also exist that are geared toward single parents and their families.

Parents Without Partners is perhaps one of the best known of these organizations. This is an association with chapters nationwide that offer support to single parents through, among other things, social and family activities. *Moms On a Mission Single* (MOMS) is another national group with local chapters that sponsor events for single parents of both genders.

To find out if there is a chapter near you, contact one of the following groups.

Parents Without Partners, Inc.
1650 South Dixie Highway
Suite 510
Boca Raton, FL 33432
561-391-8833
www.parentswithoutpartners.org

M.O.M.S.
(for single moms and dads)
475 College Boulevard
Suite 6-176
Oceanside, CA 92057-5512
760-726-7978
www.singlemoms.org

Networking also can be accomplished online with the help of Web-based organizations that are focused on single parent connections. As with any situation in which you are in touch with other people over the Internet, however, it is necessary to be very careful. Because of the nature of online communication, it is possible for people to misrepresent who they are and what their motive may be for wanting to get to know you. You may not be communicating with the person that you think you are. Do not give out personal information online, such as your home address. If you ever decide to meet someone in person after communicating with them online, do so only in a public place, and be sure that someone else, perhaps a friend or relative, knows where you are going. (Keeping all of this in mind, you will find a list of several Web-based single parent associations in Appendix C.) An online search that includes the name of your town, county, or state may help you find a local single parent association in your area.

If you are successful at networking, you may be able to fill in any gaps in your childcare arrangements with the help of other single parents that you trust. *Baby-sitting swaps* between two families can be lifesavers for single parents whose other childcare resources are limited. *Baby-sitting cooperatives* are another way to meet childcare needs. Cooperatives typically work on a point system. Members *earn* points by watching other members' children, and *spend* points when they have other members baby-sit for them. It helps to have one member serve as an administrator to keep track of each member's points account.

However you manage to meet your childcare needs as a single parent, the most important thing is to keep your morale up for your child's sake. You cannot take care of him or her if you are not taking good care of yourself. Even if you are satisfied with the day care arrangement you use while you are working, a network of other single parents can give you opportunities for adult time (whether it be with friends or on a date), as well as alone time, when you can focus on your own well-being. Do not allow yourself to go on a guilt trip over having your child in day care or with a sitter, especially if you are using the time to give yourself a break. The best way to show your child how much you care is not necessarily to spend every second of your free time with him or her, but to listen to your child, to keep the communication lines open, and to take an interest in what is going on in his or her life.

Chapter 27

Transportation During Childcare

Getting to and from an outside childcare provider is usually not an issue for younger children. Mom or Dad drops the child off on the way to work in the morning and picks him or her up on the way home later in the day. The issue is more likely to come up with older children, who have after-school activities and have to move from one location to another at the end of the school day. Even parents of those who are cared for in their own homes have to consider the child's need for transportation during the day.

If you are considering in-home childcare, such as a nanny or a relative, assess your child's need for transportation before settling on the care-giver. Can the person you are thinking about leaving your child with drive? Does she have access to a safe vehicle, either her own or yours? If not, you may want to explore other childcare options, unless you have other means of transportation for your child available.

Even if you are using a day care center or family day care for your child, you may wish to ask a relative, friend, or neighbor if they are able to drop off or pick up your child and transport him or her on a regular basis. You should discuss whether this would cause a hardship for the relative or friend, and you should offer to pay something for the service. It could be a flat per-week or per-month fee to defray automobile expenses, or it could be a mileage-based fee specifically to reimburse for the actual amount the driver expends in transporting your child. Many companies that reimburse employees for their mileage use the federal Internal Revenue Service expense deduction regulation amount—currently 40.5 cents per mile. This would be a reasonable charge for your driver's services.

In some school districts, bus service to and from your child's caregiver before and after school is a possibility. However, it is likely to be a requirement that the childcare location is on or within a reasonable distance of an existing bus route. In other words, if you wish to take advantage of bus service provided by the school district to or from your child's caregiver, you may have to choose a childcare provider that is located within the boundaries of your child's school. Check with the office of your child's school district's superintendent to see if school bus service is an option. If it is, it may be provided at minimal or no cost. If your child attends a private school, but is eligible for district-provided service, there may be a more substantial charge.

For school-aged children in most urban, many suburban, and some rural areas, commuter bus service is another means of transportation to and from school, home, and activities. Especially for many city-raised kids, taking the bus or the subway is a routine, daily activity, but it is not going to be an option for young children or for children with certain disabilities. Even with older children, it is necessary to go over safety rules regarding public transportation—particularly with regard to walking to and from, and waiting at, bus stops and train stations.

From the Expert

Children who are taking public transportation without an adult should always have a friend or classmate with them.

Private transportation may be available even in rural areas. It may take the form of taxicab service, or may be a livery service providing chartered group transportation for all of the children coming from a particular school. The advantage to using private transportation is that it is more flexible than what you can expect from a bus service. The disadvantage, however, is that it almost certainly will cost more than public transportation. In many areas of the country that do not have public transit, this may be the only transportation option for some children.

A possible advantage to using a day care center is that many of them—particularly the larger chain centers—actually have their own vans or minibuses for transporting children to and from the center, school, and their various activities. Some will limit transportation services to driving between the center and the child's school, while others are more accommodating to the child's other activities.

No matter what type of private transportation you use for your child, make sure that those who are doing the driving have valid driver's licenses and carry automobile insurance, as is required in most states. If your driver is not a family member or close friend, you should obtain written consent to check his or her driving record.

This may not be possible if you are using a taxi service, where you could have a different driver every day. In that case, you should check with your municipal government to see whether taxicabs or drivers are subject to local licensing regulations. Many cities require taxi drivers to have a special city taxicab license in order to operate a taxicab within city limits. Often, the license application authorizes the city's business license department to check the cabdriver's driving record, and perhaps his criminal record as well. Contact the business license department at city hall to see if there is a taxicab licensing requirement in your municipality.

Conclusion

According to the *Urban Institute*, almost 75% of preschool-aged children with working mothers spend part of their week in a nonparental childcare setting. Millions of other children are of school age and spend a portion of their out-of-school time—whether it is after school or over summer or winter breaks—in a childcare environment.

In and of itself, placing a child in day care is not detrimental to a child's well-being. Rather, it is the quality of the care that could affect the child's social and cognitive development. Quality is not determined by the type of care. For example, some working parents would have you believe that a nanny is the only way to go when it comes to nonparental care, and that it is irresponsible to place a child in a large day care center with dozens of other children. However, a bad nanny is much more likely to stifle a child's social and emotional growth than is a decent day care center.

The debate over whether to place a child in day care, and whether to use in-home or outside care, is completely moot for the millions of families that simply are trying to make ends meet, either financially or from a time management standpoint. For these parents, childcare alternatives are few and far between. Add to the mix an extenuating family circumstance—a single parent household, a special needs child, maybe even both—and the result can be a particularly stressful situation for a family that is already working at a disadvantage of sorts.

The best thing you can do for your children—no matter what your family's financial situation is, no matter how difficult your work schedule makes normal family life, no matter what other issues confront you as a working parent or your family in general — is to gather as much information as you can. Not only will this enable you to make the most knowledgeable decision you possibly can, but your research may lead you to resources that you never would have discovered otherwise. You may find a source of financial assistance to help you cover the cost of your child's care, or you may locate a specialized caregiver who is able to handle your unusual work schedule or your child's medical condition.

Sorting through the particular childcare issues confronting your family takes a good deal of homework, and oftentimes, chance can play a part as well. The most important consideration is your entire family's well-being, so use that as your main guide as you decide how to proceed. When in doubt, *go with your gut*. You know what is best for you and your family, so try not to let neighbors, coworkers, or other relatives make you feel as though you have made a bad decision if you are satisfied with the day care arrangement you have settled on. At the same time, if you have reasons to be worried about your child's progress in a particular childcare setting, do not hesitate to reconsider your plan.

Good luck!

Glossary

A

accreditation. The approval of a particular institution by an agency, certifying that the institution has met a certain rigorous standard of quality.

Administration for Children and Families (ACF). The federal agency, under the United States Department of Health and Human Services, that is charged with promoting the social and economic condition of families and children.

Americans with Disabilities Act (ADA). Federal legislation prohibiting discrimination in places of public accommodation—including childcare facilities—on the basis of disability or special need.

au pair. A youth, sometimes a student, from a foreign country, who agrees to care for a family's children and perhaps to perform light housework in exchange for the opportunity to live with the family and absorb the culture of the host country.

C

Child and Dependent Care Expenses Credit. A federal income tax credit that may be claimed by a taxpayer who incurs childcare expenses for the care of a dependent under the age of 13. For qualifying individuals, the credit may be as much as 35% of the childcare expenses incurred for the year.

Child Care and Development Fund. A federally funded program that helps needy families to locate and pay for childcare.

Child Care Resource and Referral Agency (CCRR). An organization that helps families to find satisfactory childcare, and that supports day care providers by assisting with training and other services that promote quality childcare.

Child Tax Credit. A federal income tax credit of up to $1,000 per qualifying child, adjusted according to the taxpayer's modified adjusted gross income.

corporal punishment. Physical discipline, such as spanking or rapping of knuckles.

D

day care center. An outside childcare provider, generally in an institutional or school-like setting, that enrolls a large number of children in different age groups and employs a number of staff members.

Dependent Care Assistance Plan (DCAP). A flexible spending plan offered by some employers that allows employees to use pretax earnings to finance childcare, resulting in tax savings for the employees.

E

Earned Income Credit. A federal income tax credit for qualified low-income taxpayers who earn income through paid employment.

F

Fair Labor Standards Act (FLSA). The federal statute governing minimum wage and overtime pay for covered employees, including domestic workers.

family day care. A smaller childcare facility, typically located in the provider's home, with little or no additional staff.

Federal Insurance Contributions Act (FICA) taxes. Federal Social Security and Medicare withholding from employees' wages.

flexible spending account. Funds that are deducted from a taxpayer's pretax income to be used for the taxpayer's childcare expenses during the course of that particular calendar year.

H

Head Start. A series of federally funded state and local programs, both public and private, that promote child development and school readiness in children up to the age of five.

I

Individuals with Disabilities Education Act (IDEA). Federal legislation requiring public schools to provide free education to eligible special needs children, in the most inclusive environment possible.

Individualized Education Program (IEP). An educational plan for special needs children, developed under mandate of the *Individuals with*

Disabilities Education Act, by a team made up of the child, his or her parents, teachers, and other appropriate persons The plan is tailored to the specific needs of the particular child.

N

nanny. A childcare provider who attends to a family's children within the family's home. May be a live-in or live-out caregiver.

National Association for Family Child Care (NAFCC). The main accrediting organization for family childcare providers.

National Association for the Education of Young Children (NAEYC). The main accrediting organization for day care centers.

National Association of Child Care Referral and Resource Agencies (NACCRRA). The organization that provides support services to more than 850 child care referral and resource agencies nationwide, and also provides contact information to families seeking quality childcare.

National Early Childhood Technical Assistance Center (NECTAC). The organization that facilitates states' implementation of requirements of the federal *Individuals with Disabilities Education Act.*

R

redirection. A method of peaceful conflict resolution for children that involves diverting an agitated or misbehaving child to an appropriate item or activity.

respondeat superior. A legal doctrine under which an employer can be held liable for damages caused by the acts of employees that occur within the course of the employer's business.

T

Temporary Assistance to Needy Families (TANF). The federal program that provides aid to low-income households (formerly known as welfare).

time out. A method of peaceful conflict resolution for children, wherein an agitated or misbehaving child is removed from the conflict situation and placed in a different setting, such as a chair in another room, for several minutes, allowing the child the opportunity to calm down or to resume acceptable behavior.

State Childcare Licensing Offices

State childcare licensing offices regulate day care centers and family day care operations. They can give you information about what is required of a day care provider, and can tell you if a particular provider has ever been cited for the violation of a state or local law.

Alabama
Child Daycare Partnership
Department of Human Resources
50 North Ripley
Montgomery, AL 36130
334-242-1425
www.dhr.state.al.us

Alaska
Child Care and Licensing Office
619 East Ship Creek Avenue
Suite 230
Anchorage, AK 99501
907-269-4500
(no website provided)

Arizona
Child Care Licensing Office
150 North 18th Avenue
Suite 400
Phoenix, AZ 85007
602-364-2539
800-615-8555
www.hs.state.az.us/als/
childcare/index.htm

Arkansas
Child Care Licensing Office
P.O. Box 1437
Slot 150
Little Rock, AR 72203
501-682-8590
800-445-3316
www.state.ar.us/childcare

California

Child Care Licensing Office
Department of Social Services
744 P Street
Mail Station 19-48
Sacramento, CA 95814
916-229-4500
(no website provided)

Colorado

Division of Child Care
Department of Human Services
1575 Sherman Street
Denver, CO 80203
303-866-5958
800-799-5876
www.cdhs.state.co.us/cyf/ccare/
    index.html

Connecticut

Child Care Licensing Office
Department of Public Health
410 Capitol Avenue
P.O. Box 340308
MS #12 DAC
Hartford, CT 06134
860-509-8045
800-282-6063
www.dph.state.ct.us/BRS/Day_
    Care/day_care.htm

Delaware

Office of Child Care Licensing
1825 Faulkland Road
Wilmington, DE 19805
302-892-5800
www.state.de.us/kids/occl.htm

District of Columbia

Child Care Licensing Office
Department of Health Regulation
    Administration
825 North Capitol Street, NE
2nd Floor
Washington, DC 20002
202-442-5888
http://dchealth.dc.gov/services/
    administration_offices/hra/
    crcfd/index.shtm

Florida

Child Care Licensing Office
Department of Children and
    Families
1317 Winewood Boulevard
B6 Room 381
Tallahassee, FL 32399-0700
850-488-4900
www5.myflorida.com/cf_web/
    myflorida2/healthhuman/
    childcare

Georgia

Bright from the Start:
    Georgia Department of
    Early Care and Learning
Ten Park Place South
Suite 600
Atlanta, GA 30303-3142
404-657-5562
http://decal.state.ga.us

Hawaii

Child Care Licensing Office
Department of Human Services
Benefit, Employment, and Support
  Services Division
820 Mililani Street
Suite 606
Honolulu, HI 96813
808-586-7050
www.state.hi.us/dhs

Idaho

Child Care Licensing Office
Department of Health and Welfare
5th Floor
P.O. Box 83720
Boise, ID 83720-0036
208-334-6559
www2.state.id.us/dhw

Illinois

Child Care Licensing Office
Department of Children and
  Family Services
406 East Monroe Street
STA 60
Springfield, IL 62701-1498
217-785-2688
www.state.il.us/dcfs/
  pr_policy.shtml

Indiana

Bureau of Child Development
  Licensing Section
Family and Social Services
  Administration
Division of Family and Children
402 West Washington Street
Room W386
Indianapolis, IN 46204-2739
317-232-1144
www.in.gov/fssa/children/bcd/
  index.html

Iowa

Child Care Licensing Office
Department of Human Services
Hoover State Office Building
1305 East Walnut
Des Moines, IA 50319
515-281-5657
800-972-2017
(no website provided)

Kansas

Bureau of Child Care and Health
  Facilities
Department of Health and
  Environment
Curtis State Office Building
1000 SW Jackson
Suite 200
Topeka, KS 66612-1274
785-296-1270
www.kdhe.state.ks.us/kidsnet

Kentucky

Child Care Licensing Office
Office of Inspector General
Division of Licensed Child Care
275 East Main Street, 5E-A
Frankfort, KY 40621
502-564-2800
http://chs.state.ky.us/oig

Louisiana

Child Care Licensing Office
Department of Social Services
Bureau of Licensing
P.O. Box 3078
Baton Rouge, LA 70821
225-922-0015
www.dss.state.la.us/
    departments/ofs/child_care_
    assistance.html

Maine

Child Care Licensing Office
State Department of Human
    Services
State House Station #11
Augusta, ME 04333
207-287-5060
www.state.me.us/dhs/bcfs/
    index.htm

Maryland

Child Care Licensing Office
Child Care Administration
311 West Saratoga Street
1st Floor
Baltimore, MD 21201
410-767-7805
(no website provided)

Massachusetts

Child Care Licensing Office
Office of Child Care Services
600 Washington Street
6th Floor
Boston, MA 02111
617-988-6600
www.qualitychildcare.org

Michigan

Division of Child Day Care
    Licensing
Family Independent Agency
Office of Children and Adult
    Licensing
7109 West Saginaw
2nd Floor
Lansing, MI 48909-8150
517-335-6124
www.michigan.gov/fia

Minnesota

Child Care Licensing Office
Department of Human Services
444 Lafayette Road North
St. Paul, MN 55155-3842
651-296-3971
www.dhs.state.mn.us/licensing

Mississippi

Child Care Licensing Office
Mississippi Department of Health
Division of Child Care Facilities
  Licensure
P.O. Box 1700
Jackson, MS 39215-1700
601-576-7613
(no website provided)

Missouri

Child Care Licensing Office
Department of Health and Senior
  Services
Bureau of Child Care
P.O. Box 570
Jefferson City, MO 65102
573-751-2450
www.dhss.mo.gov

Montana

Child Care Licensing Office
P.O. Box 202953
Helena, MT 59620
406-444-7770
www.montanachildcare.com

Nebraska

Child Care Licensing Program
Health and Human Services
  Regulation of Licensure
Credentialing Division
P.O. Box 94986
Lincoln, NE 68509-4986
402-471-1801
800-600-1289
www.hhs.state.ne.us/crl/crlindex.htm

Nevada

Child Care Licensing Office
711 East Fifth Street
Carson City, NV 89701
775-684-4400
http://dcfs.state.nv.us

New Hampshire

Bureau of Child Care Licensing
129 Pleasant Street
Concord, NH 03301
603-271-4624
800-852-3345, ext. 4624
www.dhhs.nh.gov/dhhs/bccl

New Jersey

Child Care Licensing Office
Bureau of Licensing, Department
  of Human Services
Division of Youth and Family
  Services
P.O. Box 717
Trenton, NJ 08625-0717
609-292-1018
877-667-9845
www.state.nj.us/humanservices/
  dyfs/licensing.html

New Mexico

Child Care Licensing Office
P.O. Drawer 5160
Santa Fe, NM 87502-0717
505-827-4185
800-832-1321
www.newmexicokids.org

New York
Child Care Licensing Office
Office of Children and Family
  Services
Department of Social Services
52 Washington Street
Room 338 North
Rensselaer, NY 12144
518-474-9454
800-732-5207
www.ocfs.state.ny.us

North Carolina
Regulatory Services Section
Division of Child Development
2201 Mail Service Center
Raleigh, NC 27699-2201
919-662-4499
800-859-0829
www.ncchildcare.net

North Dakota
Child Care Licensing Office
Department of Human Services
600 East Boulevard Avenue
Bismark, ND 58505-0250
701-328-2316
800-245-3736
http://lnotes.state.nd.us/dhs/
  dhsweb.nsf

Ohio
Child Care Licensing Office
State Department of Job and
  Family Services
Bureau of Child Care
3rd Floor
255 East Main Street
Columbus, OH 43215-5222
614-466-3822
866-635-3748
www.jfs.ohio.gov/cdc

Oklahoma
Child Care Licensing Office
Department of Human Services,
  Division of Child Care
Sequoyah Building
2400 North Lincoln Boulevard
P.O. Box 25352
Oklahoma City, OK 73125
405-521-3561
800-347-2276
www.okdhs.org/childcare

Oregon
Child Care Licensing Office
875 Union Street, NE
Salem, OR 97309
503-947-1400
800-556-6616
http://findit.emp.state.or.us/
  childcare.cfm

Pennsylvania

Child Care Licensing Office
Bureau of Child Day Care Services
P.O. Box 2675
Harrisburg, PA 17105-2675
717-787-8691
www.dpw.state.pa.us/ocyf/
    childcarewks/ccwFindSrcc.asp

Rhode Island

Rhode Island Department of
    Children, Youth, and Families
Day Care Licensing Unit
101 Friendship Street
Providence, RI 02903-3716
401-528-3624
www.dcyf.state.ri.us/licensing.shtml

South Carolina

Division of Child Day Care
Licensing and Regulatory Services
Department of Social Services
Room 520
P.O. Box 1520
Columbia, SC 29202-1520
803-898-7345
877-886-2384
www.state.sc.us/dss/cdclrs

South Dakota

Child Care Licensing Office
Richard F. Kneip Building
700 Governors Drive
Pierre, SD 57501-2291
605-773-4766
800-227-3020
www.state.sd.us/social/ccs/
    ccshome.htm

Tennessee

Child Care Licensing Office
Department of Human Services
Citizen Plaza
14th Floor
400 Deaderick Street
Nashville, TN 37248
615-313-4778
www.state.tn.us/humanserv

Texas

Child Care Licensing Office
Department of Protective and
Regulatory Services
Mail Code E-550
P.O. Box 149030
Austin, TX 78714-9030
512-438-3269
800-862-5252
www.tdprs.state.tx.us/Child_Care/
    About_Child_Care_Licensing/
    default.asp

Utah

Bureau of Licensing, Utah
    Department of Health
Bureau of Licensing,
    Child Care Unit
P.O. Box 142003
288 North 1460 West
Salt Lake City, UT 84114-2003
801-538-6152
888-287-3704
http://health.utah.gov/licensing

Vermont
Child Care Licensing Office
Child Care Services Division
103 South Main Street
2 North
Waterbury, VT 05671-2901
802-241-2158
800-649-2642
www.state.vt.us/srs/childcare/
  index.htm

Virginia
Division of Licensing Programs
Department of Social Services
7 North 8th Street
2nd Floor
Richmond, VA 23219
804-726-7169
800-543-7545
www.dss.state.va.us/division/
  license

Washington
Child Care Licensing Office
Department of Social and Health
  Services
P.O. Box 45480
Olympia, WA 98504-5480
360-413-3284
866-482-4325
www1.dshs.wa.gov/ca/index.asp

West Virginia
Child Care Licensing Office
350 Capitol Street
Room B18
Charleston, WV 25301-1715
304-558-1885
www.wvdhhr.org/oss/childcare/
  licensing.htm

Wisconsin
Child Care Licensing Office
Division of Children and Family
  Services
Bureau of Regulation and
  Licensing
One West Wilson Street
P.O. Box 8916
Madison, WI 53708-8916
608-266-9314
www.dhfs.state.wi.us/rl_dcfs/
  INDEX.HTM

Wyoming
Child Care Licensing Office
Department of Family Services
Hathway Building
3rd Floor
Cheyenne, WY 82002
307-777-6595
http://dfsweb.state.wy.us/child-
care.html

(Source: United States Department of Education)

Child Care Resource and Referral Agencies

Child Care Resource and Referral agencies (CCRRs) are organizations that are dedicated to supporting the development of high quality child-care and to helping families find suitable childcare arrangements.

After your own gut instinct, CCRRs are probably the most important tool you can use in your quest for good childcare solutions. What follows are listings of CCRRs throughout the country. With this contact information, you can obtain referrals to and information about childcare near both your home and your place of employment.

Publisher's Note: This appendix is ordered alphabetically by town for each state, so you can find the CCRR agency nearest to you by locating the nearest town.

ALABAMA

Children's Services
P.O. Box 670
Anniston, AL 36202
256-236-7548

Childcare Resources
1904 1ˢᵗ Avenue North
Birmingham, AL 35203
205-795-2301
800-822-2734
www.ccr-bhm.org

**Family Guidance Center
of Alabama**
2431 West Main Street
Suite 1102
Dothan, AL 36301
334-712-7777
800-499-6597
www.familyguidancecenter.org

Child Care Resource Network
P.O. Box 681025
Fort Payne, AL 35968
256-845-8238
800-593-4056

**Child Care Management Agency
of North Central Alabama**
P.O. Box 18396
Huntsville, AL 35804
256-534-5110

**South Central Alabama Child
Care Management Agency, Inc.**
P.O. Box 610
Luverne, AL 36049
334-335-6626

**GRCMA Early Childhood
Directions**
3101 International Drive
Suite 700
Mobile, AL 36616
251-473-1060
www.grcma.org

**Child Care Management
Program**
Family Guidance Center of
Alabama, Inc.
1230 Perry Hill Road
Montgomery, AL 36109
334-270-4100
800-499-6597
www.familyguidancecenter.org

Child Care Resource Center, Inc.
3766 Pepperell Parkway
Opelika, AL 36830
334-749-8400

Child Care Central
925 North Street
Talladega, AL 35160
256-362-1390

Child Development Resources
Box 870157
Tuscaloosa, AL 35487
205-348-2650

ALASKA

**Alaska Child Care Resource and
Referral Network**
c/o Child Care Connection, Inc.
Anchorage, AK 99514
907-563-2976
www.childcareconnection.org

Child Care Connection, Inc.
P.O. Box 141689
Anchorage, AK 99514
907-563-1996
800-278-3723 (In-State)
www.childcareconnection.org

C.A.R.E.S. Resource and Referrals
1908 Old Pioneer Way
Fairbanks, AK 99709
907-479-2214
www.alaskacares.org

Child Care Referrals
520 5th Avenue
Suite D
Fairbanks, AK 99707
907-459-1439
866-878-2273
http://co.fairbanks.ak.us/
childcarereferral

AEYC-SEA
P.O. Box 22870
Juneau, AK 99802
907-789-1235
888-785-1235
www.aeyc-sea.org

ARIZONA

**Association for Supportive
Child Care**
3910 South Rural Road
Suite E
Tempe, AZ 85282
602-244-2678
800-308-9000
http://arizonachildcare.org

Child & Family Resources, Inc.
2800 East Broadway Boulevard
Tucson, AZ 85716
520-325-5778
800-308-9000
www.azchildcare.org

ARKANSAS

Children of North Central Arkansas
P.O. Box 2396
Batesville, AR 72503
870-793-5233
800-737-2237 (In-State)
www.childrenofncar.org

Crowley's Ridge Development Council, Inc.
P.O. Box 1497
Jonesboro, AR 72403
870-931-6331
800-753-5827

Arkansas Resource and Referral System
101 East Capitol
Suite 106
Little Rock, AR 72201
501-682-9699
www.state.ar.us/childcare

Central Arkansas CCR&R
P.O. Box 94229
North Little Rock, AR 72190
501-771-0955
800-423-1367
www.arkansaschildren.org

North West Arkansas Child Care Resource & Referral Center, Inc.
614 East Emma
Suite 107
Springdale, AR 72764
479-751-3463
800-543-7564

CALIFORNIA

MODOC Child Care Resource and Referral
112 East 2nd Street
Alturas, CA 96101
530-233-5437

Contra Costa Child Care Council
East County Area Office
3104 Delta Fair Boulevard
Antioch, CA 94509
925-778-5437
www.cocokids.org

POEC Child Development Services
1230 High Street
Suite 114
Auburn, CA 95603
530-885-6624
800-464-3322 (In-State)
www.placercoe.k12.ca.us

Kern County Superintendent of Schools/CCCC
2000 24th Street
Suite 100
Bakersfield, CA 93301
661-861-5200
877-861-5200
http://kcsos.kern.org/cccc

Options-A Child Care and Human Services Agency
13100 Brooks Drive
Suite 100
Baldwin Park, CA 91706
626-856-5900
www.optionscc.com

Child Care Connection – Inyo County
164 Grandview Drive
Bishop, CA 93514
760-873-5123
888-999-5669 (In-State)

Choices for Children Alpine and El Dorado County
3161 Cameron Park Drive
Suite 101
Cameron Park, CA 95682
530-676-0707
877-676-0707
www.choices4children.org

Child Development Resource Center
809-H Bay Avenue
Capitola, CA 95003
831-476-8585
www.santacruz.k12.ca.us

Center for Community and Family Services
649 Albertoni Street
Suite 201
Carson, CA 90746
310-217-2935
888-421-4247
www.ccafs.org

Valley Oak Children's Services
287 Rio Lindo Avenue
Chico, CA 95926
530-895-3572

Children's Services—Colusa County Office of Education
345 Fifth Street
Suite ABC
Colusa, CA 95932
530-458-0300
www.colusa-coe.k12.ca.us

Mexican American Opportunities Foundation
972 South Goodrich Boulevard
Commerce, CA 90022
323-890-1555
www.maof.org

Contra Costa Child Care Council— Administrative Offices
1035 Detroit Avenue
Suite 200
Concord, CA 94518
925-676-5437
www.cocokids.org

Contra Costa Child Care Council— Central County Area Office
2280 Diamond Boulevard
Suite 500
Concord, CA 94520
925-676-5437
www.cocokids.org

Del Norte Child Care Council
212 K Street
Crescent City, CA 95531
707-464-8311
www.dnccc.com

City of Davis— Child Care Services
600 A Street
Davis, CA 95616
530-757-5695
800-723-3001
www.cityofdavis.org

Sierra Nevada Children's Services
P.O. Box 202
Downieville, CA 95936
530-289-3666
www.sierrachildcare.org

Imperial County Child Development Services
1398 Sperber Road
El Centro, CA 92243
760-312-6431
www.icoe.k12.ca.us

Humboldt Child Care Council
2259 Myrtle Avenue
Eureka, CA 95501
707-444-8293
www.hccc1.org

Solano Family & Children's Services
421 Executive Court North
Fairfield, CA 94534
707-863-3950
www.solanosfcs.org

Central Valley Children's Services Network
1911 North Helm Avenue
Fresno, CA 93727
559-456-1100
www.cvcsn.org

Sierra Nevada Children's Services
256 Buena Vista
Suite 110
Grass Valley, CA 95945
530-272-8866
800-655-3984 (In-State)
www.sncs.org

River Child Care Services
P.O. Box 16
Guerneville, CA 95446
707-887-1809
800-994-3613 (In-State)
www.rccservices.org

Kings Community Action Organization, Inc.
1222 West Lacey Boulevard
Suite 201
Hanford, CA 93230
559-582-4386
www.kcao.org

Community Child Care Coordinating Council of Alameda County
22351 City Center Drive
Suite 200
Hayward, CA 94541
510-582-2182
www.4c-alameda.org

Go Kids, Inc.
1111 San Felipe Road, Suite 103
Hollister, CA 95023
831-637-9205
www.gokids.org

Human Resources Council — Child Care Resources Amador County
201 Clinton Road
Suite 204
Jackson, CA 95642
209-223-1624
www.hrcccr.org

North Coast Opportunities — Rural Communities Child Care
850 Lakeport Boulevard
Lakeport, CA 95453
707-263-4688

Children's Home Society of California
Long Beach, CA 90810
310-816-3654
www.chs-ca.org

Children's Home Society of California
1300 West Fourth Street
Los Angeles, CA 90017
310-816-3690
www.chs-ca.org

Crystal Stairs, Inc.
650 West Adams Boulevard
Suite 100
Los Angeles, CA 90007
323-421-1029
888-543-7247 (In-State)
www.crystalstairs.org

Pathways
3550 West 6th Street
Suite 500
Los Angeles, CA 90020
213-427-2700
www.cfsla.org

Madera County Action Committee
1200 West Maple Street
Madera, CA 93637
559-675-8469
800-505-0404 (In-State)
www.maderacap.org

Community Connection for Children
P.O. Box 8571
Mammoth Lake, CA 93546
760-934-3343
800-317-4600 (In-State)

ICES Child Care Resource and Referral
P.O. Box 1898
Mariposa, CA 95338
209-966-4474
800-966-4474 (In-State)

Choices for Children— Alpine County
P.O. Box 215
Markleeville, CA 96120
530-694-2129
877-694-2129
www.choices4children.org

Children's Services Network of Merced County, Inc.
1520 West Main Street
Merced, CA 95340
209-722-3804
877-722-3804
209-723-1068 (fax)

Stanislaus County Office of Education Child Care Resource and Referral
1324 Celeste Drive
Modesto, CA 95355
209-558-4050
www.stan-co.k12.ca.us

Community Resources for Children
5 Financial Plaza
Suite 224
Napa, CA 94558
707-253-0376
800-696-4272
www.crcnapa.org

BANANAS, Inc.
5232 Claremont Avenue
Oakland, CA 94618
510-658-0381
www.bananasinc.org

Glenn County Office of Education Department of Child and Family Services
P.O. Box 696
Orland, CA 95963
530-865-1118
800-394-2818 (In-State)
www.glenn-co..k12.ca.us/gcoe

Child Development Resources of Ventura County, Inc.
221 Ventura Boulevard
Oxnard, CA 93036
805-485-7878
www.cdrofvtaco.org

Child Care Information Service
2698 Mataro Street
Pasadena, CA 91107
626-449-8221

Child Care Links
1020 Serpentine Lane
Suite 102
Pleasanton, CA 94566
925-417-8733
www.childcarelinks.org

Child Care Information Services
1460 East Holt Avenue
Suite 130
Pomona, CA 91767-5856
909-397-4740
800-822-5777

Plumas Rural Services
586 Jackson Street
Quincy, CA 95971
530-283-4453
800-284-3340

Early Childhood Services
Shasta County
1427 Market Street
Redding, CA 96001
530-225-2999
www.shastacoe.org

Contra Costa Child Care Council—
West County Area Office
3065 Richmond Parkway
Suite 112
Richmond, CA 94806
510-758-5439
www.cocokids.org

Riverside County Office of
Education, Children and
Family Services
P.O. Box 868
Riverside, CA 92502
951-826-6369
800-442-4927

Child Action, Inc.
9961 Horn Road
Sacramento, CA 95827
916-369-0191
www.childaction.org

Monterey County Child Care
Resource and Referral
622 East Alisal Street
Suite 6
Salinas, CA 93905
831-757-0775
www.maof.org

Human Resouces Council/
Child Care Resources
P.O. Box 919
San Andreas, CA 95249
209-754-1075
www.hrcccr.org

SBCSS—
Child Development Services
144 North Mountain View Avenue
San Bernardino, CA 92408
909-384-8046
800-722-1091 (In-State)
www.kidsncare.com

YMCA Child Care Resource
Service
3333 Camino del Rio South
Suite 400
San Diego, CA 92108
800-481-2151
www.ymcacrs.org

Children's Council of
San Francisco
445 Church Street
San Francisco, CA 94114
415-343-3300
www.childrenscouncil.org

California Child Care Resource and Referral Network
111 New Montgomery Street
7th Floor
San Francisco, CA 94105-3605
415-882-0234
www.rrnetwork.org

Wu Yee Children's Services
831 Broadway Street
2nd Floor
San Francisco, CA 94133
415-391-4956
www.wuyee.org

4C's Santa Clara County
111 East Gish Road
San Jose, CA 95112
408-487-0749
www.4c.org

EOC Child Care Resource Connection
805 A Fiero Lane
San Luis Obispo, CA 93401
805-541-2272
888-727-2272 (In-State)
www.eocslo.org

Child Care Coordinating Council
2121 South El Camino Real
San Mateo, CA 94403
650-655-6777
www.thecouncil.net

Marin Child Care Council
555 Northgate Drive
Suite 105
San Rafael, CA 94903
415-479-2273
www.mc3.org

Children's Home Society of California—Orange County
525 North Cabrillo Park Drive
Suite 300
Santa Ana, CA 92701
714-835-8252
www.chs-ca.org

Santa Barbara Family Center Child Care Resource and Referral
1124 Castillo Street
Santa Barbara, CA 93101
805-963-6631

Connections for Children Child Care Resource and Referral
2701 Ocean Park Boulevard
Suite 253
Santa Monica, CA 90405
310-452-3202
www.cfc-ca.org

Community Child Care Council of Sonoma County
396 Tesconi Court
Santa Rosa, CA 95401
707-544-3077
www.sonoma4cs.org

Infant/Child Enrichment Services
14326 Tuolumne Road
Sonora, CA 95370
209-533-0377
800-533-0377
www.icesagency.org

Family Resource and Referral Center
509 West Weber Avenue
Suite 101
Stockton, CA 95203
209-948-1553

**Lassen Child and
Family Resources**
336 Alexander Avenue
Susanville, CA 96130
530-257-9781

Child Care Resource Center, Inc.
16650 Sherman Way
Suite 200
Van Nuys, CA 91406
818-256-1000
www.ccrcla.org

**Tulare County Child Care
Resource and Referral**
7000 Doe Avenue
Suite C
Visalia, CA 93291
559-651-0862
800-613-6262

Human Response Network
P.O. Box 2370
Weaverville, CA 96093
530-623-2024
800-358-5251
www.humanresponsenetwork.org

**SISKIYOU Child Care Council,
Inc.**
P.O. Box 500
Weed, CA 96094
530-938-2748
800-938-2748 (In-State)

**North Coast Opportunities —
Rural Communities Child Care**
156 South Humboldt Street
Willits, CA 95490
707-459-6767
www.ncoinc.org

**Children's Home Society of
California — Sutter and
Yuba Counties**
990 Klamath Lane
Suite 18
Yuba City, CA 95993
530-673-7503
800-552-0400 (In-State)
www.chs-ca.org

COLORADO

Kids First
215 North Garmish
Suite 1
Aspen, CO 81611
970-920-5363
888-928-7111
www.aspenpitkin.com/kidsfirst

**City of Boulder Children, Youth,
and Families**
2160 Spruce Street
Boulder, CO 80302
303-441-3544
www.ci.boulder.co.us/cyfhhs/
children/cyf_chld.htm

Child Care Connections
125 North Parkside Drive
Colorado Springs, CO 80909
719-638-2057
800-379-6765
www.childcareconnections.net

**Early Childhood Council of
San Luis Valley**
P.O. Box 263
Creede, CO 81130
719-658-0101

Metro Denver Resource and Referral Partners City & County of Denver
Mayor's Office of Child Care
Initiatives
Denver, CO 80202
303-381-2990
www.corra.org/RRSearch/
AllAgencies.asp

Early Childhood Options
P.O. Box 3355
Dillon, CO 80435
970-513-1170
www.earlychildhoodoptions.org

Durango 4-C Council, Inc.
P.O. Box 259
Durango, CO 81302
970-247-5960
http://tchs4c.org

Southwest Office of Child Care Resource and Referral
P.O. Box 259
Durango, CO 81302
970-247-5960
www.tchs4c.org

The Early Childhood Council of Larimer County
P.O. Box 271708
Ft. Collins, CO 80525
970-377-3388
www.fortnet.org/ECC

Morgan County Family Center
800 West Platte Avenue
Suite 1
Ft. Morgan, CO 80701
970-867-9606
www.morganfamilycenter.org

CCR&R for Garfield and Eagle Counties
401 23rd Street
Suite 207
Glenn Wood Springs, CO 81601
970-928-7111
www.corra.org

Child Care Resource Network
P.O. Box 20,000-5028
US Bank Building
Grand Junction, CO 81501
970-241-1764
www.coopext.colostate.edu/
TRA/cfs

United Way of Weld County Child Care Resource & Referral
P.O. Box 1944
Greeley, CO 80634
970-353-4300
800-559-5590
www.unitedway-weld.org

Work Options Group
1455 Dixon Avenue
Suite 200
Lafayette, CO 80026
303-381-2990

Family Resources and Child Care Education
13300 West 6th Avenue
Box 22B
Lakewood, CO 80228
303-381-2990
800-436-3665
www.frcce.org

Western Slope CCRR
P.O. Box 552
Olathe, CO 81425
970-240-3323

Children First/
Pueblo Community College
900 West Orman Avenue
CC165
Pueblo, CO 81004
719-549-3411
800-894-7707
www.pueblocc.edu/advise/
children.htm

Child Care Network
P.O. Box 775376
Steamboat Springs, CO 80477
970-879-7330
888-879-7330
www.familydevelopmentcenter.org

Northeast Colorado Child Care
Resource aand Referral
P.O. Box 284
Yuma, CO 80759
970-848-3867
800-794-3867
www.ncccrr.org

CONNECTICUT

2-1-1 Child Care Infoline
1344 Silas Deane Highway
Rocky Hill, CT 06067
800-505-1000
800-505-1000
http://www.childcareinfoline.org

DELAWARE

The Family and Work Place
Connection
3511 Silverside Road
Wilmington, DE 19810
302-479-1660
800-660-6602 (Out-of-State)
www.familyandworkplace.org

DISTRICT OF COLUMBIA

Washington Child Development
Council
1420 Columbia Road, NW
Suite 201
Washington, DC 20009
202-387-0002
www.wcdconline.org

FLORIDA

Arcadia One Stop
819 North Mills Avenue
Arcadia, FL 34266
863-494-5233
www.sarasota-ymca.org

Resource Connection for Kids
302 Manatee Avenue East
Suite 200
Bradenton, FL 34208
941-745-5949
http://www.rc4k.org

Childhood Development
Services — Hernando County
20162 Cortez Boulevard
Brooksville, FL 34601
352-754-5068

Child Care Association of
Brevard County, Inc.
18 Harrison Street
Cocoa, FL 32922
321-634-3500
www.childcarebrevard.com

Childhood Development Services
5641 West Gulf To Lake Highway
Crystal River, FL 34429
352-795-2667
www.childhooddevelopment.org

Child Care Resource Network
230 North Beach Street
2nd Floor
Daytona Beach, FL 32114
386-323-2400
800-443-3262 (In-State)
www.ccrnetwork.org

Child Care of Southwest Florida, Inc.
3625 Fowler Street
Ft. Myers, FL 33901
239-278-4114
888-290-4114
www.ccswfl.org

Okaloosa-Walton Child Care Services
107 Tupelo Avenue
Ft. Walton Beach, FL 32548
850-833-9333
www.owccs.org

Child Care Resources, Inc.
515 North Main Street
Gainesville, FL 32601
352-334-1576
800-834-8111 (In-State)
www.ccresources.org

Wesley House Resource and Referral
1304 Truman Avenue
Key West, FL 33040
305-292-7150
877-595-5437
www.wesleyhouse.org

Episcopal Children's Services
100 Bell Tel Way
Suite 100
Jacksonville, FL 32216
904-726-1500
800-238-3463
www.ecs4kids.org

Jacksonville Children's Commission
421 West Church Street
Suite 201
Jacksonville, FL 32202
904-630-6408
www.jaxkids.org

Gateway School Readiness Coalition, Inc.
484 SW Commerce Drive
Lake City, FL 32025
386-752-9770
866-752-9770
www.fl-gsrc.org

Suwannee Valley 4C's
236 South Columbia Street
Lake City, FL 32056
386-758-0650
www.sv4cs.org

LifeStream Child Care Choice Services
P.O. Box 491000
Leesburg, FL 34748
352-315-3905
866-463-3905
www.childcarechoiceservices.com

Miami Dade County Child Development Services
1701 NW 30th Avenue
Miami, FL 33125
305-633-6481

Child Care of Southwest Florida, Inc.
3625 Fowler Street
Fort Myers, FL 33901
239-278-1002
www.ccswfl.org

Youth & Family Alternatives, Inc.
7524 Plathe Road
New Port Richey, FL 346543
727-835-4166
800-443-1024
www.yfainc.org

Family Central, Inc.
840 SW 81ˢᵗ Avenue
North Lauderdale, FL 33068
954-724-4609
877-522-3767
www.familycentral.org

Childhood Development Services, Inc.
1601 NE 25ᵗʰ Avenue
Suite 900
Ocala, FL 34470
352-629-0055
800-635-5437 (In-State)
www.childhooddevelopment.org

Community Coordinated Care for Children, Inc.
3500 West Colonial Drive
Orlando, FL 32808
407-522-2252
800-347-7602 (In-State)
www.4corlando.org

Early Education and Care, Inc.
450 Jenks Avenue
Panama City, FL 32401
850-872-7550
800-768-8316
www.ecskids.org

Children's Services Center
1800 North Palafox Street
Pensacola, FL 32501
850-983-5313
www.childrensservicescenter.org

Coordinated Child Care of Pinellas
6698 68ᵗʰ Avenue North
Suite B
Pinellas Park, FL 33781
727-547-5750
www.childcarepinellas.org

Port Charlotte Satellite Office
1600 Tamiami Trail
Suite 103
Port Charlotte, FL 33948
941-255-1650
www.sarasota-ymca.org

Sarasota Family YMCA, Inc.
1 South School Avenue
Suite 301
Sarasota, FL 34237
941-951-2916
800-317-4599
www.sarasota-ymca.org

Sarasota One Stop
3660 North Washington Boulevard
Sarasota, FL 34234
941-358-4200

St. John's County School Readiness Services
2980 Collins Avenue, Building A
St. Augustine, FL 32084
904-823-3559

School Readiness Coalition of Martin County
2020 SE Ocean Boulevard
Stuart, FL 34996
772-463-3212
866-273-6340 (Out-of-State)

ACS State & Local Solutions, Inc.
325 John Knox Road
Tallahassee, FL 32303
850-414-6085
www.schoolreadiness
professional.org

Florida Children's Forum
2807 Remington Green Circle
Tallahassee, FL 32308
888-352-4453
www.fcforum.org

Kids, Inc. of the Big Bend
1170 Capital Circle NE
Tallahassee, FL 32301
850-414-9800
www.kidsincorporated.org

School District of Hillsborough County Child Care Resource and Referral
207 Kelsey Lane
Suite K
Tampa, FL 33619
813-744-8941
www.sdhc.k12.fl.us

Childhood Development Services—Lake County
4113 County Road 561
Tavares, FL 32778
800-435-5210
www.childhooddevelopment.org

Venice One Stop
897 East Venice Avenue
Venice, FL 34292
941-486-2682

Family Central
3111 South Dixie Highway
Suite 222
West Palm Beach, FL 33405
561-514-3300
800-683-3327
www.familycentral.org

4C Sumter County
P.O. Box 1303
Wildwood, FL 34785
352-748-4005
800-687-5439
www.4Corlando.org

Agricultural and Labor Program, Inc.
P.O. Box 3126
Winter Haven, FL 33881
863-956-3491
www.alpi.org

Early Childhood Resources
122 Central Avenue, West
Winter Haven, FL 33880
863-385-8300
800-331-4886
www.earlychildhood.net

GEORGIA

Child Care Resource and Referral of Southwest Georgia at Albany
717 North Monroe Street
Albany, GA 31701
229-430-6868
866-833-3552

Child Care Resource and Referral Agency of West Georgia at Americus
802 Ashby Street
Americus, GA 31709
229-928-3499
800-465-0414

Child Care Resource & Referral of Northeast Georgia at Athens
452 Prince Avenue
Athens, GA 30601
706-353-1313
800-924-5085
www.communityconnection211.com

Child Care Resource and Referral of Metro Atlanta Quality Care for Children
50 Executive Park South
Atlanta, GA 30329
404-479-4240
877-722-4233 (In-State)
www.qualitycareforchildren.org

**Georgia Association of Child
Care Resource and Referral
Agencies**
50 Executive Park Drive, South
Atlanta, GA 30329
800-916-9896

**Child Care Resource and Referral
of East Georgia at Augusta**
1054 Claussen Road
Augusta, GA 30907
706-736-2122
877-228-3566
www.lsga.org

**Child Care Resource and Referral
of Coastal Georgia at Brunswick**
P.O. Box 2899
Brunswick, GA 31521
912-262-9819
800-834-9803

**Child Care Resource and Referral
of West Georgia at Columbus**
4225 University Avenue
Columbus, GA 31907
706-569-3109
800-650-2102
http://ccrrc.colstate.edu

**Child Care Resource and Referral
of Northwest Georgia at Dalton**
913 North Tennessee Street
Dalton, GA 30722
770-387-0828
800-308-1825
www.qualitycareforchildren.org

**Child Care Resource and Referral
of Northeast Georgia
at Gainesville**
P.O. Box 1358
Gainesville, GA 30501
770-718-3883
800-793-6383

**Child Care Resource and Referral
of Middle Georgia at Macon**
277 Martin Luther King Jr.
Boulevard
Macon, GA 31201
800-558-4804

**Child Care Resource and Referral
of East Central Georgia
of Swainsboro Tech**
346 Kite Road
Swainsboro, GA 30401
478-289-2275
877-495-9188
http://ccrr.swainsborotech.edu

**Child Care Resource and Referral
of West Central Georgia
at Thomaston**
115 East Main Street
Thomaston, GA 30286
706-646-6215
800-613-8546
www.flintrivertech.org/ccr&r

**Child Care Resource and Referral
of South Central Georgia
at Tifton**
P.O. Box 243
Tifton, GA 31794
229-382-9919
888-893-4582

**Child Care Resource and Referral
of South Central Georgia
at Waycross**
1235 B MacDonald Street
Waycross, GA 31501
912-338-9000
877-244-5379

HAWAII

PATCH
650 Iwilei Road
Suite 205
Honolulu, HI 96817
808-839-1988
www.PatchHawaii.org

IDAHO

Idaho CCR&R State Network
The 211 Idaho Careline
1720 Westgate Drive
Suite A
Boise, ID 83704
800-926-2588
www.idahocareline.org

IdahoSTARS—United Way
Success By 6
Region 4
1276 West River
Suite 100
Boise, ID 83702
208-345-6505
800-926-2588
www.idahostars.org

IdahoSTARS—United Way
Success By 6
Region 3
524 Cleveland Boulevard
Suite 225
Caldwell, ID 83605
800-926-2588
800-926-2588
www.idahostars.org

IdahoSTARS—United Way
Success By 6
Region 7
956 East Lincoln Road
Idaho Falls, ID 83401
208-709-1275
800-926-2588
www.idahostars.org

IdahoSTARS—
Community Action Partnership
Region 2
124 New 6th Street
Lewiston, ID 83501
800-926-2588
800-926-2588
www.idahostars.org

IdahoSTARS—Idaho State
Training and Registry System
129 West Third Street
Moscow, ID 83843
208-885-3004

IdahoSTARS—Panhandle Health
District Child Care Resources
Region 1
412 East Mullan Avenue
Suite B
Post Falls, ID 83854
800-926-2588
800-926-2588
www.idahostars.org

IdahoSTARS—United Way
Success By 6
Region 6
355 South Arthur
Pocatello, ID 83204
208-235-3119
800-926-2588
www.idahostars.org

IdahoSTARS—United Way
Success By 6
Region 5
426 Main Avenue, South
Twin Falls, ID 83301
800-926-2588
800-926-2588
www.idahostars.org

ILLINOIS

Child Care Resource and Referral Network
207 West Jefferson
Suite 301
Bloomington, IL 61701
309-828-1892
800-437-8256
www.ccrrn.com

CCR&R—John A. Logan College
700 Logan College Road
Carterville, IL 62918
618-985-5975
800-232-0908 (In-State)
www.jal.cc.il.us/ccrr/index.html

Eastern Illinois University Child Care Resource & Referral
600 Lincoln Avenue
Charleston, IL 61920
217-581-6698
800-545-7439
www.eiu.edu/~ccrr

Action For Children
4753 North Broadway
Suite 1200
Chicago, IL 60640
773-687-4000
www.actforchildren.org

Community Coordinated Child Care (4C)
155 North 3rd Street
Suite 300
Dekalb, IL 60115
815-758-8149
800-848-8727
www.four-c.org

Illinois Central College Child Care Connection
One College Drive
562
East Peoria, IL 61635
309-679-0400
800-421-4371
www.icc.edu

ChildCare Network of Evanston
1416 Lake Street
Evanston, IL 60201
847-475-2661
www.childcarenetwork
ofevanston.org

YWCA Child Care Resource and Referral
739 Roosevelt
Building 8, 210
Glen Ellyn, IL 60137
630-790-8137
www.ywcadupage.org

CHASI-Child Care Resource and Referral
2133 Johnson Road
Suite 103
Granite City, IL 62040
618-452-8900
800-467-9200
www.chasiccrr.org

McHenry County CCR&R
667 Ridgeview Road
McHenry, IL 60050
815-344-5510
866-347-2277
www.four-c.org

Project CHILD: Care Resource and Referral
P.O. Box 827
Mt. Vernon, IL 62864
618-244-2210
800-362-7257
www.rlc.edu/prochild

Child Care Resource and Referral
801 North Larkin Avenue
Suite 202
Joliet, IL 60435
815-741-1163
800-552-5626
www.childcarehelp.com

West Central Child Care Connection
510 Maine Street
WCU Building
Room 610
Quincy, IL 62301
217-222-2550
800-782-7318 (In-State)
www.wcccc.com

Young Womens Christian Association Child Care Solutions
4990 East State Street
Rockford, IL 61108
815-484-9442
800-872-9780
www.ywcachildcaresolutions.org

Community Child Care Connection, Inc.
1004 North Milton Avenue
Springfield, IL 62656
217-525-2805
800-676-2805
www.childcaresolutions.org

Child Care Resource Service
905 South Goodwin Avenue
314 Bevier Hall
Urbana, IL 61801
217-333-3252
800-325-5516
www.aces.uiuc.edu/~CCRSCare

YWCA — Child Care Resource and Referral of Lake County
2133 Belvidere Road
Waukegan, IL 60085
847-662-4247
800-244-5376
www.ywcalakecountyil.org

INDIANA

Southeastern Indiana Economic Opportunity Corporation
P.O. Box 240
Aurora, IN 47001
812-926-1585
800-755-8558
www.sieoc.org

Childhood Connections
1531 13th Street
Suite 1100
Columbus, IN 47201
812-375-2208
866-693-0672
www.childhoodconnections.org

4C of Southern Indiana Inc.
5115 Oak Grove Road
Suite A
Evansville, IN 47715
812-423-4008
866-200-5909
www.child-care.org

Early Childhood Alliance
3320 Fairfield Avenue
Fort Wayne, IN 46807
260-744-0298
800-423-1498
www.ecalliance.org

Workforce Development Services, Inc.
1776 West 37th Avenue
Gary, IN 46402
219-981-4100
www.workonenw.com

Child Care Answers
3750 North Meridian Street
1st Floor
Indianapolis, IN 46208
317-631-4643
800-272-2937
www.childcareanswers.com

Indiana Association for Child Care Resource and Referral
3901 North Meridian Street
Suite 350
Indianapolis, IN 46208
800-299-1627
800-299-1627
www.iaccrr.org

Community Action of Southern Indiana
1613 East 8th Street
Jeffersonville, IN 47130
812-288-6451
812-877-5400

Child Care Solutions
Bona Vista Programs, Inc.
P.O. Box 2496
Kokomo, IN 46904
765-452-8870
800-493-8870 (In-State)
www.bonavista.org

Connexions Resource and Referral
330 Fountain Street
Lafayette, IN 47904
765-742-7105
800-932-3302
www.cnxcare.com

Child Care Resource & Referral— HMCC
2000 North Elgin Street
Muncie, IN 47303
765-284-0887
800-554-9331
www.huffer.uwctl.org

Community Coordinated Child Care
3606 East Jefferson Boulevard
Suite 215
South Bend, IN 46615
574-289-7815
800-524-4533
www.4csindiana.org

4-C Wabash Valley
1520 North 19th Street
Terre Haute, IN 47807
812-232-3952
800-886-3952 (In-State)
www.4c-wabashvalley.com

IOWA

Center for Child Care Resources
100 University Village
Ames, IA 50010
515-294-8833
800-437-8599
www.centraliowachildcare.org

Family Resource Center
611 North West Street
Carroll, IA 51401
712-792-6440

MATURA Action Corporation Child Care Resource Center
203 West Adams
Creston, IA 50801
641-782-8431
888-482-8431
www.swiowachildcare.org

Project Concern, Inc., Child Care Resource and Referral
3505 Stoneman Road
Dubuque, IA 52002
563-557-1628
866-296-5331
www.neiowachildcare.org

Child Care Resource and Referral of Central Iowa
808 5ᵗʰ Avenue
Des Moines, IA 50314
515-286-2043
800-722-7619 (In-State)
www.childnetiowa.org
www.centraliowachildcare.org

Iowa Child Care/ Early Education Network
218 6ᵗʰ Avenue
Suite 710
Des Moines, IA 50309
515-883-1206
www.iowachildnetwork.org

Community Child Care Resource and Referral Center
500 East 59ᵗʰ Street
Davenport, IA 52803
563-324-1302
800-369-3778

Upper Des Moines Opportunity Child Care Resource and Referral
101 Robins Street
Graettinger, IA 51342
712-859-3885
800-245-6151 (In-State)
www.udmo.com

Child Care Resource and Referral of Southwest Iowa
P.O. Box 709
Harlan, IA 51537
712-755-7381
800-945-9778 (In-State)
www.swiowachildcare.org

Hawkeye Area Community Action Program, Inc.
1515 Hawkeye Drive
Hiawatha, IA 52233
319-739-1556
800-233-0054

4Cs Community Coordinated Child Care
1500 Sycamore Street
Iowa City, IA 52240
319-338-7684
http://soli.inav.net/~fourcs

S.C.I.C.A.P. Child Care Resource and Referral
1403 NW Church
Leon, IA 50144
641-446-8227
877-874-2623
www.swiowachildcare.org

Mid-Iowa Community Action, Inc.
1001 South 18ᵗʰ Avenue
Marshalltown, IA 50158
641-752-7162
www.midiaca.org

Child Care Resource and Referral
202 First Street
Suite 205
Mason City, IA 50401
641-424-9559
866-424-9559
www.neiowachildcare.org

Child Care Resource and Referral of Northwest Iowa
418 Marion Street
Remsen, IA 51050
712-786-2001
800-859-2025
http://mid-siouxopportunity.org/ccr/index.shtml

Child Care Resource and Referral of Northeast Iowa
P.O. Box 4090
Waterloo, IA 50704
319-233-0804
800-475-0804
www.NEIowaChildCare.org

KANSAS

Colby Community College Resource and Referral
1255 South Range
Colby, KS 67701
785-462-3984
888-634-9350
www.colbycc.edu

Cloud County Community College CCR&R
2221 Campus Drive
Concordia, KS 66901
785-243-9345
www.cloud.edu/childcare

Dodge City Community College Child Care Resource and Referral
1000 West Wyatt Earp Boulevard
Dodge City, KS 67801
620-227-8344
800-951-3837
www.dc3.edu/ccrra

East Central Kansas Child Care Resource & Referral
1200 Commercial
Campus Box 4037
Emporia, KS 66801
888-724-3206
www.emporia.edu/eckccrra

Care Connection Resource and Referral
2606 Fleming
Suite 5
Garden City, KS 67846
620-275-0399
800-275-2507
www.careconnection.org

Hays Area Children's Center
94 Lewis Drive
Hays, KS 67601
785-625-3257
888-351-3589
www.geocities.com/resourcereferral

Child Care Links
21 West 2nd Street
Hutchinson, KS 67501
620-669-0291
800-530-5129
www.childcarelink.org

The Family Conservancy Child Care Source
626 Minnesota Avenue
Kansas City, KS 66101
913-573-2273
800-755-0838
www.childcaresource.org

Douglas County Child Development Association
2331 Alabama Street
Suite 101
Lawrence, KS 66047
785-842-9679
www.dccda.org

Day Care Connection
8855 Long
Lenexa, KS 66215
913-529-1200
www.daycareconnection.org

Flint Hills Child Care Resource and Referral Agency
2323 Anderson Avenue
Suite 250
Manhattan, KS 66502
785-532-7197
800-227-3578
www.kccto.org/index2.html

Child Care Focus
2601 Gabriel—KUCDD
Parsons, KS 67357
620-421-6550
800-362-0390
www.childcarefocus.org

**Midwest Whole Child
  Development Group**
8001 Conser
Suite 280
Overland Park, KS 66204
913-573-2273
800-963-0009
www.mwdg.org

**YMCA Child Care Resource and
  Referral**
570 YMCA Drive
Salina, KS 67401
785-825-4861
800-586-3316
www.ymcaccrr.com

ERC Resource & Referral
1710 SW 10ᵗʰ Street
Suite 215
Topeka, KS 66604
785-357-5171
www.ercrefer.org

**Child Care Association of
  Wichita/Sedgwick County**
1069 South Glendale
Parklane Office Park
Wichita, KS 67218
316-682-3962
800-684-3962 (In-State)
www.childcareassociation.org

KENTUCKY

**Eastern Kentucky Child Care
  Coalition**
P.O. Box 267
Berea, KY 40403
859-986-5896

**Western Kentucky University
  Child Care Resource and
  Referral**
1 Big Red Way
Bowling Green, KY 42101
270-745-2216
800-621-5908
www.ttas.org

**Community Coordinated Child
  Care**
54 First Street
Elizabethtown, KY 42701
270-360-9911
800-879-0998 (In-State)
www.4cforkids.org

**Buffalo Trace Child Care
  Resource and Referral/
  Licking Valley C.A.P, Inc.**
203 High Street
Flemingsburg, KY 41041
606-845-0081
800-327-5196

**Gateway Child Care Resource
  and Referral**
203 High Street
Flemingsburg, KY 41041
606-783-7006
800-888-2770
www.lvcap.com

Kentucky Child Care Network
146 Consumer Lane
Frankfort, KY 40601
502-223-5002
877-723-5002
www.kychild.com

4C of Northern Kentucky
20 North Grand Avenue
Suite 1-A
Ft. Thomas, KY 41075
859-781-3511
800-315-7878
www.4c-cinci.org/ky.html

L.K.L.P Community Action Council
P.O. Box 340
Jeff, KY 41751
606-436-3161
800-401-4287
www.lklp.org

The Child Care Council of Kentucky
1460 Newtown Pike
Suite 101a
Lexington, KY 40511
859-254-9176
800-809-7076
www.childcarecouncilofky.com

Community Coordinated Child Care 4C
1215 South 3rd Street
Louisville, KY 40203
502-636-1358
800-928-1350
www.4cforkids.org

Audubon Area CCR&R
2000 College Drive
Madisonville, KY 42431
270-824-8684
800-689-5144
www.madcc.kctcs.edu/ccrr

Purchase Area Child Care Resource and Referral
P.O. Box 588
Mayfield, KY 42066
270-247-7171
877-352-5183
www.purchaseadd.org

Northeast Kentucky Area Development Council, Inc.
539 Hitchins Avenue
Olive Hill, KY 41164
606-286-4443
800-817-4443

Audubon Area Child Care Resource and Referral
1800 West Fourth Street
Owensboro, KY 42304
270-689-1929
877-389-7513
www.audubon-area.net

Eastern Kentucky Child Care Coalition Resource and Referral — Lake Cumberland
2387 Monticello Road
Somerset, KY 42501
606-679-0167
800-354-3703

LOUISIANA

Partnerships in Child Care
4521 Jamestown
Suite 5
Baton Rouge, LA 70808
225-926-8005
888-926-8005

Agenda for Child Care Resources
P.O. Box 51837
New Orleans, LA 70151
504-586-8509
800-486-1712
www.agendaforchildren.org

Northwestern State University Child and Family Network
1800 Warrington Place
Shreveport, LA 71101
318-677-3150
www.nsu-cfn.org

MAINE

Community Concepts, Inc.
79 Main Street
Auburn, ME 04210
207-777-1387
800-543-7008
www.community-concepts.org

Child Care Options
99 Western Avenue
Suite 6
Augusta, ME 04330
207-626-3617
www.skcdc.org

Maine Association of Child Care Resource and Referral Agencies
C/O Child Care Options
Augusta, ME 04330
888-917-1100
800-525-2229

Penquis Community Action Program Resource Development Center
262 Harlow Street
Bangor, ME 04401
207-941-2853
888-917-1100 (In-State)
www.penquiscap.org

Mid-Coast Regional Resource Development Center
34 Wing Farm Parkway
Bath, ME 04530
207-442-7963
877-684-0466
www.midcoastrdc.com

Child and Family Opportunities, Inc.
P.O. Box 648
Ellsworth, ME 04605
207-667-2467
800-834-4378
www.childandfamilyopp.org

Washington Hancock Community Agency
P.O. Box 280
Milbridge, ME 04658
207-546-7544
800-223-3632
www.whcacap.org

Aroostook County Action Program, Inc.
Resource Development Center
Presque Isle, ME 04769
207-768-3045
888-435-7881
www.acap-me.org

Carelink Resource Development Center
906 Main Street
Sanford, ME 04073
207-324-0735
888-917-1100
www.carelinkrdc.com

Cumberland County Child Care Resource Development Center
Child Care Connections
136 US Route 1
Scarborough, ME 04074
207-396-6566
888-917-1100
www.childcaremaine.org

MARYLAND

Open Door Child Care Resource Center
219 West Bel Air Avenue
Suites 4 and 5
Aberdeen, MD 21001
410-297-6592
888-297-1885
www.mdchildcare.org

Anne Arundel Child Care Connections
77 West Street
Suite 300
Annapolis, MD 21401
410-222-1728
www.mdchildcare.org/AA

Child Care Links
1101 North Point Boulevard
Suite 112
Baltimore, MD 21224
410-288-5600
www.childcarelinksinc.org

Baltimore City Child Care Resource Center
1645 Ridgely Street
Suite 200
Baltimore, MD 21230
410-539-2209
www.mdchildcare.org

Southern Maryland Child Care Resource Center
29958 Killpeck Creek Court
Charlotte Hall, MD 20622
301-290-0040
800-290-0040
www.smccrc.org

Howard County Child Care Resource Center
3300 North Ridge Road
Suite 380
Ellicott City, MD 21044
410-313-1940
www.mdchildcare.org

Child Care Choices/FCMHA
263 West Patrick Street
Frederick, MD 21701
301-695-4508
877-230-7422
www.fcmha.org

Apples for Children, Inc.
323 West Memorial Boulevard
Hagerstown, MD 21740
301-733-6914
800-924-9180
www.applesforchildren.org

Prince George's Child Resource Center
9475 Lottsford Road
Suite 202
Largo, MD 20774
301-772-8400
www.childresource.org

Montgomery County Child Care Resource and Referral
332 West Edmonston Drive
Rockville, MD 20852
301-279-1773
www.montgomerycountymd.gov

Lower Shore Child Care Resource Center
Power Professional Building
Wayne Street
Suite 500
Salisbury, MD 21804
410-548-3279
www.lowershoreccrc.org

Chesapeake Child Care Resource Center
P.O. Box 8—Chesapeake College
Wye Mills, MD 21679
410-822-5400
www.chesapeakechildcarerr.org

MASSACHUSETTS

Child Care Circuit
180 Cabot Street
Beverly, MA 01915
978-921-1631
800-660-2868
www.childcarecircuit.org

Child Care Choices of Boston
105 Chauncy Street
2nd Floor
Boston, MA 02111
617-348-6641
www.childcarechoicesofboston.org

Home Health and Child Care Services, Inc.
P.O. Box 640
Brockton, MA 02301
508-588-6070
www.hhcc.org

Child Care Resource Center, Inc.
130 Bishop Allen Drive
Cambridge, MA 02139
617-547-1063
www.ccrcinc.org

Child Care Search
2352 Main Street
Suite 102
Concord, MA 01742
978-897-6400
800-455-8326 (In-State)
www.comteam.org

Child Care Resources
76 Summer Street
Suite 345
Fitchburg, MA 01420
978-660-6269
800-660-6269 (In-State)
www.cafinc.org

FCAC Franklin Athol Child Care Services
393 Main Street
Greenfield, MA 01301
413-772-2177

Child Care Network of The Cape and Islands
115 Enterprise Road
Hyannis, MA 02601
508-778-9470
888-530-2430

Child Care Circuit
190 Hampshire Street
Lawrence, MA 01840
978-686-4288
877-823-2273
www.childcarecircuit.org

P.A.C.E. Child Care Works
4 Park Place
Room 101
New Bedford, MA 02740
508-999-9930
www.paceccw.org

Warmlines Parent Resources, Inc.
218 Walnut Street
Newtonville, MA 02460
617-244-4636
www.warmlines.org

Hampshire Community Action Commission
557 Easthampton Road
Northampton, MA 01060
413-582-4218
800-962-5511 (In-State)
www.hcac.org

Resources for Child Care
152 North Street
Suite 230
Pittsfield, MA 01201
413-443-7830
877-443-7830
www.resourcesforchilcare.net

Community Care for Kids
1509 Hancock Street.
Quincy, MA 02169
617-471-6473
www.semaccrr.org/ccfk

Preschool Enrichment Team, Inc.
293 Bridge Street
Suite 322
Springfield, MA 01103
413-736-3900
877-478-7727 (In-State)
www.preschoolenrichmentteam.org

Child Care Connection
100 Grove Street
Suite 102
Worcester, MA 01605
508-757-1503
800-278-1503
www.cccfscm.org

MICHIGAN

**Child Care Network—
Lenawee Office**
1040 South Winter Street
Suite 2020
Adrian, MI 49221
517-264-5306

**Child Advocacy 4C of
Central Michigan**
150 West Center Street
Alma, MI 48801
989-463-1422
800-552-4489 (In-State)

Child and Family Services 4C
P.O. Box 516
Alpena, MI 49707
989-354-8089
www.4c-ne.com

**Child Care Network/
Washtenaw 4C**
3060 Packard Road
Suite G
Ann Arbor, MI 48108
734-975-1840
800-777-2861
www.childcarenetwork.org

Macomb County 4C
21885 Dunham Road
Suite 12
Clinton Township, MI 48036
586-469-6993
800-621-8661 (In-State)
www.msue.msu.edu/macomb

**Child Care Coordinating Council/
Wayne County**
2151 East Jefferson Avenue
Suite 250
Detroit, MI 48207
313-259-4411

4Child Care Unlimited
1401 South Grand Traverse
Flint, MI 48503
810-232-0145
800-527-2182
www.flint4c.org

Kent Regional 4C
233 East Fulton
Suite 107
Grand Rapids, MI 49503
616-451-8281
800-448-6995
www.4cchildcare.org

**Child Care Network—
Hillsdale Office**
P.O. Box 675
Hillsdale, MI 49242
517-439-4592

Children's Resource Network
710 Chicago Drive
Suite 250
Holland, MI 49423
616-396-8151
800-332-5049
www.crn.nu

**Livingston County Community
Coordinating Council 4C**
2710 East Grand River
Suite 6
Howell, MI 48843
571-548-9112
800-260-0202
www.childcare4c.com

Child Care Network
209 East Washington Avenue
Suite 237
Jackson, MI 49201
517-817-0820
888-338-7656
www.childcarenetwork.org

Child Care Resources
3304 Mindi Lane
Kalamazoo, MI 49001
269-349-3296
www.workfamilysolutions.com

**Oakland County Child Care
  Council 4C's**
2111 Cass Lake Road
Suite 104
Keego Harbor, MI 48320
248-681-9192
www.oaklandchildcare.org

Michigan 4C Association
839 Centennial Way
Lansing, MI 48917
866-424-4532
www.mi4c.org

Office for Young Children
P.O. Box 30161
Lansing, MI 48909
517-887-4319
800-234-6996
www.ingham.org/hd/oyc

4C of Upper Peninsula
104 Coles Drive
Suite F
Marquette, MI 49855
906-228-3362
866-424-4532 (In-State)
www.4c-up.com

Child Care Concepts
1714 Eastman Avenue
Midland, MI 48640
989-631-8950

**Child Care Network—
  Monroe Office**
1051 South Telegraph
Monroe, MI 48161
734-243-7451

Saginaw Valley Regional 4C
5560 Gratiot
Suite B
Saginaw, MI 48603
989-497-0680
866-424-4532 (In-State)
www.svr4c.org

Northwest Michigan 4C Council
720 South Elmwood
Suite 4
Traverse City, MI 49684
231-941-7767
800-968-4228
www.nwmi4c.org

MINNESOTA

ACCAP—CCR&R
1201 89th Avenue NE,
Suite 345
Blaine, MN 55434
763-783-4884
www.accap.org

**Leech Lake Early Childhood
  Development**
6530 Highway 2, NW
Cass Lake, MN 56633
218-335-8257
800-551-0969

**Tri-Valley Opportunity Council
  Child Care Resource & Referral**
1424 Central Ave, NE
East Grand Forks, MN 56721
701-772-7905
800-452-3646
www.ndchildcare.org

Greater Minneapolis Day Care Association
1628 Elliot Avenue South
Minneapolis, MN 55404
612-341-1177
www.gmdca.org

Mid-West Child Care Resource and Referral
P.O. Box 695
Montevideo, MN 56265
320-269-8727
800-292-5437
www.prairiefive.com

Child Care Resource and Referral
715 11th Street North
Suite 402
Moorhead, MN 56560
218-299-7026
800-941-7003
www.lakesandprairies.net

Region 7E Child Care Resource and Referral
Pine Technical College
Pine City, MN 55063
320-629-5164
800-890-5399 (In-State)
www.ptcfaculty.edu

SCOPE Resource Center
560 Dunnell Drive
Suite 207
Owatonna, MN 55060
507-455-2560
877-455-2560

Child Care Resource and Referral, Inc.
126 Woodlake Drive SE
Rochester, MN 55904
507-287-2020
800-462-1660
www.c2r2.org

Resources for Child Caring
10 Yorkton Court
St. Paul, MN 55117
651-641-0332
www.resourcesforchildcare.org

MISSISSIPPI

Mississippi Forum on Children and Families, Inc.
737 North President Street
Jackson, MS 39202
601-355-4911
www.mfcf.org

MISSOURI

Mississippi Forum on Children and Families, Inc.
737 North President Street
Jackson, MS 39202
601-355-4911
www.mfcf.org

MONTANA

District VII Human Resources Development Council
P.O. Box 2016
Billings, MT 59103
406-247-4732
www.imt.net/~dist7hrdc

Child Care Connections, Inc.
317 East Mendenhall
Suite 3
Bozeman, MT 59715
406-587-7786
800-962-0418
www.childcareconnections.info

Community Coordinated Child Care/4C's
101 East Broadway
Butte, MT 59701
406-723-4019
800-794-4061 (In-State)
www.butte4-cs.org

Hi-Line Home Programs, Inc. Child Care Resource and Referral
605 3rd Avenue South
Glasgow, MT 59230
406-653-1219

DEAP Child Care Resource and Referral Glendive
218 West Bell, Suite 209
Glendive, MT 59330
406-377-4909
800-578-4909
www.deapmt.org

Family Connections
600 Central Plaza
Suite 225
Great Falls, MT 59401
406-761-6010
800-696-4503
www.famcon.org

Child Care Link/ District IV Human Resources Development Council
2229 5th Avenue
Havre, MT 59501
406-265-6743
800-640-6743
www.hrdc4.havre.mt.us

Child Care Partnerships
901 North Benton Avenue
Helena, MT 59601
406-443-4608
888-244-5368
www.childcarepartnerships.org

The Nurturing Center, Inc.
146 3rd Avenue West
Kalispell, MT 59901
406-756-1414
800-204-0644 (In-State)
www.nurturingcenter.org

District VI Human Resources Development Council
300 1st Avenue North
Suite 203
Lewistown, MT 59457
406-538-7488
800-766-3018
www.hrdc6.org

DEAP Child Care Resource and Referral
2200 Box Elder
Suite 151
Miles City, MT 59301
406-234-6034
800-234-6034
www.deapmt.org

Child Care Resources
P.O. Box 7038
Missoula, MT 59807
406-728-6446
800-728-6446
www.childcareresources.org

Montana Child Care Resource and Referral Network
127 East Main Street
Suite 217
Missoula, MT 59802
406-549-1028
866-750-7101
www.montanachildcare.com

NEBRASKA

Child Care Solutions
1137 South Locust Street
Grand Island, NE 68801
308-385-5182
www.esu3.org/ectc/HCCN/
ne_progs/ccs/ccs.htm

Family Service Care Connection
2101 South 42nd Street
Omaha, NE 68105
402-552-7000
www.familyservicemidlands.org

Midwest Child Care Association
5015 Dodge Street
Suite 2
Omaha, NE 68132
402-551-2379
800-876-1892
www.childcarene.org

NEW HAMPSHIRE

Child Care Resource, Referral, Recruitment, and Training
2020 Riverside Drive
Berlin, NH 03570
603-752-1113
800-445-4525
www.nhctc.edu

21C Childcare Resource and Referral
111 South Street
Claremont, NH 03743
603-543-4295
877-212-7267

Easter Seals
2 Industrial Park Drive
Building 2
Concord, NH 03301
603-226-3791
800-307-2737
www.eastersealsnh.org

Child Care Project
17 ½ Lebanon Street
Suite 2
Hanover, NH 03755
603-646-3233
800-323-5446
www.dartmouth.edu/~esaa/
ccp.html

Southwestern Community Services, Inc.
P.O. Box 603
Keene, NH 03431
603-352-7512
800-529-0005 (In-State)
www.scshelps.org

Lakes Region Community Services
635 Main Street
Laconia, NH 03246
603-284-7311
866-261-7555
www.lrcsc.org

Easter Seals
555 Auburn Street
Manchester, NH 03103
603-621-3501
800-870-8728
www.eastersealsnh.org

Nashua Area CCR&R
19 Chestnut Street
Nashua, NH 03061
603-883-7726
800-852-0632 (In-State)

Strafford County Child Care Connections
P.O. Box 607
Farmington, NH 03835
603-335-3849
888-440-4914 (In-State)
http://straffordctyrnr@aol.com

Rockingham Community Action Child Care Services
8 Centerville Drive
Salem, NH 03079
603-893-8446
800-310-8333 (In-State)

NEW JERSEY

Camden County Division for Children
P.O. Box 88, Lakeland Road
Blackwood, NJ 08012
856-566-7231
http://camdencounty.com/
    health/healthserv/children.html

Tri-County Community Action Agency
110 Cohansey Street
Bridgeton, NJ 08302
856-451-8100
www.tricountycaa.org

Burlington County Community Action Program
718 South Route 130
Burlington, NJ 08016
888-554-2077

Child Care Services of Monmouth County
P.O. Box 1234
Neptune, NJ 07754
732-918-9901
800-734-4810
www.ccrnj.org

Bergen County Office for Children
1 Bergen County Plaza
2nd Floor
Hackensack, NJ 07601
201-336-7150

New Jersey Association of Child Care Resource and Referral Agencies
Bergen County Office for Children
Hackensack, NJ 07601
201-336-7176
800-332-9227

Community Coordinated Child Care of Union County
225 Long Avenue
Building 15
Hillside, NJ 07205
973-923-1433
800-834-1184 (In-State)
www.ccccunion.org

Urban League of Hudson County
253 Martin Luther King Drive
Jersey City, NJ 07305
201-451-8888
www.ulohc.org

Children's Home Society of New Jersey
761 River Avenue
Lakewood, NJ 08701
732-905-6363
866-905-6363 (In-State)
www.chsofnj.org

Programs for Parents
20 Church Street
Montclair, NJ 07042
973-744-4677
800-713-9006

Programs for Parents, Inc.
33 Washington Street
6th Floor
Newark, NJ 07102
973-744-4677

**NORWESCAP Child and Family
Resource Services**
186 Halsey Road
Suite 1
Newton, NJ 07860
973-383-3461
866-793-3149
www.norwescap.org

**Atlantic County Women's Center-
Child Care Network**
P.O. Box 311
Northfield, NJ 08225
609-646-1180

North Jersey 4Cs
101 Oliver Street
Paterson, NJ 07501
973-684-1904
www.nj4c.com

**Catholic Charities-Diocese of
Metuchen-UCC**
103 Center Street
Perth Amboy, NJ 08886
732-324-4357
877-224-6364
www.childcareinfo.info

Child and Family Resources, Inc.
111 Howard Boulevard
Mount Arlington, NJ 07856
973-398-1730
www.childandfamily-nj.org

EIRC-Cape May County
4005 Route 9 South
Rio Grande, NJ 08242
609-886-5164
800-329-2273
www.eirc.org

**Tri-County Community Action
Partnership**
14 New Market Street
Salem, NJ 08079
856-935-7739

EIRC-Gloucester County
606 Delsea Drive
Sewell, NJ 08080
856-582-7000
www.eirc.org

Child Care Connection, Inc.
1001 Spruce Street
Suite 201
Trenton, NJ 08638
609-989-8101
800-231-1639
www.childcareconnection-nj.org

NEW MEXICO

Choices for Families, Inc.
2727 San Pedro NE
Suite 113
Albuquerque, NM 87110
505-884-0208

**YWCA/Cariño Child Care
Resource and Referral**
210 Truman NE
Albuquerque, NM 87108
505-265-8500
800-219-3999
www.ywca.org/newmexico

Family Resource Center
4601 College Boulevard
Farmington, NM 87401
505-566-3825
www.newmexicokids.org

Project Success
200 College Road
Gallup, NM 87301
505-722-2640
www.newmexicokids.org/
TTA_Centers

La Vida Institute
255 West Hadley
Las Cruces, NM 88005
505-527-1149

877-527-1168
www.newmexicokids.org

**Luna Community College—
Child Care Resource and
Training Project**
P.O. Box 1510
Las Vegas, NM 87701
505-454-2539
800-588-7232
www.luna.cc.nm.us

**ENMU Child Care Training and
Technical Assistance**
ENMU Education Building
Station 11
Portales, NM 88130
505-562-2850
800-287-2536
www.newmexicokids.org

Family Resource and Referral, Inc.
704 South Sunset
Suite A
Roswell, NM 88203
505-623-9438
800-447-9005

**Eight Northern Indian Pueblos
Council, Inc.**
P.O. Box 969
San Juan Pueblo, NM 87566
505-852-4265

**Santa Fe Community College/
Early Childhood Training and
Technical Assistance Program**
6401 Richards Avenue
Santa Fe, NM 87508
505-428-1344
866-209-6116 (In-State)
www.sfccnm.edu/sfcc/pages/
   98.html

La Familia Resource Center
P.O. Box 680
Silver City, NM 88062
505-538-6483
800-872-9668

Taos Family Resource Center
1335 Gusdorf Road
Suite Q
Taos, NM 87571
505-758-1395
http://newmexicokids.org

NEW YORK

**Fulmont Community Action
Agency, Inc.**
1200 Riverfront Center
Amsterdam, NY 12010
518-842-5713
www.fulmont.org

**NYS Child Care Coordinating
Council, Inc.**
230 Washington Avenue Extension
Albany, NY 12203
518-690-4217
www.nyscccc.org

**Child Care Council of
the Finger Lakes, Inc.**
17 East Genesee Street
4th Floor
Auburn, NY 13021
315-255-6994
www.cccfl.org

**Orleans Community Action
Committee—Child Care
Resource and Referral**
5073 Clinton Street
Batavia, NY 14020
585-343-7727

Accord Corporation, Child Care Services Division
15 Martin Street
Wellsvillle, NY 14895
585-593-0792
800-498-2277
www.accordcorp.org

Steuben Child Care Project
117 East Steuben Street
Suite 11
Bath, NY 14810
607-776-2126
800-553-2033
www.proactioninc.com

Family Enrichment Network
P.O. Box 880
Binghamton, NY 13902
607-723-8313
800-281-8741
www.familyenrichment.cc

Child Development Support Corporation
352-358 Classon Avenue
2nd Floor
Brooklyn, NY 11238
718-398-6730
888-469-5999
www.cdscny.org

Child Care Coalition of the Niagara Frontier
2635 Delaware Avenue
Suite A
Buffalo, NY 14216
716-877-6666
www.wnychildren.com

Schoharie County Community Action Program
795 East Main Street
Cobleskill, NY 12043
518-234-2568
www.sccapinc.org

Schoharie County Community Action Program, Inc.
795 East Main Street
Suite 5
Cobleskili, NY 12043
518-234-2568
www.sccapinc.org

Child Care Council of Suffolk
60 Calvert Avenue
Commack, NY 11725
631-462-0303
http://resourcereferral@
    childcaresuffolk.org

Delaware Opportunities, Inc.
Child and Family Development
    Division
47 Main Street
Delhi, NY 13753
607-746-2165

Cortland Area Child Care Council
111 Port Watson Street
Cortland, NY 13045
607-753-0106
www.cortlandchildcare.org

Adirondack Com Action Program
P.O. Box 848
Elizabethtown, NY 12932
518-873-3207

Chemung County Child Care Council, Inc.
571 East Market Street
Suite 205
Elmira, NY 14901
607-734-3941
www.chemchildcare.com

Child Care Council of Nassau, Inc.
925 Hempstead Turnpike
Suite 400
Franklin Square, NY 11010
516-358-9288
www.childcarenassau.org

Southern Adirondack Child Care Network
88 Broad
Fort Edward, NY 12828
518-798-7972
800-807-3224
www.saccn.org

Southern Adirondack Child Care Network, Inc.
88 Broad Street
Glens Falls, NY 12801
518-798-7972
800-807-3224 (In-State)

Child Care Council of Orange County, Inc.
40 Matthews Street
Suite 103
Goshen, NY 10924
845-294-4012
800-827-1751
www.childcarecounciloc.org

Child Care Council of Columbia and Green Counties
Suite 207 Fairview Plaza
Hudson, NY 12534
518-822-1944
800-494-1944

Day Care and Child Development Council of Tompkins County
609 West Clinton Street
Ithaca, NY 14850
607-273-0259
www.daycarecouncil.org

Chautauqua Child Care Council
560 West 3rd Street
Jamestown, NY 14701
716-366-8176
800-424-4532
www.chautauquaopportunities.com

Family of Woodstock, Inc.
P.O. Box 3516
Kingston, NY 12402
845-331-5197
www.familyofwoodstockinc.org

Child Care Council, Inc.
5604 Big Tree Road
Lakeville, NY 14480
800-754-6317
www.childcarecouncil.com

Sullivan County Child Care Council, Inc.
P.O. Box 186
Ferndale, NY 12734
845-292-7166
www.scchildcare.com

Franklin Day Care Development Office
26 Raymond Street
Malone, NY 12953
518-483-5151

Putnam County Child Care Council, Inc.
935 South Lake Boulevard
Suite 15
Mahopac, NY 10541
845-621-5619
www.putchild.org

Orleans Community Action Commitee
409 East State Street
Albion, NY 14411
585-343-7727
www.ocacinc.org

Capital District Child Care Coordinating Council
91 Broadway
Menands, NY 12204
518-426-7181
800-521-5437
www.cdcccc.org

Schuyler County Child Care Coordinating Council
P.O. Box 312
Montour Falls, NY 14865
607-535-7964
www.sccccc.org

The Child Care Council, Inc. — Wayne County
1173 East Union Street
Newark, NY 14513
800-201-6402
www.childcarecouncil.com

Child Care, Inc.
322 8th Avenue
New York, NY 10001
212-929-4999
www.childcareinc.org

Chinese-American Planning Council, Inc.
365 Broadway
Ground Floor
New York, NY 10013
212-941-0030
888-469-5999

Committee for Hispanic Children and Families
140 West 22nd Street
Suite 301
New York, NY 10011
212-206-8043
888-469-5999
www.chcfinc.org

Day Care Council of New York, Inc.
12 West 21st Street
3rd Floor
New York, NY 10010
212-206-7818
888-469-5999
www.dccnyinc.org

Community Child Care Clearinghouse of Niagara
1521 Main Street
Niagara Falls, NY 14305
716-285-8572
800-701-4543 (In-State)

Chenango County Child Care Coordinating Council
19 Eaton Avenue
Norwich, NY 13815
607-336-2809

St. Lawrence Child Care Council
318 Ford Street
Ogdensburg, NY 13669
315-393-6474

ACCORD Corporation
84 Schuyler Street
Belmont, NY 14813
585-593-0792
800-498-2277
www.accordcorp.org

Catholic Charities of Delaware and Otsego Counties
15 South Main Street
Oneonta, NY 13820
607-432-0061

Oswego County Child Care Council, Inc.
157 West 1st Street
Oswego, NY 13126
315-343-2344

Child & Family Resource, Inc.
100 East Main Street
Penn Yan, NY 14527
315-536-1134
800-881-5786 (In-State)

Child Care Coordinating Council of the North Country, Inc.
194 U.S. Oval
P.O. Box 2640
Plattsburgh, NY 12901
518-561-4999
800-540-2273

Child Care Council of Dutchess, Inc.
70 Overocker Road
Poughkeepsie, NY 12603
845-473-4141
888-288-4148
www.childcaredutchess.org

Western New York Child Care Council, Inc.
595 Blossom Road
Suite 120
Rochester, NY 14610
585-654-4720
www.childcarecouncil.com

Mid-York Child Care Coordinating Council, Inc.
143 West Dominick Street
Rome, NY 13440
315-339-8450
888-814-5437
www.mycccc.org

Child Care Council of the Finger Lakes, Inc.—Seneca County
10 State Street
Seneca Falls, NY 13148
315-568-0945
www.cccfl.org

Child Care Resources of Rockland, Inc.
235 North Main Street
Suite 11
Spring Valley, NY 10977
845-425-0009
www.childcarerockland.org

Child Care Solutions
3175 East Genesee Street
Suite 5
Syracuse, NY 13224
315-446-1220
888-729-7290
www.childcaresyracuse.org

Jefferson/Lewis Child Care Project
518 Davidson Street
Watertown, NY 13601
315-782-8475
800-287-8904
www.capcjcorg.verizons
   upersite.com

Child Care Council of Westchester, Inc.
470 Mamaroneck Avenue
White Plains, NY 10605
914-761-3456
www.childcarewestchester.org

NORTH CAROLINA

Stanly County Partnership for Children
P.O. Box 2165
Albemarle, NC 28002
704-982-2038
www.stanlypartnership.org

Randolph County Partnership for Children CCR&R
125 South Park Street
Asheboro, NC 27203
336-328-1400
www.randolphkids.org

Buncombe County Child Care Services
59 Woodfin Place
Asheville, NC 28801
828-255-5726
www.buncombecounty.org/
   governing/depts/childcare

The Children's Council Child Care Resource and Referral
290 Queen Street
Boone, NC 28607
828-262-5424
http://thechildrenscouncil.org

Transylvania County Child Development
299 South Broad Street
Brevard, NC 28712
828-884-3116
www.transylvania.lib.nc.us/ childcare

Child Care Resource and Referral of Pender County
P.O. Box 429
Burgaw, NC 28425
910-259-9978

Child Care Connections
P.O. Box 2243
Burlington, NC 27216
336-227-9653

Mitchell-Yancey Child Care Resource and Referral
P.O. Box 1387
Burnsville, NC 28714
828-682-0717

Child Care Services Association
P.O. Box 901
Chapel Hill, NC 27514
919-403-6950
866-406-6950
www.childcareservices.org

Child Care Resources, Inc.
4601 Park Road
Suite 500
Charlotte, NC 28209
704-348-2181
800-532-9634
www.childcareresourcesinc.org

Child Development Program
PSC Box 8009
Cherry Point, NC 28533
252-466-3595

Sampson County Partnership for Children
211 West Main Street
Clinton, NC 28328
910-592-9399
www.scpcsmartstartexpress.org

Partnership for Children of Lincoln and Gaston Counties
1012 Philadelphia Church Road
Dallas, NC 28034
704-922-0900
www.pfclg.com

Albemarle Child Care Resource and Referrals
1403 Parkview Drive
Elizabeth City, NC 27909
252-333-3206
http://Wecare4kids.org

Child Care Solutions
351 Wagoner Drive
Suite 200
Fayetteville, NC 28303
910-860-2277
www.ccpfc.org

Family Resources Inc., CCR&R
P.O. Box 1619
Forest City, NC 28043
828-286-3411
www.frrc.org/main/index.htm

Wayne Child Care Resource and Referral
800 North William Street
Goldsboro, NC 27530
919-735-3371
www.waynesmartstart.org

Regional Child Care Resources and Referral
1200 Arlington Street
Greensboro, NC 27406
336-378-7700
www.ucdccip.org

Childlinks
111B Eastbrook Drive
Greenville, NC 27858
252-792-9840
www.mppfc.org

Franklin Granville Vance Child Care Resource and Referral
P.O. Box 142
Henderson, NC 27536
888-244-2480
www.fgvpartnership.org

Children and Family Resource Center/CCR&R
P.O. Box 1105
Hendersonville, NC 28793
828-692-3847
www.childrenandfamily.org

Children's Resource Center
1985 Tate Boulevard SE
Hickory, NC 28602
828-328-8228
www.childrensresourcecenter.org

Duplin County Child Care Resource and Referral
P.O. Box 989
Kenansville, NC 28349
910-296-2000
www.duplinsmartkids.com

Dare County Child Care Resource and Referral
P.O. Box 2539
Kill Devil Hills, NC 27948
252-441-4737
www.darekids.org

Stokes Partnership for Children
P.O. Box 2319
King, NC 27021
336-985-2676
800-559-5606
www.stokespfc.com

Lenoir/Greene Child Care Resource and Referral
1465 Highway 258 North
Kinston, NC 28504
252-526-5000
www.lenoirgreenesmartstart.org

Northampton Partnership for Children
P.O. Box 997
Jackson, NC 27845
252-534-9921
www.northamptonsmartstart.org

Child Care Resource and Referral Onslow County
308 Western Boulevard
Jacksonville, NC 28546
910-938-0336
www.onslowkids.org

Ashe County Child Care Resource and Referral
626 Ashe Central School Road
Unit 2
Jefferson, NC 28640
336-982-8870

Child Care Directions, Inc.
P.O. Box 911
Laurinburg, NC 28353
910-276-3367
www.ccdirections.org

Choices in Child Care
602 Morganton Boulevard
Lenoir, NC 28645
828-426-2422

Child Care Connection of Davidson County, Inc.
4766 East US Hwy 64
Lexington, NC 27292
336-249-0216

Harnett County Child Care Resource and Referral
P.O. Box 1089
Lillington, NC 27546
910-893-7597
http://harnett.ces.state.nc.us/childcare/ccr&r.htm

Child Care Directions, Inc.
P.O. Box 3265
Lumberton, NC 28359
910-671-8335

Children's Services Network
54 College Drive
Marion, NC 28752
828-652-0637
www.mcdowelltech.cc.nc.us/child.html

Madison County Partnership for Children, CCR&R
P.O. Box 545
Marshall, NC 28253
828-649-1364

CCR&R of Carteret County Partnership for Children
305 Commerce Avenue
Suite 102
Morehead City, NC 28557
252-727-0445
www.carteretkids.org

Child Care Connections of Burke County
P.O. Box 630
Morganton, NC 28680
828-439-2328

Surry County Early Childhood Partnership
P.O. Box 7050
Mt. Airy, NC 27030
336-786-1880
www.surrychildren.org

Hertford County Partnership for Children, CCR&R Services
P.O. Box 504
Murfreesboro, NC 27855
252-398-4124
www.hertfordpartnership.org

Craven County Child Care Resource and Referral
628 Hancock Street
New Bern, NC 28560
252-672-5921

Avery County Partnership for Children
P.O. Box 1455
Newland, NC 28657
828-733-7325
http://averypartnership.org

Wilkes Child Care Resource and Referral
P.O. Box 788
North Wilkesboro, NC 28659
336-838-0977
www.wilkessmartstart.com

Child Care Networks
P.O. Box 1531
Pittsboro, NC 27312
919-542-6644
www.childcarenetworks.org

Washington County Child Advocacy Council, Inc.
125B West Water Street
Plymouth, NC 27962
252-793-5437
www.washingtonchildadvocacy.org

Halifax-Warren Child Care Resource and Referral
1139 Roanoke Avenue
Roanoke Rapids, NC 27870
252-535-4715
www.hwss.org

Richmond County Partnership for Children
Child Care Avenues, Inc.
P.O. Box 1944
Rockingham, NC 28380
910-997-2273
www.richmondsmartstart.org/
  cca.htm

Down East Partnership for Children Child Care Resource and Referral
P.O. Box 1245
Rocky Mount, NC 27802
252-985-4300
www.depc.org

Person County Partnership for Children Child Care Resource and Referral
P.O. Box 1791
Roxboro, NC 27573
336-599-3773
www.personpartnershipfor
  children.org

Child Care Connections
Salisbury, NC 28147
704-630-9085
www.rowan-smartstart.org

Brick City CCR&R
P.O. Box 3873
Sanford, NC 27330
919-774-9496

Child Care Choices
1200 South Pollock Street
Selma, NC 27576
919-202-4893
www.childcarechoices-jc.org

Child Care Resource and Referral of Brunswick County
P.O. Box 2232
Shallotte, NC 28459
910-755-3362
877-422-7710
www.smartstart-bruns.org

Child Care Connections of Cleveland County
P.O. Box 1739
Shelby, NC 28151
704-487-7778
www.ccckidsbiz.org

Child Care Resources of Alleghany
P.O. Box 1643
Sparta, NC 28675
336-372-2846

Child Care Connections, Inc. of Moore County
P.O. Box 1139
Southern Pines, NC 28388
910-692-6123
www.childcareconnections.org

Iredell County Partnership for Young Children, Inc.
132 East Broad Street
Statesville, NC 28677
704-878-9980
www.iredellsmartstart.org

Alexander County Child Care Resource & Referral
P.O. Box 1661
Taylorsville, NC 28681
828-632-3799

Child Care Central
404-A North Main Street
Troy, NC 27371
910-576-0112
www.brighterfutures.org

Anson County Partnership for Children CCR&R
117 South Greene Street
Wadesboro, NC 28170
704-694-2038
www.ansonsmartstart.org

Child Connections
211 B North Market Street
Washington, NC 27889
252-975-4647
www.beaufortcountykids.org

Southwestern Child Care Resource and Referral
P.O. Box 250
Webster, NC 28788
800-662-4158 (In-State)
828-586-5561

Rockingham County Partnership for Children
P.O Box 325
Wentworth, NC 27375
336-342-9676
www.rcpfc.org

Southeastern Child Care Resource and Referral
P.O. Box 151
Whiteville, NC 28472
910-642-8189

ChildLinks — Martin County
224 Green Street
Williamston, NC 27892
252-792-9840
www.mppfc.org

Creative Child Care Solutions, Inc.
228 Eastwood Road
Suite A-3 PMB-193
Wilmington, NC 28403
910-799-8914

The Child Advocacy Commission
P.O. Box 4305
Wilmington, NC 28406
910-791-1057
888-556-5624
www.childadvocacywilm.org

Wilson County Partnership for Children
P.O. Box 2661
Wilson, NC 27893
252-206-4235
www.wilson-coforchildren.org

Bertie County Partnership for Children, Inc.
P.O. Box 634
Windsor, NC 27983
252-794-3438
www.bertiesmartstart.org

Work Family Resource Center, Inc.
313 Indera Mills Court
Winston-Salem, NC 27101
336-761-5100
800-937-7610
www.ccrr.org

Yadkin County Partnership for Children
P.O. Box 39
Yadkinville, NC 27055
336-679-7833

Caswell County Partnership for Children
P.O. Box 664
Yanceyville, NC 27379
336-694-1538
www.caswellchildren.org

NORTH DAKOTA

**Lutheran Social Services Child
Care Resource and Referral**
1616 Capitol
Bismarck, ND 58501
888-223-1510
www.ndchildcare.org/splash

Sitting Bull College
1341 92nd Street
Fort Yates, ND 58538
701-854-3861

OHIO

**Child Care Connection,
A Program of Info Line, Inc.**
474 Grant Street
Akron, OH 44311
330-376-7706
800-407-5437
www.infolineinc.org

**COAD Child Care Resource
Network Central Office**
1 Pinchot Lane
Athens, OH 45701
740-594-8499
800-577-2276 (In-State)
www.coadinc.org/ece

4C
1924 Dana Avenue
Cincinnati, OH 45207
513-221-0033
800-256-1296
www.4c-cinci.org

Child Care Choices
P.O. Box 439
110 Island Road
Circleville, OH 43113
937-644-1010

Starting Point
2000 East 9th Street
Suite 1500
Cleveland, OH 44115
216-575-0061
800-880-0971
www.starting-point.org

Action for Children
78 Jefferson Avenue
Columbus, OH 43215
614-224-0222
www.actionforchildren.org

**Ohio Child Care Resource
Referral Association**
80 Jefferson Avenue
Columbus, OH 43215
614-849-0500
www.occrra.org

**Children's Hunger Alliance/
Child Care Works**
3077 Kettering Boulevard
Suite 300
Dayton, OH 45439
937-534-0600
800-340-0600
www.childcareworksohio.org

**Northwestern Ohio Community
Action Commission**
1933 East 2nd Street
Defiance, OH 43512
419-784-2150
800-686-2964 (In-State)
www.nocac.org

**Action for Children —
Delaware County**
39 West Winter Street
Delaware, OH 43015
740-369-0649
www.actionforchildren.org

Child Care Choices
120 Harding Way East
Suite 107
Galion, OH 44833
419-468-7587
800-922-4453
www.childcarechoices.org

Child Care Finder
239 West Main Street
Lancaster, OH 43130
740-687-6833

YW Child Care Connections
616 South Collett Street
Suite 203
Lima, OH 45805
419-225-5465
800-992-2916
www.carelinkservices.com

Child Care Network
P.O. Box 230
London, OH 43140
740-852-0975
www.actionforchildren.org

Child Care Resource Center
5350 Oberlin Avenue
Lorain, OH 44053
440-960-7187
800-526-5268 (In-State)
www.ccrcinc.com

COAD Child Care Resource Network
1500B Greene Street
Marietta, OH 45750
740-373-6996
800-577-2276 (In-State)
www.coadinc.org/ccrnpage.htm

Child Care Network
Marysville, OH 43040
937-644-1010
800-248-2347

www.co.union.oh.us/djfs

Pathways of Licking County
1627 Bryn Mawr Drive
Newark, OH 43055
740-345-6166
www.pathwayslc.org

COAD Child Care Resource Network, SDA 5
1243 Monroe Street, NW
New Philadelphia, OH 44663
330-364-8882
800-577-2276 (In-State)
www.coadinc.org/ccrnpage.htm

COAD Child Care Network
500 Chillicothe Street
Suite 203
Portsmouth, OH 45662
740-354-6527
800-577-2276 (In-State)

Shelby County Department of Job and Family Services
129 East Court Street
Sidney, OH 45365
937-498-4981
800-915-0090
www.occrra.org

Child Care Connections
P.O. Box 59
Springfield, OH 45501
937-323-4211
800-915-0090
www.uwccc.org

Child Care Choices
814 West Main Street
Tipp City, OH 45371
937-667-1799
866-667-4799 (In-State)
www.child-care-choices.org

YW Child Care Connections
1018 Jefferson Avenue
Toledo, OH 43624
800-632-3052
www.ywcatoledo.org

OKLAHOMA

**ECU Child Care Resource and
  Referral**
200 Fentem Hall
Ada, OK 74820
580-310-5303
800-862-5593
www.ecok.edu/ccrra

**Delaware Tribe Child
  Development**
220 NW Virginia Avenue
Bartlesville, OK 74003
918-336-7567
866-254-9864
www.dtcd.org/child_care_links.htm

**Child Care Association—
  Choctaw Nation**
16th and Locust
P.O. Box 1210
Durant, OK 74701
580-924-8280
www.choctawnation.org

**Southeastern Child Care Resource
  and Referral**
PMB 4232
Durant, OK 74701
580-745-3176
888-320-5205
www.sosu.edu/childcare

**Child Care Finders Resource and
  Referral**
2615 East Randolph
Enid, OK 73701
580-548-2318
800-401-3463
www.childcarefinder.org

**Great Plains Child Care Resource
  and Referral Center**
901 South Broadway
Hobart, OK 73651
580-726-2172
888-878-4417
www.gpccrr.org

Rainbow Fleet CCR&R
3024 Paseo
Oklahoma City, OK 73103
405-525-3111
800-438-0008
www.rainbowfleet.org

**Cherokee Nation Child Care
  Resource Center**
P.O. Box 948
Tahlequah, OK 74465
918-458-6230
888-458-6230
www.cherokeekids.net

Child Care Resource Center
18 North Norwood
Tulsa, OK 74115
918-834-2273
www.ccrctulsa.org

OREGON

Family Connections
6500 Pacific Boulevard SW
Albany, OR 97321
541-917-4899
800-845-1363
http://linnbenton.edu/family
  resources/familyconnections

Caring Options of CAT, Inc.
10 Sixth
Suite 205B
Astoria, OR 97103
503-325-1053
866-504-2273
www.clatsoponestop.org/home.htm

Child Care Resource and Referral
1916 Island Avenue
La Grande, OR 97850
541-963-7942
800-956-0324
wwwtrainingemployment.org

Child Care Resource & Referral, Training, and Employment Consortium
113 West Jefferson
Burns, OR 97720
541-573-6676
800-895-0641
www.trainingemployment.org

Care Connections
1988 Newmark Avenue
Coos Bay, OR 97420
541-888-7957
800-611-7555
www.socc.edu

Child Care Resource and Referral, Training, and Employment Consortium
P.O. Box 85
Enterprise, OR 97828
541-426-2020
800-956-0324
wwwtrainingemployment.org

Lane Family Connections
4000 East 30ᵗʰ Avenue
Eugene, OR 97402
541-463-3954
800-222-3290 (In-State)
www.lanecc.edu/lfc/index.htm

CCR&R of Multnomah and Clackamas — Mt. Hood Council of Camp Fire
5427 Glen Echo Avenue
Gladstone, OR 97207
503-548-4400
866-227-5529
www.campfireusamthood.org

Metro Child Care Resource and Referral
912 NE Kelly Avenue
Suite 239
Gresham, OR 97030
800-695-6988
www.metroccrr.org

Umatilla Morrow Child Care Resource & Referral
110 NE 4ᵗʰ Street
Hermiston, OR 97838
541-564-6878
800-559-5878
www.umchs.org

Child Care Resource and Referral of Washington County
Community Action
Hillsboro, OR 97123
971-223-6100
800-624-9516
www.communityaction4u.org

Klamath/Lake Child Care Resource and Referral
1803 Avalon Street
Klamath Falls, OR 97603
541-882-2308
800-866-9835
http://oregonchildcare.org/ccrrs/sda13.htm

Child Care Resource and Referral
1916 Island Avenue
La Grande, OR 97850
541-963-7942
800-956-0324
www.trainingemployment.org

The Job Council Child Care Resource Network
673 Market Street
Medford, OR 97504
541-776-1234
800-866-9034
www.jobcouncil.org/child_care.html

Family Care Resource and Referral
P.O. Box 425
Moro, OR 97039
541-565-3200
877-279-8262 (In-State)

Family Care Connection for Lincoln County
29 SE 2ⁿᵈ Street
Newport, OR 97365
541-265-2558
800-603-2728
http://extension.oregonstate.edu

Child Care Resource and Referral, TEC
190 East Lane
Ontario, OR 97914
541-889-7864
800-694-4558

Child Care Resource and Referral of Multnomah and Clackamas Counties
1006 SE Grand Avenue
Suite 100B
Portland, OR 97214
503-548-4400
866-227-5529 (In-State)
www.ccrr-mc.org

Portland Community College — Child Care Services
PCC Sylvania SY 246
Portland, OR 97219
503-977-4366

Child Care Resources — Cocaan
2303 SW First
Suite A
Redmond, OR 97756
541-548-2380
888-298-2672
www.cocaan.org

Family Connections of Douglas County
815 SE Oak Avenue
Roseburg, OR 97470
541-672-7955
800-443-0812 (In-State)
www.familyconnectionsof
   douglascounty.com

Child Care Information Service
2475 Center Street NE
Salem, OR 97301
503-585-2491
800-289-5533
www.open.org/ccis

Caring Options Program of CAT, Inc.
310 Columbia Boulevard
St. Helens, OR 97051
503-397-3511
www.oregeonchildcare.org

Child Care Partners
400 East Scenic Drive
The Dalles, OR 97058
541-298-3107
800-755-1143 (In-State)
www.cgcc.or.us

Caring Options Program of CAT, Inc.
3600 East 3ʳᵈ Street
Tillamook, OR 97141
503-842-3267
866-486-4391
www.clatsoponestop.org/home.htm

PENNSYLVANIA

Community Services for Children, Inc.
1520 Hanover Avenue
Allentown, PA 18109
610-868-4636
800-528-7222
www.cscinc.org

**CCIS of Blair County/
Child Care Connection**
3001 Fairway Drive
Suite D
Altoona, PA 16602
814-949-9110
800-750-0610 (In-State)

**Child Care Information Services
of Northampton County**
2200 West Broad Street
Bethlehem, PA 18018
610-419-4500
866-800-3880 (In-State)

**Child Care Information Service of
Columbia County**
3119 Old Berwick Road
Bloomsburg, PA 17815
570-784-0963
866-784-2247 (In-State)

Child Care Network, Inc.
1416 Trindle Road
Suite 201
Carlisle, PA 17103
717-243-1830
800-358-8725

**Child Care Information Services
of Adams, Franklin and Fulton
Counties**
600 Norland Avenue
Suite 2
Chambersburg, PA 17201
717-263-6549
800-682-5702 (In-State)

**Child Care Information Services
of Clearfield**
10438 Clearfield Curwensville
Highway
Clearfield, PA 16830
800-422-5807

**Child Care Information Service of
Montour County**
398 Wall Street
Danville, PA 17821
570-275-3996
www.montourchildcare.com

**Bucks Child Care Information
Service**
70 West Oakland Avenue
Suite 102
Doylestown, PA 18901
215-348-1283
800-371-2109 (In-State)
www.buckschildcare.com

**Child Care Information Service of
Cambria County**
300 Prave Street
Suite 101
Ebensburg, PA 15931
814-472-6341
800-492-9292
www.cciscambria.com

**Child Care Information Service of
Cameron, Elk, McKean, and
Potter Counties**
P.O. Box 389
Emporium, PA 15834
814-486-1974
800-638-4670 (In-State)

**Child Care Information Services
of Erie County**
155 West 8th Street
Suite 316
Erie, PA 16501
814-451-6676

**Child Care Information Service of
Bedford County**
10241 Lincoln Highway
Everett, PA 15537
814-623-2002
888-465-9304

Child Care Information Service of Mercer County
1600 Roemer Boulevard
Farrell, PA 16121
800-564-7600
724-346-6171

Child Care Information Services of Venango County
24 Front Street
Franklin, PA 16323
814-437-1906
800-892-3448
www.dpw.state.pa.us/child/childcare

Child Care Information Service of Adams County
153 North Stratton Street
Gettysburg, PA 17325
717-334-7634
800-232-6562 (In-State)

CCIS of Westmoreland County
766 East Pittsburgh Street
Suite 202
Greensburg, PA 15601
724-836-4580
800-548-2741
www.cciswestmoreland.com

Pennsylvania Child Care Association
2300 Vartan Way
Suite 103
Harrisburg, PA 17110
717-657-9000
www.pacca.org

Child Care Information Service of Huntingdon County
52 Juniata Avenue-Rear
Huntingdon, PA 16652
814-643-4980

Child Care Information Service of Indiana County
1055 Oak Street
Suite A
Indiana, PA 15701
724-349-8830
800-327-3070
www.childcareinfoservice.org

Carbon County Child Care Agency
76 Susquehanna Street
Jim Thorpe, PA 18829
570-325-2226
888-212-0483

Child Care Information Service of Armstrong County
124 Armsdale Road
Suite 211
Kittanning, PA 16201
724-763-8490
888-808-6529
www.armstrongcap.com

Child Care Information Service of Mifflin County
152 East Market Street
Suite 101
Lewistown, PA 17044
717-242-4346
866-803-4346
www.sumcd.org

Child Care Information Service of Crawford County
378 Chestnut Street
Meadville, PA 16335
814-337-8055
800-682-6118 (In-State)

Child Care Information Service of Snyder/Union County
14 South 11th Street
Mifflinburg, PA 17844
570-966-2216
866-996-2216
www.sumcd.org

Child Care Information Service of Juniata County
12 Weatherby Way Road
Mifflintown, PA 17059
717-436-8613

Child Care Information Service of Pike County
Shohola, PA 18458
570-296-3447
877-475-2273 (In-State)

Child Care Information Service of Lawrence County
1001 East Washington Street
Suite 3
New Castle, PA 16101
724-658-8874
888-774-9130

Montgomery County Office of Child Day Care Services
P.O. Box 311
Norristown, PA 19404
640-278-3707
800-281-1116 (In-State)
www.montcopa.org/ccis

CCIS of Allegheny County
305 Wood Street
2nd Floor
Pittsburgh, PA 15222
412-261-2273
www.ywcapgh.org

CCIS — Northeast
1926 Grant Avenue
Philadelphia, PA 19152
215-333-1560
www.philadelphiachildcare.org

CCIS of Philadelphia — South/Center City
1500 South Columbus Boulevard
2nd Floor
Philadelphia, PA 19147
215-271-0433
888-461-5437
www.philadelphiachildcare.org

Child Care Information Services of Philadelphia County — West/Southwest
3901 Market Street
Philadelphia, PA 19104
215-382-4762

Child Care Information Services — North
642 North Broad Street
6th Floor
Philadelphia, PA 19130
215-763-0100
www.philadelphiachildcare.org

Philadelphia Child Care Resources Northwest
6350 Greene Street
Philadelphia, PA 19144
215-842-4820
888-461-5437
www.philadelphiachildcare.org

Philadelphia Information Services
3901 Market Street
Box 1969
Philadelphia, PA 19104
888-461-5437
www.philadelphiachildcare.org

**Child Care Information Services
  of Schuylkill County**
2335 West End Avenue
Pottsville, PA 17901
570-624-7950
800-216-1938
www.ccis-schuylkill.org

**Child Care Information Service of
  Clarion and Jefferson Counties**
105 Graceway
Punxsutawney, PA 15767
814-938-3302
800-648-3381 (In-State)
www.jccap.org

**Child Care Information Services
  of Berks County**
P.O. Box 16050
Reading, PA 19612
610-987-8444
800-257-3038

**Child Care Information Service of
  Lackawanna County**
345 Wyoming Avenue
Scranton, PA 18503
570-963-6644

**Child Care Information Service of
  Susquehanna County**
1356 North Washington Avenue
Scranton, PA 18509
570-341-0811
800-559-6020 (In-State)
www.cciswaynesusq.com

**Child Care Information Service of
  Wayne County**
1356 North Washington Avenue
Scranton, PA 18509
570-341-0811
800-559-6020 (In-State)
www.cciswaynesusq.com

**Child Care Information Services
  of Centre County**
2565 Park Center Boulevard
Suite 100
State College, PA 16801
814-231-1352
888-440-2247
www.cdfc.org

**Monroe County Children and
  Youth Services**
730 Phillips Street
Stroudsburg, PA 18360
570-420-3590
866-284-5829 (In-State)

**Child Care Information Service of
  Somerset County**
300 North Center Avenue
Somerset, PA 15501
814-445-9260
800-428-8920 (In-State)

**Child Care Information Service of
  Northumberland County**
601½ Pennsylvania Avenue
Sunbury, PA 17801
570-988-4452
800-692-4332 (In-State)
www.dpw.state.pa.use/child/
  childcare

**Child Care Information Service of
  Bradford and Sullivan County**
P.O. Box 189
Towanda, PA 18848
570-265-1760
888-369-3599

**Child Care Information Service of
  Wyoming County**
Route 29
Box 29
Tunkhannock, PA 18657
570-836-1826

Child Care Information Service of Fayette County
137 North Beeson Avenue
Uniontown, PA 15401
724-425-1818
800-443-0888 (In-State)

Child Care Information Service of Warren and Forest Counties
1209 Pennsylvania Avenue West
Warren, PA 16365
814-726-1361
www.wfcaa.org

Child Care Information Service of Greene County
22 West High Street
Waynesburg, PA 15370
724-852-5277
888-355-2247

Child Care Information Service of Tioga County
P.O. Box 766
Wellsboro, PA 16901
570-724-5766
800-242-5766 (In-State)
www.tiogahsa.org

Child Care Information Service — Chester County
GSC610 Westtown Road
Suite 310
West Chester, PA 19380
610-344-5862
www.chesco.org/cyf/childcare_
  search.html

CCIS of Luzerne County
P.O. Box 2631
Wilkes-Barre, PA 18703
570-822-6500
800-922-6264

Child Care Information Service of Clinton County
P.O. Box 3568
Williamsport, PA 17707
800-346-3020

Child Care Resource Developers of Central Region
P.O. Box 3568
Williamsport, PA 17701
570-327-6949

Child Care Information Service of Lycoming County
2138 Lincoln Street
Williamsport, PA 17701
570-327-5429

Child Care Consultants, Inc.
13 West Market Street
York, PA 17401
717-854-2273
800-864-4925
www.childcareconsultants.org

RHODE ISLAND

Options for Working Parents
30 Exchange Terrace
4th Floor
Providence, RI 02903
401-272-7510
800-244-8700 (In-State)
www.optionsforworking
  parents.com

SOUTH CAROLINA

Child Care By Choice/ United Way of Aiken County
P.O. Box 699
Aiken, SC 29801
803-648-8331
877-919-2828
www.childcarebychoice.org

Interfaith Community Services of South Carolina, Inc.
P.O. Box 5150
Columbia, SC 29250
803-252-8390
800-879-2219
www.midnet.sc.edu/icsofsc

United Way of Greenville County Success By 6, Child Care Resource and Referral
24 Vardry Street
Suite 404
Greenville, SC 29601
864-467-4800
877-467-4800
www.unitedwaygc.org

Child Care Resource and Referral/ Trident United Way
P.O. Box 63305
North Charleston, SC 29419
843-747-9900
877-227-3454
www.tuw.org

Success By 6-United Way of Sumter, Clarendon and Lee Counties, Inc.
215 North Washington Street
Sumter, SC 29150
803-773-7935
www.charityadvantage.com/ sumtersuccessby6

SOUTH DAKOTA

Early Childhood Partners
1500 North Main Street
Aberdeen, SD 57401
605-229-8505

Family Resource Network
South Dakota State University
Box 2218
Brookings, SD 57007
605-688-5730
800-354-8238
http://frn.sdstate.edu

Pierre Area Referral Service
118 East Missouri
Pierre, SD 57501
605-224-8731

Black Hills Parent Resource Network
730 East Watertown Street
Rapid City, SD 57701
605-394-5120

Early Childhood Connections
809 South Street
Suite 304
Rapid City, SD 57701
605-342-6464
888-999-7759 (In-State)
www.earlychildhood connections.com

Child Care Service/ Rosebud Sioux Tribe
P.O. Box 430
Rosebud, SD 57570
605-747-5264

C.H.I.L.D. Services
1115 West 41st Street
Sioux Falls, SD 57106
605-333-0663

Help! Line Center
1000 North West Avenue
Suite 310
Sioux Falls, SD 57104
605-339-4357
www.helplinecenter.org

TENNESSEE

Southeast Child Care Resource and Referral
c/o Signal Centers, Inc.
Signal Centers
Chattanooga, TN 37404
866-296-3422
www.signalcenters.org

Mid-Cumberland Child Care Resource and Referral
c/o Developmental Services of
Dickson County
Clarksville, TN 37040
931-648-3695
866-446-6006

Upper Cumberland Child Care Resource and Referral
Upper Cumberland CC
Resource Center
Cookeville, TN 38505
931-372-3780
888-621-5753 (In-State)
www.tntech.edu/ucccrc

South Central Child Care Resource and Referral
C/O Community Development
Center
Fayetteville, TN 37334
931-438-2322
866-776-2811

East North Child Care Resource and Referral
The Michael Dunn/Henry Center
Harriman, TN 37748
865-882-5289

Southwest Child Care Resource and Referral
c/o Kiwanis Center for
Child Development
Jackson, TN 38305
901-664-4233
800-858-2738
www.vethda.org

Upper East Child Care Resource and Referral
301 Louis Street
Kingsport, TN 37660
866-215-2936
www.uethda.org

East South Child Care Resource and Referral
University of Tennessee at
Knoxville
Knoxville, TN 37996
865-974-1363

Northwest Child Care Resource and Referral
Child Care Resource Center at U.T.
Martin, TN 38238
731-881-7868
877-424-6080

Shelby County Child Care Resource and Referral
2430 Poplar Avenue
Memphis, TN 38112
901-324-3637
www.shelbycountycorr.org

Davidson County Child Care Resource and Referral
c/o Tennessee State University
Nashville, TN 37203
615-963-7258

TEXAS

Family Connections
825 East 53rd ½ Street
Building E-101
Austin, TX 78751
512-478-5725
877-433-2057
www.familyconnectionsonline.org

Child Care Group
8585 North Stemmons Freeway
Suite 500 South
Dallas, TX 75247
214-631-2273
800-441-7865
www.childcaregroup.org

YWCA Child Care Resource and Referral
1600 North Brown Street
El Paso, TX 79902
915-533-7528
888-533-9590 (In-State)
www.ccrronline.org

Camp Fire USA First Texas Council
2700 Meacham Boulevard
Ft. Worth, TX 76137
817-831-5060
www.firsttexascampfire.org/ moreinfo.htm

Collaborative for Children, Inc.
3800 Buffalo Speedway
Suite 300
Houston, TX 77098
832-615-1234
888-833-6805
www.initiativesforchildren.org

Children's Connections, Inc.
2514 82nd Street
Suite G
Lubbock, TX 79413
800-456-4862

City of San Antonio Children's Resources Division
1222 North Main
Suite 400
San Antonio, TX 78212
210-246-5270
866-271-6797
www.sanantonio.gov

Family Service Association— Smart Start Connections
421-2 6th Street
San Antonio, TX 78215
210-299-2480
800-332-3264 (In-State)
www.family-service.org

Child Care, Inc.
1000 Lamar Street
Suite 432
Wichita Falls, TX 76301
940-766-4332

UTAH

Child Care Resource and Referral
Bridgerland Utah State University
6510 Old Main Hill
Logan, UT 84322
435-797-1552
800-670-1552
www.usuchild.usu.edu

Child Care Resource and Referral Western Region
88 East Fiddler's Canyon Road
Suite H
Cedar City, UT 84720
435-628-4843
888-344-4896 (In-State)
www.childcarehelp.org

Child Care Resource and Referral Northern Region
1309 University Circle
Ogden, UT 84408
801-626-7837
888-970-0101 (In-State)
http://programs.weber.edu/ccrr

UACCRRA/CCR&R
Mountainland-163
Utah Valley State College
800 West University Parkway
Orem, UT 84058
801-863-8220
http://webbie.hsq.usu.edu/
    usuchild

Child Care Resource and Referral Eastern Region
451 East 400 North
Price, UT 84501
435-613-5619
www.ceu.edu/childcare

Child Care Resource and Referral Metro
124 South 400 East
Suite 400
Salt Lake City, UT 84111
801-355-4847
866-438-4847
www.cssutah.org/childcare

VERMONT

Bennington County Child Care Association
P.O. Box 829
Bennington, VT 05201
802-447-3778
www.bccca.net

Windham Child Care Association
130 Birge Street
Brattleboro, VT 05301
802-254-5332
866-254-5332 (In-State)
www.windhamchildcare.org

Addison County Child Care Services
Mary Johnson Children's Center
81 Water Street
Middlebury, VT 05753
802-388-4304

The Family Center of Washington County
32 College Street
Suite 100
Montpelier, VT 05602
802-828-8771

NEKCA Parent Child Center
P.O. Box 346
Newport, VT 05855
802-334-4072
887-722-6680

Springfield Area Parent Child Center
2 Main Street
North Springfield, VT 05150
802-886-5242
www.sapcc2.com

**Child Care Support Services/
Vermont Achievement Center**
P.O. Box 6283
Rutland, VT 05702
802-747-0033
800-775-2390 (In-State)

The Family Center
27 Lower Newton Street
St. Albans, VT 05478
800-427-6574

Umbrella, Inc.
970 Memorial Drive
St. Johnsbury, VT 05819
802-748-8645
800-916-8645 (In-State)

Child Care Resource
181 Commerce Street
Williston, VT 05495
802-863-3367
800-339-3367 (In-State)
www.childcareresource.org

VIRGINIA

**Alexandria Office for Early
Childhood Development**
2525 Mount Vernon Avenue
Alexandria, VA 22301
703-838-0750

Arlington Child Care Office
3033 Wilson Boulevard
Suite 500A
Arlington, VA 22201
703-228-1685
www.co.arlington.va.us/dhs/
services/family

**People, Inc. of Southwest
Virginia Child Care Resource
and Referral**
1173 West Main Street
Abingdon, VA 24210
276-623-9000
877-933-5373
www.peopleinc.net

Child Development Services
HQBN, HQMC, Henderson Hall
Arlington, VA 22214
703-614-7332

**Caroline County CCR&R,
Cooperative Extension**
P.O. Box 339
Bowling Green, VA 22427
804-633-6550
866-543-7852 (In-State)

**Children, Youth and Family
Services**
116 West Jefferson Street
Charlottesville, VA 22902
434-296-4118
866-543-7852

**Fairfax County Office for
Children**
Child Care Assistance and Referral
12011 Government Center
Parkway
8th Floor
Fairfax, VA 22035
703-449-8484
800-451-1501
www.fairfaxcounty.gov/childcare

The Childcare Network
1907 Charles Street
Suite E
Fredericksburg, VA 22401
540-373-3275
866-543-7852
www.thechildcarenetwork.org

RADA Child Care Connect
112 Beech Street
Suite 3
Gate City, VA 24251
276-386-6549
877-222-5437 (In-State)

ChildCare Connection
411 Stone Spring Road
Harrisonburg, VA 22801
540-433-4531
800-377-4453 (In-State)

Intercounty Childcare Connection
Child Net of Virginia Cooperative
   Extension
P.O. Box 6
King And Queen, VA 23085
804-693-9446
866-336-9181
www.iccc-va.org

**ChildCare Connection of Page
   County**
P.O. Box 12
Stanley, VA 22851
540-743-1273
877-599-1273 (In-State)

**Loudoun County Department of
   Social Services**
102 Heritage Way NE
Suite 200
Leesburg, VA 20176
703-777-0353
www.loudoun.gov/services/
   childcare/index.htm

**Child Care Link and Resource
   Center**
2600 Memorial Avenue
Suite 201
Lynchburg, VA 24501
434-528-5437
866-285-5437 (In-State)
www.alliancecva.org

The Planning Council
130 West Plume Street
Norfolk, VA 23510
757-627-3993

Kidcare Resource and Referral
Memorial Child Guidance Clinic
200 North 22nd Street
Suite 140
Richmond, VA 23225
804-282-6078
www.mcgcva.com

**Virginia Child Care Resource and
   Referral Network**
Richmond, VA 23225
804-285-0846
866-481-1913
www.vaccrrn.org

**Child Care Link—
   Council of Community Services**
P.O. Box 598
Roanoke, VA 24004
540-985-0131
800-354-3388
www.councilofcommunity
   services.org

**CHILDNET/
   Virginia Cooperative Extension**
P.O. Box 156
Saluda, VA 23149
804-693-9446
866-336-9181

Child and Family Connection
312 Waller Mill Road
Suite 500
Williamsburg, VA 23185
757-229-7940
www.childandfamilyconnection.org

**Child Care Options Prince
William County Department of
Social Services**
15941 Donald Curtis Drive
Suite 180
Woodbridge, VA 22191
703-792-7609
www.co.prince-william.va.us/dss

**Child Care Quality Initiative of
Virginia Cooperative Extension**
600 North Main Street
Suite 100
Woodstock, VA 22664
540-459-6149
877-603-6145
www.ext.vt.edu/offices

WASHINGTON

**Coastal Community Action
Program CCR&R**
117 East 3rd Street
Aberdeen, WA 98520
360-533-5605
www.coastalchildcare.org

The Opportunity Council
1111 Cornwall
Suite C
Bellingham, WA 98225
360-734-5121
800-649-5121
www.oppco.org

**Child Care Resource and Referral
of Kitsap County**
105 National Avenue North
Bremerton, WA 98312
360-405-5827
www.resourceandreferral.org

**Volunteers of America Western
Washington CCR&R —
Snohomish County**
P.O. Box 839
Everett, WA 98206
425-258-4213
800-633-3183
www.voaww.org

**Lower Columbia Community
Action Child Care Resource and
Referral**
P.O. Box 2129
Longview, WA 98632
360-425-3430
800-383-2101
www.childcareanswers.org

**Catholic Family and Child
Service**
414 South Burress
Moses Lake, WA 98837
800-597-8308

**Volunteers of America Resource
and Referral — Skagit County**
1934 East College Way
Mt. Vernon, WA 98273
360-416-8299
800-503-0011
www.voaww.org

Child Care Action Council
P.O. Box 446
Olympia, WA 98507
360-754-0810
800-845-0956 (In-State)
www.familysupportctr.org/CCAC

**Benton-Franklin Community
Action Child Care Resource and
Referral**
710 West Court Street
Pasco, WA 99301
509-545-4042
800-583-1112
www.bfcac.org

The Parent Line/Lutheran Community Services Northwest
301 Lopez Street
Port Angeles, WA 98362
360-452-5437
www.lcsnw.org/parentline

WSU Child Care Resource and Referral
P.O. Box 643454
Pullman, WA 99164
800-440-2277
www.wsu.edu/CCRR

Child Care Resources
1225 South Weller
Suite 300
Seattle, WA 98144
206-329-1011
www.childcare.org

Family Care Resources— Northwest Regional Facilitators
315 West Mission Avenue
Suite 24
Spokane, WA 99201
509-484-0048
800-446-2229
www.nrf.org

Washington State Child Care Resource and Referral Network
917 Pacific Ave
Suite 600
Tacoma, WA 98402
253-383-1735
http://childcarenet.org

Tacoma/Pierce County Child Care Resource and Referral
747 Market Street
Room 836
Tacoma, WA 98402
253-591-2025
www.cityoftacoma.org/34Childcare

CCR&R-Educational Service District # 112
2500 NE 65th Avenue
Vancouver, WA 98661
360-750-9735
800-282-0874
www.firststeps.esd112.org

Child Care Resource and Referral of Walla Walla Community College
500 Tausick Way
Walla Walla, WA 99362
509-527-4333
877-527-4333
www.wwcc.edu/parent/ccr&r

Catholic Family and Child Service Child Care Resource and Referral
23 South Wenatchee Avenue
Suite 320
Wenatchee, WA 98801
509-662-6761
800-261-1094 (In-State)
www.4people.org

Catholic Family aand Child Service CCR&R
5301 Tieton Drive
Suite C
Yakima, WA 98908
509-965-7109
800-793-4453

WEST VIRGINIA

Connect Child Care Resource and Referral Agency
910 Quarrier Street
Suite 317
Charleston, WV 25301
304-344-8290
888-595-8290
www.wvdhhr.org

Link Child Care Resource and Referral
611 7th Avenue
Suite 200
Huntington, WV 25701
304-523-9540
800-894-9540
www.wvdhhr.org/link/

Choices CCR&R
4421 Emerson Avenue
Suite 102
Parkersburg, WV 26104
304-485-2668
866-966-2668 (In-State)
www.wvdhhr.org/choices

Mountain Heart Child Care Services
P.O. Box 1509
Oceana, WV 24870
800-834-7082

Central Child Care of West Virginia
411 D Street
South Charleston, WV 25303
304-382-0797

Child Care Resource Center
1025 Main Street
Suite 510
Wheeling, WV 26003
304-232-1603
800-585-1603

WISCONSIN

Child Care Resource and Referral, Inc.
1051 North Lynndale Drive
Suite 2
Appleton, WI 54914
920-734-0966
800-749-5437 (In-State)
www.getconnectedforkids.org

Project Bridges Child Care Resource and Referral
201 Hospital Road
Eagle River, WI 54521
715-479-0337
800-470-5833
www.northwoodsresources.org/ Bridges.htm

Child Care Partnership Resource and Referral Center
P.O. Box 540
Eau Claire, WI 54702
715-831-1700
800-782-1880 (In-State)

Southwest Wisconsin Child Care Resource and Referral, Inc.
1222 Lincoln Avenue
Fennimore, WI 53809
608-822-4453
800-267-1018
www.swwiccrr.com

Community Childcare Connections
621 Pine Street
Green Bay, WI 54301
920-432-8899
888-713-5437 (In-State)
www.ccconnections.org

Northwest Wisconsin Child Care Resource and Referral
16076 West Highway 63
Hayward, WI 54843
800-733-5437

South Central Child Care Resource and Referral, Inc
1900 Center Avenue
Janesville, WI 53546
608-741-3426
888-713-5437
www.scccrr.com

Family Resources, Inc.
P.O. Box 1897
La Crosse, WI 54602
608-784-4519
800-873-1768
www.laxfamilyresources.org

Community Coordinated Child Care, Inc.
5 Odana Court
Madison, WI 53719
608-271-9181
800-750-5437
www.4-c.org

4C-Community Coordinated Child Care, Inc.
116 East Pleasant Street
Lower Level
Milwaukee, WI 53212
800-713-5437
www.4c-milwaukee.org

Child Care Resource and Referral, Inc.
105 Washington Avenue
Suite 114
Oshkosh, WI 54902
920-426-8920
800-316-8884 (In-State)
www.childcarerr.com

Family Connections, Inc.
2508 South 8th Street
Sheboygan, WI 53081
920-457-1999
800-322-2046
www.familyconnectionscc.org

Mid-Wisconsin Child Care Resource & Referral
23 Park Ridge Drive
Suite 11
Stevens Point, WI 54481
715-342-1788
800-930-5437 (In-State)

Child Care Resource and Referral Services
9400 Durand Avenue
Sturtevant, WI 53177
262-884-9890
www.wisconsinccrr.org

Child Care Connection, Inc.
301½ Grand Avenue
Wausau, WI 54403
715-848-5297
800-848-5229 (In-State)
http://childcareconnectionrr.org

Child Care Resource and Referral of Central Wisconsin, Inc.
210 East Jackson Street
Wisconsin Rapids, WI 54494
715-423-4114
800-628-8534

WYOMING

Child Care Finder— Central West Office
P.O. Box 2455
Casper, WY 82602
800-578-4017
www.childrens-nutrition.com

Children and Nutrition Services, Inc.
P.O. Box 2455
Casper, WY 82602
307-266-1236
800-578-4017
www.childrens-nutrition.com

Child Care Finder— Southeastern Wyoming Office
P.O. Box 5423
Cheyenne, WY 82003
307-638-2091
www.childrens-nutrition.com

Child Care Finder—
  Northwestern Wyoming Office
P.O. Box 108
Powell, WY 82435
307-754-8457
800-578-4017
www.childrens-nutrition.com

Child Care Finder—
  Southwestern Wyoming Office
P.O. Box 4445
Marbleton, WY 83113
307-276-5460
800-578-4017

Child Care Finder—
  Northeastern Wyoming Office
245 Broadway
Box 5
Sheridan, WY 82801
307-673-0265
800-578-4017
www.childrens-nutrition.com

(Source: National Association of Child Care Resource and Referral Agencies;
www.childcareaware.org)

Appendix C

Websites

The Internet can be a goldmine of information for working parents seeking solutions to the challenges of finding a quality childcare situation. If you do not have access to the World Wide Web in your own home, you should be able to get online at your local library, or perhaps even at a school in your area. In some areas, Internet cafes provide computer access along with a cappuccino. If your employer is online, you may be able to do some research at your workplace. If there are rules prohibiting computer use for personal purposes, ask your human resources director if you can have access before or after work. Some websites that may help you in your search for childcare answers follow.

General Childcare Issues
About.com
www.childcare.about.com
> *Community website providing helpful advice and tips on a large variety of topics*

American Academy of Pediatrics
www.healthychildcare.org
> *Professional association for 6,000 pediatricians; provides information relating to children's health*

Childcare.gov
www.childcare.gov
> *Clearinghouse of federal agency resources relating to childcare*

Child Care Aware
www.childcareaware.org
> *NACCRRA-operated initiative assisting families trying to locate quality childcare in their area*

Child Care and Early Education Research Connections
www.childcareresearch.org/discover/index.jsp
>*Organization promoting quality childcare by providing resources to early childhood researchers*

Child Care Law Center
www.childcarelaw.org
>*Advocacy organization geared toward providing quality childcare to low-income families and special needs children through the use of legal systems*

Families and Work Institute
www.familiesandwork.org
>*Nonprofit research organization focusing on work/life issues*

The Family and Workplace Connection
www.familyandworkplace.org
>*Organization providing childcare information to families and training to childcare professionals*

Nation's Network of Child Care Resource and Referral (NACCRRA)
www.naccrra.org
>*Nationwide network of local child care and referral agencies; provides resources for families in the search for quality childcare*

National Association for the Education of Young Children
www.naeyc.org
>*Organization providing accreditation for day care centers*

National Association for Family Child Care
www.nafcc.org
>*Organization providing accreditation for family day care homes*

National Child Care Association
www.nccanet.org
>*Professional association for the interests of private, licensed childcare providers*

National Child Care Information Center
www.nccic.org
>*Clearinghouse for families, providers and researchers for early childhood information*

National Institute of Child Health and Human Development
www.nichd.nih.gov
>*Agency of the National Institutes of Health, dedicated to promoting research for the protection of children's health*

National Network for Child Care
www.nncc.org
>*Internet resource providing links to publications relating to various childcare issues*

National Resource Center for Health and Safety in Child Care

http://nrc.uchsc.edu
Clearinghouse of information for parents and providers relating to childcare safety issues

United States Consumer Product Safety Commission
www.cpsc.gov
Government agency providing information concerning safety of products for consumer use; specializes in product recall information

United States Office of Personnel Management
www.opm.gov/family/wrkfam
Human resources agency for employees of the federal government

United States General Services Organization Office of Child Care
www.gsa.gov
Government agency administering federal facilities providing childcare

Urban Institute
www.urban.org
Nonpartisan social policy research organization

USA Child Care
www.usachildcare.org
Organization advocating for quality childcare for low- to middle-income families

Work At Home Magazine
www.WAHM.com
Online community and resource center for parents working at home

Work At Home Moms Wellness and Organization Center
www.internetbasedmoms.com/wellness-center
Business-centered Internet community for parents working from home

Zero to Three
www.zerotothree.org
Advocacy organization promoting development of infants and toddlers

Au Pairs

Au Pair Foundation
www.aupairfoundation.org
Organization providing matching services for au pairs and U.S. families

Au Pair in America
www.aupairinamerica.com
Matching organization for au pairs and American families

United States Department of State Exchange Visitor Program
www.exchanges.state.gov/education/jexchanges/private/aupair.htm
Resources and information connected with the U.S. Exchange visitor Program

Child Abuse

National Clearinghouse on Child Abuse and Neglect Information
www.nccanch.acf.hhs.gov
   Information website for reporting child abuse

Nannies

4 Everything Nanny
www.4nanny.com
   Information and resources for families seeking in-home childcare

4Nannies.com
www.4nannies.com
   Online search tool for families seeking nannies

International Nanny Association
www.nanny.org
   Professional association for nannies, agencies, and nanny training programs

Nanny.com
www.nanny.com
   Resources for families, nannies, and nanny agencies

Nanny Locators
www.nannylocators.com
   Online nanny/family matching service

Nanny Network
www.nannynetwork.com
   Online directory of nanny agencies

National Alliance of Professional Nanny Agencies
www.theapna.org
   Association of nanny placement agencies

National Association of Nannies
www.nannyassociation.com
   Professional association for nannies, nanny agencies and other industry members

Part-time and Backup Childcare

Afterschool.gov
www.afterschool.gov
   Network of federal resources supporting children during the after-school hours

Afterschool Alliance
www.afterschoolalliance.org
   Advocacy organization devoted to bringing attention to the need for after-school programs

After School Scene
www.afterschoolscene.com
> *Website geared toward school-aged children to promote appropriate after-school activities*

Bringing Yourself to Work
www.bringingyourselftowork.com
> *Training model for staff of after-school programs designed to improve relationships between caregivers and students*

National Association for Sick Child Daycare
www.nascd.com
> *Organization advocating development of quality back-up childcare for sick children*

Paying for Childcare

Child Care and Development Fund
www.nccic.org/statedata/dirs/devfund.html
> *Information website for state child care and development block grant programs*

Head Start Bureau
www.acf.hhs.gov/programs/hsb/hsweb/index.jsp
> *Government website providing information, statistics, and contacts relating to the federal Head Start Program*

Internal Revenue Service
www.irs.gov
> *Government website with online forms and publications relating to all areas of tax liability, tax credits, deductions, and filing requirements*

State Child Care Subsidy Agencies
http://nccic.org/statedata/statepro/index.html
> *Contact information for state agencies providing subsidies for qualified families needing childcare*

Veterans Administration Child Care Subsidy Program
www.va.gov/VAchildcare
> *Eligibility and application information for Veterans Administration childcare benefits*

Single Parenting and Childcare

Making Lemonade—The Single Parent Network
www.makinglemonade.com
> *Online support community for single parents*

Single Parent Central
www.singleparentcentral.com
> *Publications and other resources for single-parent families*

Single Parents
www.single-parents.net
  Resources for single parents

Single Parents Network
www.singleparentsnetwork.com
  Online support community for single parents

Special Needs Childcare
About.com
www.specialchildren.about.com
  Online community resource for issues relating to special needs children

Council for Exceptional Children
www.ideapractices.org
  Professional organization promoting education in special needs and gifted children

Easter Seals
www.easterseals.com
  Support organization for people with special needs or disabilities and their families; provides childcare for children with special needs

Internet Resource for Special Children
www.irsc.org
  Online information clearinghouse

National Dissemination Center for Children with Disabilities
www.nichcy.org
  Information and resource clearinghouse for issues related to children with disabilities, including the Individuals with Disabilities Education Act

Office of Special Education Programs
www.ed.gov/about/offices/list/users/osep/index.html
  Federal agency administering the Individuals with Disabilities Education Act

Appendix D

Sample Forms

Table of Forms

Sample Childcare Employment Agreement 280

Parental Consent to Obtain Emergency Medical Treatment 286

Authorization to Obtain Background Check 287

SAMPLE CHILDCARE EMPLOYMENT AGREEMENT

Parties to Agreement
This agreement is made _____(*today's date*), between _____
_____ (*name/s and address of
parent/s*), hereinafter "Employer," and _____
(*name and address of nanny*), hereinafter "Employee."

Start Date of Employment
Employment will start on _____ (*first date nanny is to work for parents*),
hereinafter referred to as the "Start Date."

Compensation
Employer will pay Employee $_____ per week (*or day, hour, etc.*).
Compensation will be payable every other Friday, beginning with the second
Friday after the Start Date.

[If the nanny is live-in, you might add the something along the lines of the following:

Employee also shall receive, as part of Employee's compensation, exclusive use of
the assigned bedroom/bath suite designated as the Employee's quarters, along
with three meals every day, as prepared by either Employee as part of Employee's
duties, or by Employer as part of the family meal. Employee shall be provided a
telephone for personal use, with telephone line to be shared with Employer's
family. Any personal long-distance charges Employee incurs shall be Employee's
own responsibility.]

[If the nanny is live-in, you may wish to add something similar to the following paragraph:

Relocation Expenses
In addition to compensation as set forth above, Employer will pay reasonable
expenses incurred by Employee in relocating to Employer's home, up to the amount
of $_____. In order to receive reimbursement for these costs, Employee will pres-
ent Employer receipts for any such expenses claimed. Within seven days after receiving these receipts, Employer will make a determination as to the reasonableness of
the expenses, and will then immediately provide reimbursement to Employee.

or, if you do not wish to be responsible for any relocation costs:

Employee shall be solely responsible for payment of Employee's costs incurred in
relocating for this position, and Employer will have no liability whatsoever for
any such expenses, whether incurred by Employee in relocating to Employer's
home or incurred by Employee in vacating Employer's home upon termination
of this contract.]

Work Schedule
Employee will work from _____ a.m. until _____ p.m., Monday through Friday.

Paid Holidays
The following days will be paid holidays every year:
New Year's Day
Memorial Day
Independence Day
Labor Day
Thanksgiving
Day after Thanksgiving
Christmas Day
Employee's Birthday

In the case of New Year's Day, Independence Day, Christmas Day, and Employee's Birthday, if the holiday falls on a Saturday, the Friday immediately before the holiday will be a paid holiday; if the holiday falls on a Sunday, the Monday immediately after the holiday will be a paid holiday.

Either Parent May Give Instructions/Authorization
Employee is entitled to rely on the instructions, consent, and approval of either parent under this agreement, and may not be disciplined for following the instructions, consent, and approval of one parent against the other parent's wishes. Employee will, however, use best efforts to inform both parents immediately if there is a discrepancy between their instructions.

Vacation
Employee will be entitled to two weeks of paid vacation per year. For the first year of employment only, Employee must complete six months of employment before vacation may be taken. Vacation time that is not used during the year will not carry over to a later year. The scheduling of one yearly vacation week will correspond with Employer's own vacation plans. The scheduling of the other yearly vacation week will be by mutual agreement between Employer and Employee. No vacation may be taken without at least two weeks' notice to Employer by Employee.

Sick Days
Employee will be entitled to _____ paid sick days per year. For the first year of employment only, Employee must complete six months of employment before sick time may be taken. If Employee must take sick time prior to six months of employment during the first year, or if Employee must take more than _____ sick days in one calendar year, those sick days will not be paid.

Taxes

Employer will deduct from Employee's pay all (*include or exclude as necessary for your state*) income, Social Security, Medicare, and/or any and all other employment taxes and deductions required by state or federal law, and will remit the same to the appropriate agency or agencies on behalf of Employee.

Insurance

Employer will pay to insure Employee as an additional driver of Employer's automobile. Employer will pay up to $_____ per month toward the premium for a health insurance policy covering Employee; the health insurance policy will be of Employee's choosing. Employee will be responsible for all premiums exceeding the amount Employer has agreed to pay, and likewise, Employee will be responsible for any and all deductibles that she is required to pay for health care.

Overtime

Employer will compensate Employee for any extra hours worked, beyond those set out above, at a rate of $_____ per hour.

Pay Increases/Reviews

Employer will provide Employee with a review every year on the anniversary of Employee's Start Date. At that time, Employer may increase Employee's salary for the following year.

Duties

Employee will be responsible for Employer's _____ (*number of children*) children, _____ (*children's names*). Should Employer have additional children, Employee will be compensated with additional salary of $_____ per hour per additional child.

Employee's duties will consist of the following:

Employee will be responsible for, and will directly supervise, the children at all times while Employee is scheduled to work.

Employee will serve breakfast, lunch (or will pack a lunch, if necessary, for school-age children), and an afternoon snack to the children, using food that is provided by Employer and according to menu instructions given by Employer. Should Employer require simple dinner-related tasks to be performed by Employee (for example, placing a dinner entrée in the oven and turning the oven on), Employee will perform those tasks. However, Employee is not required to prepare the dinner meal. Employee may dine with the children and is welcome to share whatever meal they are having.

Employee will, as is appropriate for the particular age of each child, assist or supervise the children in preparing for school and in other routine daily activities, including but not limited to the following.

- Dressing
- Washing up
- Toileting
- Brushing teeth
- Packing up homework and school supplies
- Cleaning up breakfast and/or lunch dishes
- Doing homework
- Picking up toys, art supplies, etc.

Employee will follow all house rules as set out by Employer, and will require the children to follow the rules as well. Employee will use discipline as allowed by Employer, namely, time-outs and redirecting. Under no circumstances will Employee use corporal punishment upon the children.

Employee will transport the children to activities, in Employer's vehicle, as necessary according to Employer's instructions. Employee will not transport the children without prior approval of Employer. Employee will not transport any children other than Employer's children without prior approval of Employer. Employee will not allow others to transport Employer's children without prior approval of Employer.

Employee will facilitate the children's learning, social development, and physical fitness through daily activities geared toward these purposes. Activities may include but are not limited to:

- reading, whether reading aloud to the children, having the children read aloud, or providing the children time to read to themselves if they are able;
- math as is age-appropriate;
- appropriate outside play, under constant supervision of Employee;
- creative activities, such as arts and crafts, skit or puppet show production, or music making;
- helping with appropriate household tasks, such as making own beds and setting the table;
- playdates with other children, only if set up in advance by Employer and the parents of the other child; and,
- nap or quiet time, as appropriate for the children's ages and for a reasonable period of time each day.

Employee will perform light housekeeping as may be necessary during the day, including but not limited to the following:

- following meals: cleaning up all dishes, wiping down kitchen counters and tables, sweeping kitchen floor;
- once daily, preferably late afternoon unless otherwise noted: vacuuming children's play area; emptying kitchen garbage can, run dishwasher and put away clean dishes as necessary, make up children's beds (morning);

- laundry as necessary to prevent staining or ruination of linens or clothing due to mishaps occurring while children are under Employee's care; and,
- sweeping or mopping of other areas, running of carpet steam cleaner, vacuuming, or any other housework as may be necessary during the course of the day due to mishaps or activities of the children.

Employee will administer any necessary medications to the children, strictly following the instructions of Employer. No over-the-counter or other medicines may be given without the prior approval of Employer.

Employee will not be responsible for the following:
- any laundry other than as specified above;
- yardwork or snow removal;
- cleaning of closets; and,
- washing of bathrooms or floors, other than as specified above.

House Rules
Employee will abide by the following house rules.
(*Set out all rules that the nanny is expected to follow; examples might include:*
- *no visitors;*
- *no long distance telephone calls; and,*
- *no television for the children until homework is completed.*)

Activities and Outings; Expenses
Employee may take the children on outings and to participate in activities if approved in advance by Employer. Where possible, Employer will pay for these activities in advance or will provide Employee with the necessary funds to pay for the activities. If payment in advance is not possible for whatever reason, Employee will pay for the activity and will submit a receipt to Employer, at which time Employer will be responsible for reimbursing Employee. Employee is not to make purchases of items for the children without the prior approval of Employer.

Emergencies
Employer will provide Employee, at the time of this contract, with a properly executed Consent to Obtain Medical Treatment for each of the children, so that emergency medical care may be obtained as necessary. In case of emergency, Employee will call 911 immediately, and then will call Employer at either of the parents' provided telephone numbers. Employer will provide Employee with telephone numbers as necessary to apprise Employee of Employer's whereabouts at all times.

Grievances

Employee may feel free to make known any complaints Employee may have regarding either the employment agreement, the Employer's policies, or the Employer or children themselves, and Employer will take these grievances into consideration and attempt to reach a workable solution.

Likewise, Employer may make Employee aware of any complaints regarding Employee's job performance. Employer may make either a verbal or written complaint, but upon a second written complaint, Employee will be considered to be on notice that a third complaint will result in immediate termination of the employment agreement.

Termination of Agreement

Either party may terminate this agreement upon the giving of three weeks' written notice to the other party. In the case where the Employer finds it necessary to terminate the agreement with fewer than three weeks' notice to Employee, Employer will pay the Employee in full for the entire three-week notice period. However, in the case of conduct by the Employee that is neglectful or harmful to the children, of conduct amounting to theft by the Employee, or upon a complaint about Employee's job performance that follows two prior written complaints, Employer may terminate the agreement without notice and without compensation past the date of termination.

[If the nanny is live-in, you may want to add verbiage here stating how much time she will have to vacate the premises upon termination. Typically, the amount of time will be the same as the notice period, unless the termination is for cause.]

Signed: _____ Date: _____
        (Employer)

        _____ Date: _____
        (Employer)

        _____ Date: _____
        (Employee)

PARENTAL CONSENT TO OBTAIN
EMERGENCY MEDICAL TREATMENT

_____ (*names of parents*), parents or legal guardians of _____ (*name of child*), hereby give consent and authority to _____ (*name of nanny*), hereinafter "Childcare Provider," to obtain emergency medical or dental treatment for _____ (*name of child*), if necessary in Childcare Provider's best judgment, while _____ (*child*) is in the care of Childcare Provider. Such treatment may include, but is not limited to: requesting paramedic or ambulance assistance; emergency room, urgent care, or doctor visit; diagnostic or other medical testing; X-rays; administration of anesthesia or medication; insertion of intravenous drip; other procedures or hospital stays as may be medically advisable.

Consent and authority granted herein is effective from _____ to _____.

Signed: _____ Date: _____

Signed: _____ Date: _____

AUTHORIZATION TO OBTAIN BACKGROUND CHECK

Employee, _____ (*Employee's name*), of _____ (*Employee's address*), _____ (*Employee's date of birth*), _____ (*Employee's Social Security number*), _____ (*Employee's driver's license number and state of issuance*), hereby consents and authorizes Employer, _____ (*Employers' names*), of _____ (*Employers' address*) to obtain the following information, as a prerequisite to an offer of employment by Employer to Employee:

Consumer Credit Report
Criminal Background Check
Educational Background Check
Employment Background Check
Department of Motor Vehicles Driving History Check

Employee authorizes Employer to contact such individuals, agencies, institutions, and organizations as Employer deems necessary in order to obtain the referenced reports and background checks. Furthermore, Employee releases and holds harmless any such individual, agency, institution, and organization from liability for providing such information to Employer.

_____   _____
Employee   Date

Index

4-H, 95

A

abuse, 12, 22, 28, 36, 42, 44, 73, 155, 159, 161, 162, 163, 164, 166, 167, 169
    addressing, 163
accredited, 19, 22, 23, 31, 32, 33, 34, 82, 99, 195
adequate classification, 16, 37, 38, 77, 85, 140
adjusted gross income, 112, 113, 114, 196
    AGI, 112
Administration for Children and Families, 117, 118, 195
advances your profession, 6
after-school care, 93, 94, 95, 96
Agent Au Pair, 80
alternatives, 11, 13, 19, 41, 193
American Camp Association, 99, 100
American College of Early Childhood Education, 54
American Institute for Foreign Study, 80
Americans with Disabilities Act (ADA), 179, 180, 195
Application for Employer Identification Number, 74
au pairs, 13, 14, 74, 79, 80, 81, 82, 83, 143, 146, 152, 154, 158, 160, 168, 171, 195
    costs, 83
    locating, 80
AuPairCare Inc., 80

B

baby-sitting cooperatives, 187–188
baby-sitting swaps, 187
babysitters, 13, 14, 54
background checks, 28, 29, 35, 36, 51, 52, 57, 61, 62, 63, 64, 93, 100, 107, 178, 181, 183
backup childcare, 105, 106, 107, 158
Boys and Girls Clubs, 95
Bureau of Educational and Cultural Affairs, 80

C

Calibar Training Institute, 54
camps, 97, 98, 99, 100
    costs, 100
career path, 6
child abuse, 155, 159, 161, 162, 163, 164, 166, 169
    avoiding, 161, 162
Child and Dependent Care Expenses Credit, 8, 112, 113, 114, 134, 135, 136, 196
Child Care and Development Block Grant, 117
Child Care Aware, 96
Child Care Resource and Referral (CCRR), 22, 23, 28, 33, 101, 115, 196
Child Tax Credit, 8, 111, 112, 196
church, 23, 24, 53, 63, 95
Citizenship and Immigration Services, 77

Consumer Product Safety
  Commission, 46, 161
cost/benefit analysis, 5, 6
credit reporting agencies, 64
Cultural Care Au Pair, 81
Cultural Homestay International, 81
curriculum, 22, 40, 56

D

day care centers, 2, 11, 12, 15, 16, 19,
  21, 22, 23, 24, 25, 26, 28, 29, 31, 32,
  33, 46, 91, 94, 102, 106, 107, 142,
  152, 153, 171, 178, 179, 198
  checking out potential, 33
  costs, 24
  daily activities checklist, 39
  director and staff checklist, 35
  disadvantages, 22
  emergencies checklist, 46
  interactions with the staff checklist,
    44
  locating, 22
  miscellaneous concerns checklist,
    47
  policies checklist, 41
  preliminary questions checklist, 34
  premises checklist, 37
  safety and security concerns check-
    list, 45
  visiting, 151
Department of Education, 176
Department of Health and Human
  Services, 32, 117, 195
Department of Justice, 180
Department of State, 80, 82
Dependent Care Assistance Plans, 133,
  135, 196
directors, 31, 33, 35, 36, 44, 45, 46, 53,
  94, 100, 133, 140, 157, 166
discipline, 14, 31, 36, 42, 59, 61, 70, 85,
  100, 162, 196
Domestic Workers United, 55

E

Earned Income Credit, 75, 114, 115,
  197
Earned Income Credit Advance
  Payment Certificate, 75
emergencies, 36, 39, 41, 45, 46, 47, 71,
  72, 105, 106
Employee's Withholding Allowance
  Certificate, 74
employer assistance, 133, 135
Employer Identification Number, 74
Employer-Provided Child Care Credit,
  134
employment agreement, 51, 65, 66, 67,
  68, 70, 71, 72, 73
Employment Eligibility Verification,
  77
employment issues, 67, 69, 71, 73, 75,
  77
English Nanny and Governess School,
  55
Equifax, 64
EurAuPair Intercultural Child Care
  Programs, 81
Exchange Visitor visas, 80
Experian, 64
Exploring Cultural and Educational
  Learning/Au Pair Registry, 81

F

Face The World Foundation/Au Pair
  Foundation, 81
Fair Labor Standards Act (FLSA), 77,
  197
family day care, 12, 15, 19, 21, 22, 23,
  27–31, 33, 34, 35, 40, 44, 49, 91, 94,
  103, 105, 106, 139, 142, 145, 146,
  152, 157, 158, 170, 178, 179, 189, 197
  checking out potential, 33
  costs, 29
  daily activities checklist, 39
  director and staff checklist, 35
  disadvantages, 27, 28
  emergencies checklist, 46

interactions with the staff checklist, 44

locating, 28

miscellaneous concerns checklist, 47

policies checklist, 41

preliminary questions checklist, 34

premises checklist, 37

safety and security concerns checklist, 45

unlicensed, 29, 30

visiting, 151

family issues, 87

Federal Insurance Contributions Act (FICA), 7, 8, 75, 76, 197

federal unemployment tax, 76

fees, 6, 7, 47, 51, 109

field trips, 32, 40, 47

flex-time, 10

flexible spending accounts, 134, 135

Form 1040, 7, 74, 112, 114

Form 1040A, 114

Form 2441, 114

Form I-9, 77

Form SS-4, 74, 75

Form W-2, 74, 75

Form W-3, 74, 75

Form W-4, 74

Form W-5, 75, 115

G

government assistance, 76, 85, 111, 113, 115, 117, 119, 121, 123, 125, 127, 129, 131

grandparents, 14, 76, 83, 86, 88, 106, 186

guilty parent syndrome, 9

H

Head Start, 117, 118, 119, 127, 197

I

IEP, 197

Immigration and Naturalization Service (INS). *See Citizenship and Immigration Services*

in-home care, 2, 19, 27, 49, 57, 142, 143, 161, 166, 168, 178, 180

application, 58

employment issues, 65

helping your child adjust, 142, 143

hiring process, 57

interview, 59

checklist, 60

maintaining a good relationship with the childcare Provider, 146, 147, 148

problems, 169

terminating the childcare relationship, 168

independent contractor, 65, 181

individual program, 22

individualized education program, 175, 197

Individuals with Disabilities Education Act (IDEA), 29, 59, 67, 91, 139, 160, 172, 175, 176, 183, 197–198

infants, 11, 15, 24, 29, 32, 36, 38, 41, 43, 61, 82, 86, 87, 103, 152, 172, 176

insurance, 5, 40, 62, 68, 69, 76, 77, 87, 180, 191, 197

InterExchange Au Pair, 82

Internal Revenue Service (IRS), 7, 74, 75, 111, 112, 114, 115

Publication 15, 75

Publication 503, 114

Publication 926, 75

International MOMS Club, 184

J

J-1 visa, 80

job sharing, 10

Journal of Applied Developmental Psychology, 15

Junior Achievement, 95

L

level of care, 16, 32

licensing, 19, 30, 31, 32, 33, 34, 178, 191

M

medical payments insurance, 68
Middlesex Community College
    Childcare Specialist/Nanny
    Certificate, 55
minimum wage, 17, 77, 78, 97, 109, 197
Moms On a Mission Single
    (M.O.M.S.), 186, 187
monitoring the childcare situation, 153
Montessori, 26
Mothers & More National Office, 184
MUMS: National Parent to Parent
    Network, 184

N

nannies, 2, 10, 13, 14, 15, 27, 51–77, 79,
    105, 106, 109, 142, 143, 145, 146,
    147, 148, 152, 153, 154, 158, 160,
    166, 168, 169, 170, 171, 173, 178,
    179, 182, 189, 193, 198
    agencies, 51
    employment agreement, 65
    hiring process, 57, 58, 59, 60, 61, 62,
        63, 147
    insurance, 68
    locating, 51, 52
    nanny,
    training programs, 13, 54
nanny cams, 152, 153, 160
National AfterSchool Association, 96
National Association for Family Child
    Care (NAFCC), 12, 33, 198
National Association for the Education
    of Young Children (NAEYC), 22,
    32, 33, 198
National Association of Child Care
    Resource and Referral Agencies
    (NACCRRA), 23, 115, 198
National Early Childhood Education
    Technical Assistance Center
    (NECTAC), 176, 177, 198
National Institute of Child Health and
    Human Development (NICHD), 15
National Organization of Mothers of
    Twins Clubs, 184

National Resource Center for Health
    and Safety in Child Care (NRC),
    32, 161
neglect, 22, 28, 73, 159, 161, 163, 166
    addressing, 163
net cash benefit, 8, 9
networking, 24, 95, 152, 183, 186, 187
night shift, 101, 102, 103
nighttime care, 101, 102, 103
Northwest Nannies Institute, 55

O

occasional childcare, 91
Office of Special Education and
    Rehabilitative Services, 176
on-site day care, 134
out-of-home care, 13, 16, 19, 31, 33, 35,
    37, 39, 41, 43, 45, 47, 139, 143, 145,
    147, 177
    evaluating, 31
    helping your child adjust, 139, 140,
        141, 142
    maintaining a good relationship
        with the childcare Provider,
        145, 146
overtime, 66, 67, 77, 147, 197

P

Parents Without Partners, 186, 187
park districts, 95, 98
part-time childcare, 91
paying for childcare, 109, 173
personal injury liability insurance, 68
prekindergarten, 11
preschools, 12, 13, 21, 23, 25
    academic vs. play-based, 25
primary earner's income, 6
property damage liability, 68

Q

quality, 1, 2, 10, 15–19, 22, 28, 29, 30,
    31, 33, 34, 35, 36, 41, 52, 91, 93, 101,
    107, 151, 178, 185, 193, 195, 196, 198

R

references, 36, 44, 51, 58, 62, 63, 94, 96, 100, 170, 178, 183
regular paycheck, 6
regulations, 12, 30, 31, 32, 35, 37, 46, 117, 191
relatives, 14, 23, 28, 60, 62, 85, 86, 87, 88, 89, 101, 102, 106, 182, 194
    ability, 86
    availability and reliability, 86
    compensation, 88
resolving problems, 155, 156, 157, 158

S

Schedule H, 74, 75
sexual harassment, 169, 170
short-notice sitters, 91
sick child day care, 107
single parents, 2, 101, 185, 186, 187, 188, 193
    finding support, 185
sitters, 91, 94, 97, 182
Social Security, 6, 7, 9, 14, 58, 63, 74, 76, 77, 114, 197
Social Security Administration, 74
Southeast Community College Early Childhood Education, 56
special needs child, 175, 177, 178, 179, 180, 193
specialized childcare, 175
    costs, 180
    evaluating special needs childcare options, 178
staff, 12, 16, 17, 21, 22, 24, 28, 29, 31, 32, 35, 36, 37, 38, 41–47, 93, 94, 96, 99, 100, 146, 157, 162, 163, 171, 177, 178, 196, 197
staff-to-child ratio, 35
stay-at-home moms (SAHMs), 94, 181
subsidized childcare, 18, 111
    employer provided subsidies, 134, 135
substandard classification, 15, 16, 31
Sullivan University Professional Nanny Diploma, 56
summer breaks, 97, 98, 99, 193

T

taxes, 2, 6, 7, 8, 14, 62, 65, 67, 74–77, 97, 109–115, 134, 135, 136, 137, 197
    credits, 111
    qualified childcare expenses, 134
Temporary Assistance to Needy Families (TANF), 116, 117, 120, 121, 122, 199
terminating the childcare relationship, 169, 171
    by the provider, 170
toddlers, 11, 24, 32, 35, 38, 46, 61, 86, 140, 157, 176
Transmittal of Wage and Tax Statements, 74
transportation, 6, 70, 85, 101, 189, 190, 191
    costs, 6
TransUnion, 64
travel, 6, 185
tweens, 86, 95

U

unemployment tax, 76
uninsured/underinsured motorist liability insurance, 68
Urban Institute, 193
USAuPair, Inc., 82

V

Vincennes University Professional Nanny Certificate, 56

W

Wage and Tax Statement, 74
welfare, 116, 117, 125, 128, 130, 199
work-at-home moms (WAHMs), 181, 182, 183
working part-time, 10

Y

YMCA, 53, 95, 98

About the Author

Linda H. Connell received her undergraduate degree in psychology from the University of Illinois at Urbana, and her law degree from Notre Dame Law School. After law school, she practiced municipal law for several years before deciding that she preferred legal writing and research to litigation. She joined the editorial staff of a publisher of legal study materials, and worked there until shortly after she started her family, when she decided to go into business for herself as a freelance writer and editor.

Ms. Connell has faced the quality childcare dilemma from before the arrival of her first child, both as a parent employed outside of the home and as a work-at-home mother. She has made the cost/benefit analysis, has experienced the search for a good provider, and terminated several caregiver arrangements. As a result, she has a great interest in helping other parents navigate the uncertainties connected with such an important family decision.

Ms. Connell lives with her family in the Chicago area. This is her fourth book.